SEEING THINGS

SEEING THINGS

VIRTUAL AESTHETICS IN VICTORIAN CULTURE

AMANDA SHUBERT

CORNELL UNIVERSITY PRESS
Ithaca and London

First published 2025 by Cornell University Press

Librarians: A CIP catalog record for this book is available from the Library of Congress.

ISBN 9781501783678 (hardcover)
ISBN 9781501784941 (paperback)
ISBN 9781501783685 (pdf)
ISBN 9781501783692 (epub)

GPSR EU contact: Sam Thornton, Mare Nostrum Group B.V., Mauritskade 21D, 1091 GC, Amsterdam, NL, gpsr@mare-nostrum.co.uk.

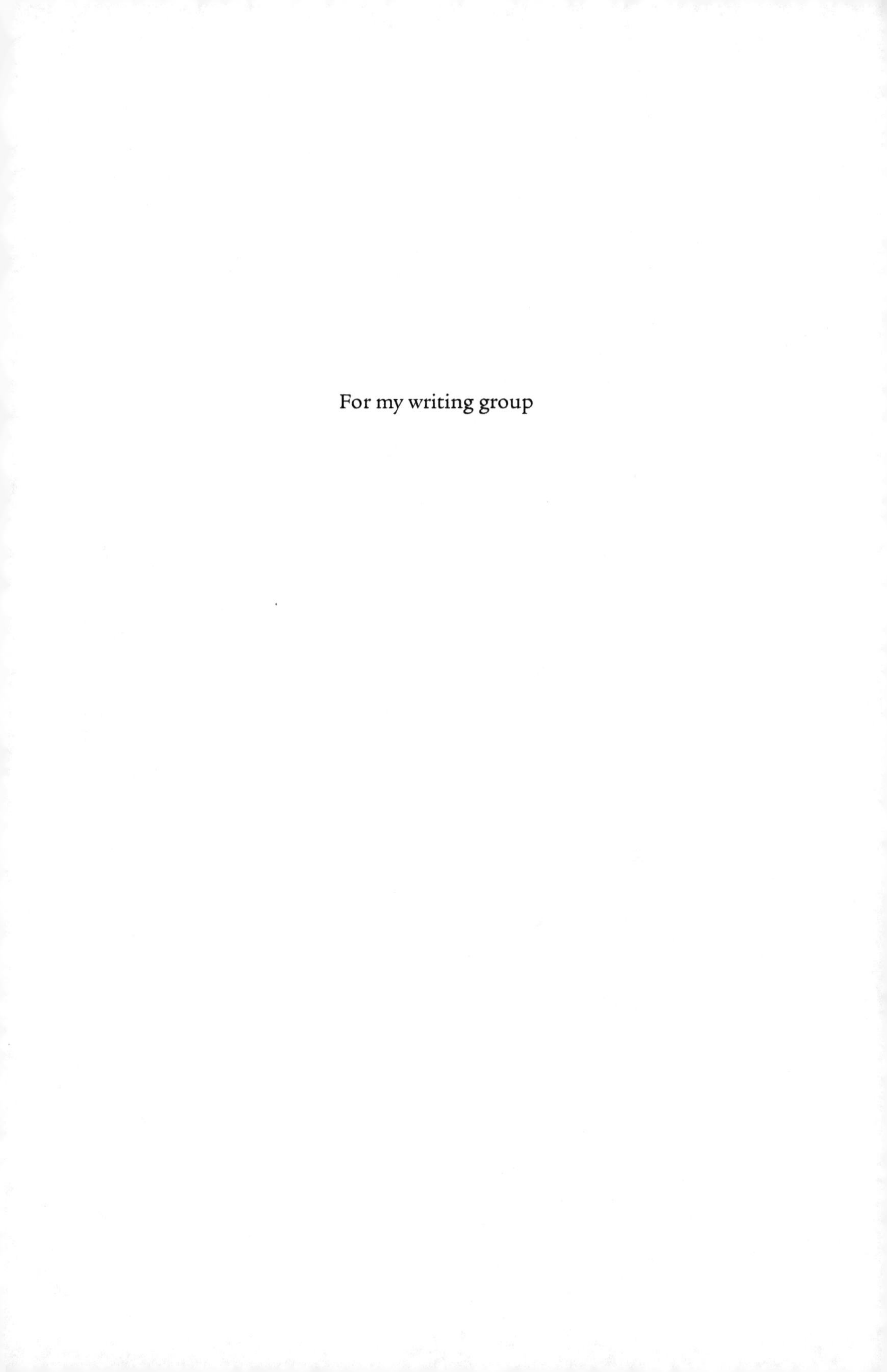

For my writing group

Contents

SEEING THINGS

Introduction

What Was the Virtual?

Did filmgoers really jump out of their seats when they saw a train pulling into the station? This famous story about the first screening of Auguste and Louis Lumière's *Arrival of a Train at La Ciotat* (1896) tells us that audiences panicked and raced for the exits as if they were about to be run over (figure I.1). Film historians will tell you that this never happened.[1] Why would people accustomed to magic lantern shows, technological optical illusions, and the moving pictures of the Mutoscope respond to projected moving images with terror? Did you run screaming the first time you saw a three-dimensional (3D) film or put on a virtual reality (VR) headset? Nineteenth-century spectators were no more naïve than we are. Their visual and technological media culture had trained them in an aesthetic principle that was comparatively new at the time but already deeply rooted—a principle that you may recognize as conditioning your own practices of media spectatorship. That is, Victorian media taught people how to see things that are not there.

This book is a cultural history of virtual aesthetics before the arrival of that first train and, with it, the beginning of cinema. It tells the story of when, how, and why the experience of "seeing things" became an indelible part of Victorian mass culture that set the terms not only for early cinema spectatorship but also for how we relate to film, television,

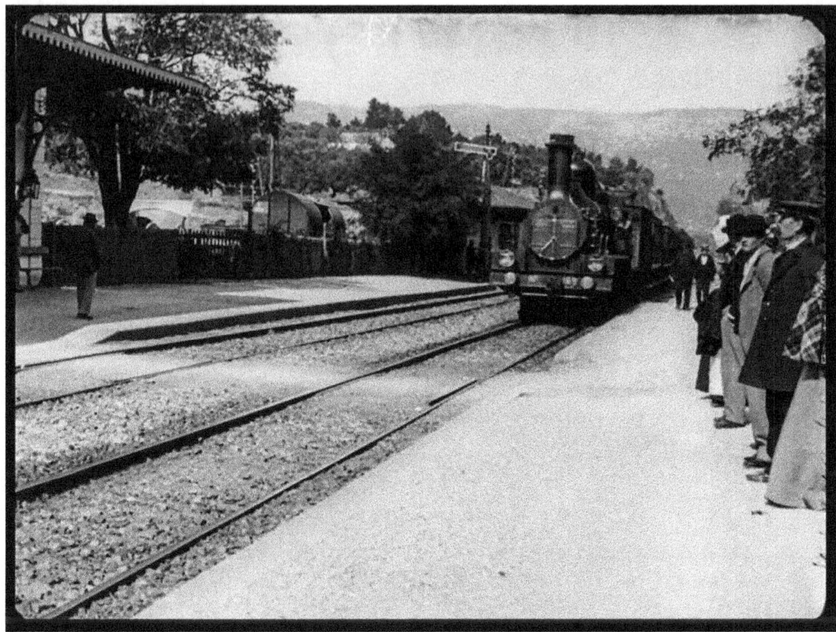

FIGURE I.1. Film still from *Arrival of a Train at La Ciotat.* Auguste Lumière and Louis Lumière, 1896.

and digital media today. "Virtual aesthetics" is my term for the technological aesthetics of visual or perceptual encounters with things that are not really there, an aesthetic form and experience that became increasingly popular over the course of the nineteenth century both as an attraction in and of itself and an object of imaginative inquiry. Virtual aesthetics is not only the grounds for the visual and perceptual effects of cinema but also for the popular nineteenth-century media culture most often described as "precinematic"—a culture that included stereoscopes, zoetropes, flip-books, and optical stage magic. What holds these media together—and what distinguishes them from related forms of technologically produced visual media like photography or lithography that were on the rise during the same period—is that they all create virtual images. That is, they all exploit physiological and technological optics to create images that do not have a tangible form but that we can see all the same. Contingent and ephemeral, the moving images of the zoetrope and 3D images of the stereoscope come into being at the interface of a technological apparatus and a spectator's embodied visual perception. This book tells the story of how these virtual media collided with the practice of fiction—especially the novel—and how this collision produced an imaginary of the virtual as an experience and condition of mediation that continues to inform our lives today.

This book is both a history and a theory of virtual aesthetics, one that turns to an archive of literary, visual, and technological media to excavate an idea that was not yet fully nameable but could still be articulated through diverse frames—an idea in the messy and vigorous process of coming into being. This book is rooted in Victorian studies, and it argues that the "Victorian" is characterized by the emergence of the virtual. Between 1830 and 1900, a transformational period that spans the rise of optical technology as mass cultural entertainment and the invention of cinema, "seeing things" was redefined as an enlightened mode of spectatorship and a paradigmatic media aesthetic of Western modernity. Instead of a symptom of insanity or proof of supernatural forces at work in the world, seeing things that are not there was newly constructed as a reflexive, scientifically literate, and culturally sophisticated experience of technological mediation that brought spectators into contact with the mutually constitutive relationship between their perceiving selves and the world they inhabited. In this sense, "seeing things" was more than an aesthetic experience: it was an aesthetic expression of a civilizational ideal that defined the capacity to see but not believe, to be entertained without being deceived, as a sign of Western supremacy. In novels and short stories, popular science writing and travelogues, and the design and marketing of optical media, optical spectatorship offered the experiential and imaginative grounds for writers, inventors, and showmen to conceptualize virtuality as simultaneously a characteristic of and means through which modern people could apprehend modern life in an expanding global empire.

My account of Victorian virtual aesthetics is based in the analysis of nineteenth-century optical media culture, which was itself composed of a wide range of devices and exhibition formats. Of these, the best known today is probably the magic lantern, which was used by showmen in museums, lecture halls, and theaters to project painted or photographic slides that dissolved one into the next, effecting stunning visual transformations. With its shaky gray pictures, early cinematography literally paled in comparison with the virtuosic oil paintings executed by the best slide painters in mouthwateringly vibrant colors.[2] But the magic lantern was only one of many Victorian optical formats to use light and lenses for visual transformations. Dioramas back-projected light onto a painted screen to create astonishing views that shifted from day to night, season to season, or scene to scene, and optical conjuring used light reflected or refracted from hidden lenses and mirrors to make objects appear and disappear. In the home, families could create virtual images with optical toys that included smaller-scale versions of theatrical equipment, such as the toy magic lantern or the polyorama panoptique, a perspective box for transforming views like those of the diorama, as well as an entirely new class of toys like the thaumatrope, kaleidoscope, and stereoscope that were designed to demonstrate principles of optics. For instance, thaumatropes are paper disks you can spin by twirling a piece of string attached at both ends between your thumb and forefinger. The act of spinning composites the pictures on each side into a single virtual image through an effect that nineteenth-century scientists attributed to persistence of vision.[3] Phenakistoscopes and zoetropes exploited the same principle to create the first moving images. The stereoscope demonstrated the relationship between binocular vision and depth perception by adding an illusion of perspectival depth to photographs.

At the heart of the book is my belief that Victorian literary culture and optical media can help explain each other and that by reading them together we can discover emergent conceptions of the virtual that are not legible in either archive alone. This book is a work of visual studies and media aesthetics that applies what W. J. T. Mitchell calls "the pictorial turn," or "the rediscovery of the picture as a complex interplay between visuality, apparatus, institutions, discourse, bodies, and figurality," to the analysis of virtual images and the aesthetic, technological, and ideological discourses that shaped the way they were perceived.[4] I follow in the footsteps of scholars of Victorian media aesthetics like Rachel Teukolsky, Susan Zieger, and Isobel Armstrong who offer us rich, capacious studies of visual culture by working across media, texts, and formats and treating literary production as an archive of theories of visuality.[5] This book adopts a multimedia and mass culture approach to virtual aesthetics as, in Teukolsky's words, a means of recuperating "the actual cultural expression of nineteenth-century aesthetic phenomena" that is so often obscured by disciplinary fragmentation and the separation of "high" and "low" art forms.[6] In addressing the heterogeneity of virtual aesthetics at the intersection of varied texts, objects, performances, and sites, I am not trying to advance a singular aesthetic of the virtual. I seek instead to describe a wide-reaching imaginary of the virtual grounded in the experience of optical spectatorship and conceptualized in a broad range of cultural production.

Although my archive encompasses a diverse set of materials, I have a particular interest in the novel and the way it reflects on and fantasizes about the aesthetics of the virtual image. My purpose here is not to position novels as master texts that can "explain" the aesthetics of optical technology or to position optical technology as "cultural context" for readings of novels but rather to generate theories of virtual aesthetics at the intersection of both media forms. I approach Victorian novels and other fictional and nonfictional print media as an archive of discourses about optical technology, and optical technology as a framework through which print media conceptualized the virtual. In this way, this book responds to Nicholas Dames's call for literary studies scholars to "reimagine the novel as a technology" by proposing that Victorian novels took up the mantle of optical technology to portray themselves as technologies of perception.[7] Across the case studies in this book, we will see examples of how Victorian novelists not only elaborated imaginaries of the virtual that we find in optical media culture but also incorporated the embodied visual and perceptual effects of optical media as models for theorizing the novel's distinct media effects. In other words, the Victorian novel understood itself as a technology that produces virtual experience.

This book is thus part of a long tradition in Victorian literary studies that views the novel as a profoundly visual and intermedial genre. Many scholars have turned to Victorian "new media" like photography and telegraphy as models for how novels might, as Richard Menke puts it, "turn real life into pictures, reality into fictional information."[8] Scholars such as Helen Groth, John Plunkett, Joss Marsh, and Meegan Kennedy have looked at the relationship between nineteenth-century optical technology and literature, with an overarching concern about the relationship between the novel and technologies of visual projection like the dissolving views of the magic lantern, phantasmagoria shows, Pepper's Ghost, and the projection microscope.[9] Meanwhile, a new strain of novel studies exemplified by the work of Alison Byerly, John Plotz, and Jules Law has taken up "virtuality" and "virtual reality" as key terms for exploring the immersive, participatory, projective, and imaginative qualities of Victorian fiction.[10] It is surprising, however, that the notion of virtuality in Victorian fiction has still never been explored in the context of the visual media that created virtual images.[11] This is where my book makes its contribution. To understand the novel as a technology of visualization, one that is attuned to the phenomenological affordances of narrative for constructing an imaginative visual experience, we must look to the novel's relationship to the virtual media that made the act of spectatorship central to the production of the image.

My account of virtual aesthetics is also grounded in the political work that its media formats, practices, and experiences performed. I argue specifically that the Victorian imaginary of the virtual comes into being through, and in service of, British civilizational ideology. Over the course of the nineteenth century, scientific writing, optical shows, and novels constructed virtual aesthetics as a product and crowning expression of Britain's civilizing empire. Optical technology was simultaneously a triumph of Western scientific advancement—a sign of British civilizational and epistemic superiority—and a sublation of the so-called native magic or superstition represented as characterizing the backward religions and cultures of regions conquered by the West.[12] As I will demonstrate in chapter 1, the scientific literature that helped to popularize optical technology and stage magic relied on a binary view of spectatorship that used colonial and patriarchal frameworks to distinguish so-called rational spectators—those who could appreciate optical illusions while recognizing their technological basis—from superstitious fools. The first chapter lays out the case for virtual aesthetics' civilizational politics, and the following chapters continue to trace the ways that the virtual spectator was constructed along colonial, national, racial, gendered, and class lines. Thus, my book not only reimagines the novel as an optical technology; it also reimagines optical technology as a kind of fiction that produced civilizational imaginaries through its content and modes of spectatorship.

To develop its account of virtual aesthetics, this book employs mixed methods that allow the chapters to move fluidly across varied media forms. I pair literary studies with media archaeology, a branch of media history that values hands-on archival research as a way of excavating, historicizing, and analyzing the experiential dimensions of media objects and challenging the technological determinism that undergirds contemporary media discourse.[13] While media archaeology encompasses diverse methods and approaches, Jussi Parikka and Erkki Huhtamo argue that the field is unified by "discontent with 'canonized' narratives of media culture and history" and the drive to correct such narratives with "alternate histories of suppressed, neglected, and forgotten media that do not point teleologically to the present media-cultural condition as their perfection."[14] My study of nineteenth-century media of the virtual image, an archive of materials that could be characterized as ephemeral mass culture, is an example of this kind of "alternate history." This book incorporates research conducted in British archives of nineteenth-century optical media, including the Victoria and Albert Museum, the National Media Museum, and the Bill Douglas Cinema Museum, where I saw and operated examples of many of the devices I discuss in this book.

This archival research could also reasonably be called play. I employ an experimental method of media archaeology that Andreas Fickers and Annie van den Oeve call "re-enactment," or handling, interacting, and playing with media technologies "to re-sensitize [the researcher] to the sensorial and performative dimensions of media use."[15] For me, this involved playing with optical devices—peering into them, spinning them, projecting from them—to document and interpret their range of visual and perceptual effects and the sensations and affects they provoked in me. Play is an especially critical method for what Meredith Bak calls "the ludic archive" of optical toys, toys that were designed for play and work by "'play[ing]' with the senses."[16] Building on Bak's work, I argue that optical media also constitutes a virtual archive, or an archive of virtual images that are only visible at the interface of the spectator and the apparatus and that therefore cannot be reduced to objective, material form. In other words, because virtual images do not exist outside the experiences of performance and play, performance and play are required to study them.

In addition to a means of visual analysis, archival play is a historical method. Rather than reconstructing historical media experience, I use the evidence of my own experience as a kind of raw and unprocessed secondary source. Archival play is how I know that the virtual image of the thaumatrope does not move but flickers; that your eyes get tired after looking through the stereoscope for too long; and, in one mortifying case, that a phenakistoscope can snap in half while you are spinning it. Rather than discussing such playful experiences directly in the chapters of the book, I have treated them as phenomenological data points that inform the way I write about virtual aesthetics. They help me make historical claims about how Victorian spectators interacted with virtual images that are attuned to the embodied experience of play and attentive to the range of visual, perceptual, and somatic effects that optical media can create. This ludic methodology has also allowed me to identify points of convergence between optical and literary constructions of virtuality by tracing aesthetic modalities like the composition of an image through spinning, the embodied labor of optical peeping, and the potentially destructive physical power of the spectator over the optical apparatus. Each of these insights has sensitized me to the operations of Victorian literary texts and allowed me to develop richer accounts of virtual aesthetics. For example, you will find that the dialectical relationship between stillness and motion, stasis and circling, in optical toys undergirds my reading of *The Mayor of Casterbridge* in chapter 5. You may catch a hint of both my stereoscope fatigue and my phenakistoscope accident in chapter 3, when I describe the mad scientist at the heart of Fitz-James O'Brien's short story "The Diamond Lens," whose microscopic exertions lead him to fall asleep on top of his instrument and destroy it.

As these examples show, the question of what media "do" encompasses more than their objective technical capacities. I understand the affects, experiences, even fantasies that media produce as part of their history, a method of inquiry that media archaeologists like Erkki Huhtamo, Siegfried Zielinski, and Eric Kluitenberg have called the analysis of "imaginary media."[17] My book is a cultural history not just of virtual media themselves but also of how virtual media are imagined—a cultural history of the virtual imaginaries that we find in optical spectatorship and representations of optical spectatorship alike. The stereoscope does not make it possible to leave the body behind and enter the virtual image's scopic field, but these imaginative affordances, evidenced in Victorian advertisements and cartoons, are still part of the history and culture of the medium. In this way, the methods of literary studies and media archaeology begin to converge. The close reading of imaginative texts like novels opens new archives of media discourse—new imaginaries of media—that are easily overlooked by more traditional media historians. In addition to the imaginary affordances of virtual media, my book discusses virtual media that are truly imaginary—impossible media that have never existed outside cultural discourse and that come into being to express and embody fantastical ideas about mediation. These, too, have a history, one that allows us to better understand what virtuality meant in the Victorian age and the cultural uses to which the idea of the virtual was put.

A Brief Word on Terminology

Although I focus on the visual culture of the nineteenth century, I will break with convention by refraining from labeling these optical devices and shows as precinematic. "Precinematic" is a misleading term for the visual media created before the invention of cinema because it implies that cinema superseded and replaced them. This is untrue: if you have ever played with a flip-book or kaleidoscope, you know that nineteenth-century optical technology is alive and well, finding new roles and meanings in contemporary life.[18] To call these media precinematic is to imply that cinema was the obvious and natural end point of the nineteenth-century's explorations in virtual aesthetics and thus to close down avenues of inquiry that reveal the deeply noncinematic ways that these media created and conceptualized virtuality. This book seeks to recover a virtual aesthetics that was interrupted by cinema's ascension to the status of modernity's paradigmatic media technology.

In my book, you will encounter, among other things, exhibitions of ghosts, a magic mirror of ink, a diamond that is actually an optical technology, and a moving picture ouroboros that spins in a circle. All these media relate to the virtual moving image aesthetics of the cinema in some way; if I have done my job well, each of them will cast the history of cinema in a new light. But they will also compel diverse, sometimes conflicting conceptions of virtual aesthetics that challenge any clear narrative of technological or cultural development. I take cinema as a heuristic that opens a nineteenth-century culture of virtual aesthetics that is far stranger, richer, and more meaningful than the term "precinematic" will ever convey.

What Was the Virtual?

It would be easy to assume that my case for a Victorian media aesthetics of virtuality hinges on an act of strategic presentism, one in which I am (at best) reading the virtual interfaces, realities, and environments of our contemporary media ecology backward into the nineteenth century and (at worst) retrofitting Victorian aesthetics to the digital age. This is far from the case. I approach the virtual as a distinct media aesthetic of Victorian culture. I have generated my theory of Victorian virtual aesthetics from a historical analysis of nineteenth-century optical media technologies, practices of spectatorship, and cultural discourse, and I offer an account of the virtual that is deeply—to some extent, inextricably—placed within this context. How virtuality migrates and evolves and to what extent the aesthetic formations I discuss in this book prefigure or become the virtual technologies and experiences of today are fascinating questions beyond the scope of the book. My book is not asking what the virtual *is* but rather what the virtual *was* as an aesthetic and cultural framework in nineteenth-century British culture.

What was the virtual? As a way of answering this question, let me direct us to an essay published in *The National Magazine* in 1856 called "How to See Pictures." "We assume it to be a self-evident truth," the article begins, "that every man of healthy constitution, physical and mental, possesses a capacity for studying and enjoying works of art."[19] To explain how the average person might overcome the "artificial impediments" to their birthright of artistic appreciation, the author offers an analogy to another way of "see[ing]" another kind of "picture": the image produced by an optical toy called the pseudoscope. This device, proposed by Charles Wheatstone just a few years before the essay appeared, reverses the user's depth perception so that convex objects appear concave and concave objects appear convex. "Yet the instrument has this further peculiarity," the author of "How to See Pictures" remarks, "that its ordinary effect fails when you first look through it." Only after a few moments, "by a flash of light, as though you had grown wiser under a miracle," does the optical illusion occur, "the hollow of the cup bulging outwards." This transformation in the spectator's vision is "exactly analogous to the change which takes place in the perception of a man in the interval after he has made some acquaintance with objects of art, and before he has become familiarized with any new school."[20] Anchored by this reassuring example of spectatorial perseverance, the essay goes on to instruct readers in how to overcome deficits in their artistic education by looking closely at works of art. Just as the hollow cup suddenly bulges outward, so will a painting in an unfamiliar style become beautiful, if only the spectator will patiently wait for the "miracle" of their own visual perception to make them wise.

My theory of virtual aesthetics also rests on the question of how Victorians saw pictures. Rather than how they saw paintings, I am interested in how they saw a kind of picture that, as the article suggests, was in many cases *more* familiar, *more* profoundly mass cultural, and offered an easier and more immediately gratifying experience of visual novelty. I call this kind of picture a virtual image, or an image created by optical technology. Readers of this book are probably more familiar with looking at paintings than playing with toys like the pseudoscope. In this respect, the central premise of "How to See Pictures"—that looking at a pseudoscope can help us understand how to look at paintings—probably seems somewhat strange, as if the premise itself should be viewed through the pseudoscope and so flipped inside out. Written in the first decades of the optical toy boom, when devices like the pseudoscope began to appear in middle-class homes just as televisions would a century later, "How to See Pictures" makes apparent how relatable and ordinary the experiences of using optical toys and seeing virtual images were for Victorians. By comparing virtual spectatorship to looking at painting, the article offers us an example of how the virtual image's particular configuration of technology, embodiment, and perception made possible new ways of thinking about aesthetic experience. In other words, "How to See Pictures" points to a mid-century virtual aesthetics that is grounded in but ultimately transcends the experience of seeing the virtual images of optical technology.

What exactly Victorian virtual aesthetics looked like is a richly interpretive and historical question that the chapters of this book will endeavor to answer, each in their own way. But what virtual images looked like is comparatively simple and concrete, and I can explain it succinctly here. "Virtual images" refers to a class of images created at the interface of optical technology and a spectator's embodied visual perception. My use of the term is modeled on that of the film historian Tom Gunning, from whose profound body of work on nineteenth-century optical devices and spectacles this book takes inspiration.[21] For Gunning, a virtual image is a technological and perceptual image that arises when one or more spectators use, play with, or are exposed to an optical device that manipulates their vision. A virtual image is ephemeral and contingent; "[its] existence consists in its appearance and effects rather than its materiality."[22] When I use the term "virtual image," I am not projecting onto the optical culture of the nineteenth century a piece of contemporary jargon. I am challenging, as does Anne Friedberg, the assumption that "virtual" refers "only to electronically mediated or digitally produced images" as well as "its unquestioned equation with 'virtual reality.' "[23] Friedberg's work shows that the term "virtual" has been in use to describe the images seen through a lens or in a mirror since the seventeenth century; this English-language usage was popularized in the early nineteenth century by Sir David Brewster, the inventor of the kaleidoscope and lenticular stereoscope, whose writings on optical illusions and technology I discuss at some length in chapter 1.[24] In *A Treatise on Optics* (1831), for instance, Brewster distinguishes between real and virtual images: real images are seen directly by the eye, whereas virtual images are seen through the mediation of a lens.[25] While nineteenth-century optical usage referred primarily to lens- and mirror-based technologies, I follow Gunning in using the term more expansively to encompass all perceptual and technologically mediated optical illusions, like those created by paper-based

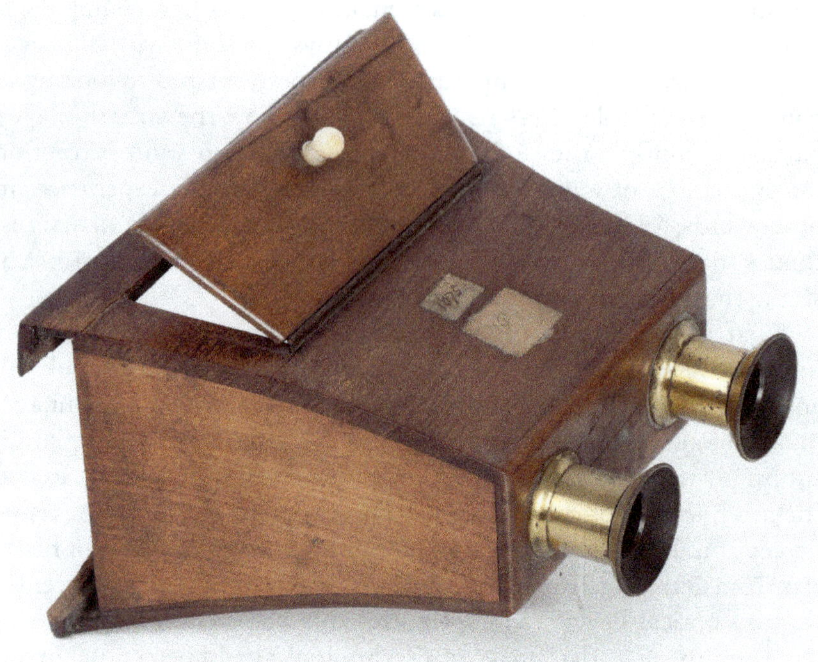

FIGURE I.2. The Brewster stereoscope. Courtesy of the University of Padua.

optical toys such as the zoetrope and flip-book. Rather than reflecting, refracting, or projecting images, these toys create a stream of composite moving images.

To understand what a virtual image looks like in practice, let us turn to the stereoscope. The stereoscope was the better-known and more commercially successful sibling of Wheatstone's pseudoscope, the case study of virtual images used in "How to See Pictures." It was refined in the middle of the nineteenth century by Brewster, who transformed it into a ubiquitous household toy that one scientific popularizer described as "a piece of domestic equipment without which no drawing room was thought complete" (figure I.2).[26] While the pseudoscope reverses depth perception, the stereoscope simulates depth perception, allowing the viewer to see a flat picture as if it were 3D. This 3D image is an example of what I call a virtual image. It does not exist anywhere except in the encounter between the perceiving subject and the technological apparatus. You cannot touch the 3D image that you see through the lenses of the stereoscope because it is not really "there." Yet it does exist, in its visual appearance and perceptual effects, for as long as you are looking through the lenses.

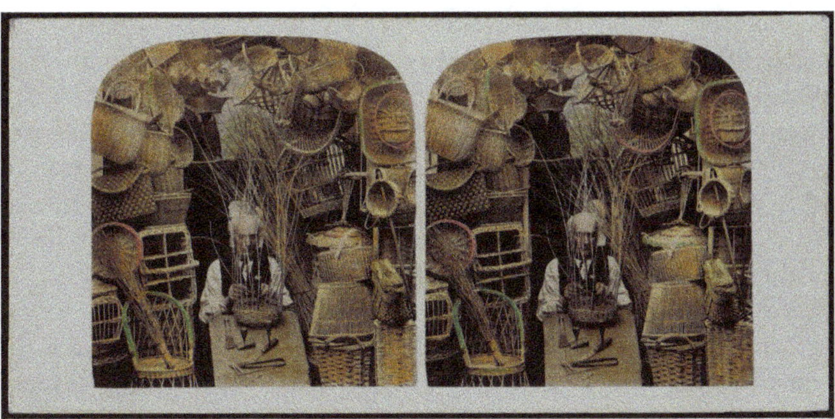

FIGURE I.3. Stereograph of "The Brighton Fancy Basket Maker" by W. H. Mason, Great Britain, 1860s. © Victoria and Albert Museum, London.

Consider the hand-colored stereograph of the fancy basket maker in Brighton (figure I.3). When you look at the image printed in the book, you see two seemingly identical pictures of an old man with white hair, wearing a white shirt and brown waistcoat, in the middle of a sea of wicker. Baskets hang over his head, piled on either side of him, and one partly obscures his face as he weaves it together. By touching the page, you can touch the picture—its existence is confirmed by its materiality. But if you place the page in a stereoscope and peep at the stereograph through its lenses, a different image appears—a singular image endowed with an illusion of depth and relief. The wicker fronds of the basket that the man is weaving open out toward you, like a static variation on the Lumière film and its onrushing train. The textures and dimensions of the baskets on the wall explode, vivid and sharp. The small distances between things, like the man's hands and the basket he is working on, expand as if they have suddenly been rendered on the receding planes of a pop-up book. The black void behind the man suddenly becomes visible in new ways; no longer just negative space, its contrast with the vital presence of the man and the baskets makes it seem almost concave, like a corridor. This is a virtual image, and if you reached out to touch it, it would not be there at all. You could touch the stereograph or the lenses of the stereoscope, of course. But you could not touch the inky depths of the corridor or the prickly edges of the wicker fronds. Their depths and dimensions are purely virtual effects.

The stereograph of the fancy basket maker is a helpful case study because it grounds the virtual image in the materiality and corporeality of Victorian media culture. Stereographs, which usually consist of pieces of cardstock with two nearly identical photographs printed or pasted side by side, are examples of what Teukolsky calls "the small-scale printed matter of the Victorian media revolution."[27] The stereograph of the fancy basket maker is therefore illustrative twice over of what Bill Brown has termed the "material unconscious" of Victorian mass culture, both as an ephemeral media object and a representation of the thingness of Victorian life, wicker baskets and all.[28] While the process of seeing through or with a stereoscope was often imaginatively associated with transcending time, space, and body—as if the spectator could become Ralph Waldo Emerson's "transparent eyeball" and roam across the Earth through a mobile virtual gaze—stereoscope spectatorship was in fact deeply corporeal. It involved not just the eyes but the hands, which hold the device and select the stereographs, and not just the body but its placement in the domestic environs of the parlor. Playing with a stereoscope is not just a way of seeing but also a form of doing that, like basket weaving itself, involves the work of hands and eyes.[29] Our basket maker therefore reminds us that the immateriality of the virtual image is always in dialectical relation to the materiality of technology and vision, the fantasy of virtual travel to the armchair in which it occurs. At the same time, he foregrounds an aesthetic dimension of Victorian mass culture that is often elided in the many scholarly accounts of its profound, almost overbearing thingness: that such thingness both gave rise to and could be experienced through the dematerializing aesthetics of the virtual.

This book explores two types of optical mass culture that created virtual images. The first is the optical show, with examples such as optical conjuring, optical ghost shows, and cinema. These were public spectacles that used optical technology, sometimes exhibiting the device as a key part of the attraction and other times obscuring the process of technological mediation to create a sense of mystery and magic. The second type of optical mass culture is the optical toy, or household optical device, a category that includes the stereoscope, phenakistoscope, and flip-book. Optical toys are a kind of philosophical toy, an early modern nomenclature meant to distinguish instruments of measurement (mathematical instruments) from those that facilitate the study of nature through distortion.[30] Optical toys distort vision to reveal the properties of vision: the stereoscope and pseudoscope demonstrate the principles of depth perception, while the zoetrope and flip-book demonstrate an illusion of motion that nineteenth-century scientists called persistence of vision. Although they originate in experimental science, the toyness of optical toys was evident in their commercialization and use as playthings both by adults and children.[31]

The historical parameters of the book reflect the period when these toys and spectacles became part of Victorian mass culture. Some of the devices and shows I discuss existed before 1830—in chapter 4, we will even take a substantial detour back to the 1790s—but in the 1830s, several of the most formative optical devices and formats of the nineteenth century would be invented. The 1830s also saw the rise of a new mode of scientific popularization embodied in commercial museums of science and technology like London's National Gallery for Practical Science, Blending Instruction and Amusement (founded in 1832) and Royal Polytechnic Institution (founded in 1838), and in optical treatises and showmen's memoirs that sought to explain optical illusions for a broad audience with the aim of defeating superstition. While optical magic and technology had a place in the eighteenth-century home, it was usually confined to the education and amusement of elites.[32] The 1830s saw a concerted effort to democratize optical literacy and optical play by bringing it into middle-class homes and bringing the middle classes into the hallowed halls of scientific endeavor—all for a reasonable fee. Over the course of the next few decades, the virtuality of optical media would become so common that it began to generate new ways of seeing and thinking about seeing in the culture at large. It is not a coincidence that many of the novels I discuss in this book were, like "How to See Pictures," published in the 1850s, roughly a generation after the optical popularization efforts of the 1830s. The ease with which "How to See Pictures" explains painting by reference to virtual spectatorship is not the result of the mere existence of optical toys but the cultural saturation of virtual aesthetics in everyday life.

My emphasis on optical media as mass culture is therefore notably different from the approach taken by Jonathan Crary in *Techniques of the Observer*, his landmark study of nineteenth-century technological vision.[33] Crary understands the technological reconstruction of visual experience undertaken by optical devices like the phenakistoscope and stereoscope to signal a new form of perception distinct to Western modernity, a regime that he calls "subjective vision." For him, the rise of virtual images creates a sudden and seismic rupture in the historical experience of vision. This line of argument has been justly critiqued for positing a single historical spectator without consideration to gender, race, or class and for overlooking the aesthetic and technological continuities between nineteenth-century technologies and earlier forms of visual media.[34] It also overstates the cultural significance of elite scientific discourse by relying for its primary evidence of epistemic transformation on a handful of men reporting on their laboratory discoveries. My book does not make the case that the invention of virtual image technologies overturned dominant models of visual perception by making vision untrustworthy for the first time in history. It makes the more modest and empirically supported claim that, by the mid-nineteenth century, the popularization of optical technologies that create virtual images and the democratization of theories of optical perception offered writers and showmen a new set of frameworks for thinking about aesthetic experience in terms of visual and perceptual mediation. The media I explore not only generated many ways of seeing virtual images but also many ways of thinking about seeing as a virtual experience. Instead of collapsing these different practices and ideas into a singular model for Victorian virtuality, my chapters survey a variety of virtual media imaginaries to show how they are distinct as well as some of the ways that they intersect.

My media archaeological approach to optical mass culture also distinguishes this book from existing studies of the virtual in Victorian fiction. The last fifteen years have seen a burst of scholarly works in Victorian studies that define the properties of Victorian fiction as forms of "virtuality," "virtual reality," "virtual travel," "virtual aesthetics," and "virtual play."[35] These terms are often defined in reference to contemporary digital media, internet culture, and video games to generate descriptive accounts of the fictionality of Victorian novels or the phenomenological affordances of narrative. For instance, Alison Byerly draws on contemporary formulations of virtual reality to conceptualize Victorian realism as a technology of "virtual travel" that facilitates "a transference of imaginative experience into a perception of physical experience" and "a projection of the self into a fictive environment."[36] Byerly's definition of "virtuality" is robust, particular, and induced from the media effects of both novels and travel media like guidebooks that "generate an almost physical sense of presence within the fictional world—a sense of locatedness and embodiment—that depends on a strategic positioning of the reader."[37] Not all accounts of Victorian virtuality are so crisp. Jules Law calls the virtual "a specific form of representation that both foregrounds and requires the mediation of technology"; John Plotz makes it synonymous with a state of "semi-detachment" that positions the reader of novels simultaneously in the real world and the world of imagination; and Timothy Gao defines it as "fictional experiences and actions, or fictional realities which can be experienced and acted upon."[38] As a media effect of Victorian novels, the properties of virtuality are difficult to distinguish from those of existing literary critical terms like "realism," "fictionality," "imagination," "representation," "reflexivity," and "mediation."

This book offers greater conceptual and historical precision by presenting the virtual as a category of image production and visual experience grounded in the optical culture of the mid-nineteenth century. This kind of precision also makes it possible to think more capaciously about the imaginative uses to which the virtual was put by novelists, showmen, travel writers, and scientific popularizers, from writers like George Eliot and Thomas Carlyle, who identified the media effects of the literary narrative with those of optical technology, to those like Elizabeth Gaskell and Wilkie Collins, who conceptualized the virtual as a framework for forms of civilizational affect and imperial ways of knowing. It may be true that "the categories underpinning our current concept of virtual reality were elaborated in the middle of the nineteenth century," as Law writes.[39] But rather than moving backward from this current concept, itself so slippery, so overdetermined, so impossible to define neatly, the five chapters that make up this book describe a Victorian aesthetic of the virtual without worrying too much about how it does or does not relate to the intensely technologically mediated world we live in today. I hope this refusal of historical determinism, as well as the delight this book takes in obscure, obsolete, and imaginary media experiences, makes my account of what the virtual *was* even more generative for readers who want to figure out what the virtual *is*.

Victorian Virtual Aesthetics: Five Ways

The five chapters of this book each offer an account of virtual aesthetics that I find at the intersection of nineteenth-century optical media culture and literary production. Each chapter centers on an optical media format or performance, a set of Victorian literary texts, and a political framework in which they resonate. Chapter 1 sets the scene for this study by arguing that scientific popularizers invented an aesthetic of the virtual when they sought to teach readers and audiences how to divorce the apprehension of optical illusions from the belief in magic. Through readings of popular scientific treatises and works on rational magic, I identify the construction of a discourse of virtual spectatorship that I call the pedagogy of disenchantment and analyze how it defined and justified virtual aesthetics according to a civilizational logic. The pedagogy of disenchantment mobilized the colonial, racial, and patriarchal specter of magic panic—or irrational and superstitious fear at the sight of virtual images—to portray disenchanted virtual spectatorship as a practice of epistemic self-sovereignty. We see this dynamic play out in *Cranford* (1853), Elizabeth Gaskell's novel about a community of unmarried and widowed women in northern England, in which a traveling magic show inspires a female-specific magic panic in the town. I argue, however, that Gaskell subverts what she reads as the masculinist pedagogy of disenchantment by exposing the patriarchal and racial logic that undergirds it. Instead portraying magic panic as an intrinsically feminized moral and intellectual failing, the novel makes visible the ways that the pedagogy of disenchantment deployed the aesthetics of optical magic in the service of imperial domination.

The next two chapters continue to explore the relationship between virtual aesthetics and empire by asking how imaginary virtual media expressed the cultural fantasy of seeing across time and space. Chapter 2 centers on an Egyptian magic trick popularized in English letters by the Egyptologist and travel writer Edward William Lane. The mirror of ink supposedly allowed a boy to see images of dead or absent persons in a drop of ink poured into his hand, an illusion that Lane immediately understood through the technological framework of lens- and mirror-based optical magic. In the hands of Victorian writers and thinkers like Harriet Martineau and Richard Francis Burton, the mirror of ink was explained through sciences of mind like mesmerism, hypnotism, clairvoyance, and telepathy that enable persons to see things that are not there in the form of mental images. By reading these imperial and racializing constructions of the mirror of ink as a medium for virtual sight, I argue that it also generated an imaginary of the novel as a technology of virtual visual experience. In *Adam Bede* (1859), a novel that many literary scholars read as a theory of realist verisimilitude, George Eliot compares the reader's visualization of the diegesis to the traveler's visualizations in the mirror of ink. In other words, like Eliot's more experimental gothic tale *The Lifted Veil*, *Adam Bede* brings together the optical, mesmeric, and imperial attributes of the mirror of ink to imagine the realist novel as a virtual technology that makes the reader see things that are not there.

Chapter 3 continues this exploration of virtual aesthetics as an extension of vision—what H. G. Wells, in a short story from 1896, calls "real vision at a distance"—this time by focusing on the imaginary affordances of a real object. In 1851, a legendary Indian diamond called the Koh-i-noor was put on display in the Crystal Palace as part of the Great Exhibition. By tracing the history of audience disappointment with the diamond exhibit (audience members were disappointed by the Koh-i-noor's reported refusal to sparkle or shine), I excavate a discourse of diamonds as optical media that operate through the reflection and refraction of light and argue that it fueled an imaginary of colonial diamonds as media for virtual contact with the scenes of empire. This imaginary is made explicit in two literary works inspired by the display of the Koh-i-noor at the Great Exhibition. "The Diamond Lens" (1859), a short story by the Irish American writer Fitz-James O'Brien, imagines a plundered colonial diamond that is ground into a microscopic lens so powerful it reveals a world inside a drop of water. In *The Moonstone* (1868), Wilkie Collins' detective mystery, a stolen Indian diamond intoxicates its English spectators, creating frightening and pleasurable new visions and sensations. Both stories appropriate the effects of real optical devices like the stereoscope to reimagine the Koh-i-noor as a technological optical medium that acts as a visual prosthetic for the apprehension of colonial spaces through its sparkling surfaces and virtual depths.

The final chapters of the book move from the visual culture of empire to ask how virtual aesthetics shaped representations of the nation. Chapter 4 asks how the phantasmagoria—one of the most famous optical shows of the nineteenth century—became a figure for French revolutionary history and populist nationalism in both French and British thought. Invented in Paris on the cusp of the Reign of Terror, the phantasmagoria used a hidden magic lantern in a dark room to project images that seemed to move among the audience. In the context of mass violence and public execution, the phantasmagoria was often portrayed as a ghostly assembly where the living could encounter the historical dead returning to life. I trace the genealogy of the phantasmagoria as a figure for the historical return of the repressed in the work of three men who wrote about the French Revolution: Étienne-Gaspard Robertson, the Belgian showman who claimed credit as the inventor of the phantasmagoria in Paris and portrayed his spectral moving images as a resurrection of those killed in the revolution; Thomas Carlyle, who used the phantasmagoria as a figure for revolutionary historical change in *The French Revolution: A History*; and Charles Dickens, who read both Robertson and Carlyle closely before writing *A Tale of Two Cities*, a novel set during the Reign of Terror in which the historical past is "recalled to life" in ghostly form. All three writers conceptualize nationalism and national history in phantasmagorical terms.

Chapter 5 turns to the invention of moving pictures in spinning optical toys. I focus on the phenakistoscope, the first toy to create virtual moving images in a circular and repeating format, an effect that would be reproduced over the course of the century in new devices like the zoetrope and praxinoscope. These are typically read as precinematic media that led to the creation of cinema through their transformation of static pictures into an unbroken series of virtual moving images. I argue that this perspective overlooks a fundamental fact about the history of moving pictures: that it does not begin with the unfolding linear action we associate with the cinema but instead with the representation of repetitive and cyclical action. This format, with its distinctly ahistorical temporality, deserves to be theorized on its own terms. By reading the phenakistoscope alongside the novels and short stories of Thomas Hardy and Charlie Chaplin's *Modern Times* (1934), I trace an alternative genealogy of moving pictures focused on the virtual aesthetics of the loop and argue that the phenakistoscope's circular format gave rise to an imaginary of capitalist labor structured by recursion and repetition that challenged modernity's logic of industrial progress. After several chapters tracing the use of virtual aesthetics to represent the far reaches of empire, express Orientalist imaginaries, and stage the epic dramas of nineteenth-century European history, Hardy returns us to where we began with *Cranford* in chapter 1: the hyperlocal time and place of mid-century provincial England. His engagement with optical toys and the emergent culture of cinema offers us a virtual aesthetics of everyday life.

A brief epilogue returns us to the film with which we began—Auguste and Louis Lumière's *Arrival of a Train at La Ciotat*, a film that is commonly understood to announce the arrival of cinema on the world stage. By this point, I hope you will be able to see cinema's arrival in a new way. Rather than a radical break with the technological and visual culture of the nineteenth century, my book recontextualizes cinema as an epiphenomenon of Victorian virtual aesthetics. Cinema is one outcome of the vibrant nineteenth-century cultural imaginary of the virtual—one format out of many that turned the experience of seeing things that are not there into a paradigmatic expression of Western modernity.

Chapter 1

Magic Panic

The Pedagogy of Disenchantment

There is nothing more familiar to us today than looking at things that are not there. Between our phones and computers and the long history of cinema and television, we are thoroughly acculturated to a technological visual regime based on moving, dynamic, and mimetic virtual images. But in the early nineteenth century, as the field of physiological optics grew and optical technology became more popular and accessible, how people should engage in the spectatorship of virtual images and understand the presence of optical illusion in ordinary perceptual experience and everyday life were vast, open questions. This chapter investigates the construction of a popular scientific discourse of virtual spectatorship that I call the pedagogy of disenchantment, which defined and justified virtual aesthetics according to a civilizational logic. "Pedagogy of disenchantment" is my term for the project of cultivating modern and rational spectators through the eradication of superstition and supernatural belief and the development of practices of reflexivity and skepticism toward visual evidence. This pedagogy not only sought to teach spectators how to see and respond cognitively and emotionally to virtual images; it also advanced the European civilizational logic with which these competencies were imbricated.

This approach reformulates a key framework in nineteenth-century media history. Since the late 1980s, historians of film and media have argued forcefully that Victorian audiences were sophisticated and discerning, drawn to virtual images for their aesthetics of wonder and astonishment.[1] For example, in a foundational essay, Tom Gunning challenged the myth of the naïve spectator of early cinema that I invoked in the introduction of this book, a spectator "whose reaction to the image is one of simple belief and panic" and whose encounter with virtual images reduces them "to a state usually attributed to savages in their primal encounter with the advanced technology of Western colonialists, howling and fleeing in impotent terror before the power of the machine."[2] For Gunning, this myth of early film spectatorship is an ideological construction that supports the apparatus theory of cinema as a disciplinary tool wielded against passive, complacent, and easily manipulated subjects. However, media historians tend to overlook the ways that the disenchanted virtual spectatorship that Gunning ascribes to early film audiences was itself an ideological construction. If magic panic is associated with "savages," as Gunning suggests and as this chapter's historical archive will bear out, then disenchantment was not merely a fact of Victorian spectatorship but a profoundly troubling civilizational ideal.[3]

The intention of this chapter is not to challenge the idea that nineteenth-century spectators were disenchanted but to reframe the terms of the conversation.[4] Rather than asking how spectators responded to virtual images, a question that risks flattening all Victorian audiences into a single historical type, I ask how spectators were being trained to respond to virtual images and what this tells us about the ways that virtual aesthetics was theorized in the first half of the nineteenth century. Across a rangy archive that includes scientific treatises, books of magic tricks, cartoons, and fiction, the pedagogy of disenchantment turned magical and optical spectatorship into an interpretive process that could go one of two ways. The first was toward recognition of an illusion as such, a form of self-reflexivity that relies on a basic understanding of the capacity of prestidigitators and optical conjurers to trick the eye. This disenchanted interpretation of an illusion aligned the capacity to be entertained—to enjoy trickery, as an aesthetically and perceptually amusing experience—with scientific rationalism, bourgeois respectability, and Western modernity. The second, considered primitive and dangerous, was an inability to recognize the technical or technological origins of an illusion, an intellectual failure that leads ineluctably to belief in the supernatural origins of the illusion and an infantile state of panic. We need not take these two interpretative stances at face value, as accurate representations of actual experiences of historical spectatorship. Disenchantment and superstition can clearly coexist, as we will see in numerous examples scattered across this book.[5] Instead of reproducing the dichotomy between the rational and irrational, and between disenchantment and superstition, this chapter considers why nineteenth-century British writers, showmen, and scientific popularizers were so committed to presenting virtual spectatorship in dichotomous terms. When reframed in this way, it becomes clear that scientific and literary mobilizations of the pedagogy of disenchantment constructed the aesthetic appreciation of virtual images as a simultaneously practical and metaphorical form of sovereignty, one that served to justify colonial and patriarchal regimes of discipline and control.

To make this case, the chapter centers on two early to mid-nineteenth-century discussions of the pedagogy of disenchantment in magic spectatorship. The first is *Letters on Natural Magic* (1832), the seminal nineteenth-century treatise on scientific and technological magic that advances what I describe as the first fully fledged theory of virtual aesthetics. Written by the optical inventor and scientific popularizer David Brewster, *Letters on Natural Magic* argued that disenchanted spectators—spectators both divested of supernatural belief and cognizant of the optical principles undergirding visual illusions—are uniquely capable of deriving aesthetic pleasure from virtual images. For Brewster, being entertained requires protecting oneself from fraud and imposture, turning the aesthetic experience of virtual images into both a sign and expression of political agency and discernment. In this context, superstitious responses like panic, confusion, and fear mark one as unable to govern oneself in the modern world and as susceptible to despotism and tyranny. While Brewster nominally presents virtual spectatorship as accessible to any person willing to be taught, his version of virtual aesthetics is marked by a gendered and racial colonial imagination that contrasts sovereign individuals with weak dependents.

This gender and racial subtext is made explicit in *Cranford* (1853). Written by Elizabeth Gaskell for Charles Dickens's weekly magazine *Household Words*, *Cranford* is an episodic novel that concerns the lifeways and beliefs of a group of genteel women in a small northern English town in the first half of the nineteenth century. Rarely discussed in scholarship on the novel is what I consider its centerpiece: a three-chapter narrative arc concerning the arrival of a mysterious Oriental conjurer and the outsized panic of the townswomen after witnessing his rather old-fashioned magic tricks.[6] I read these chapters as a response to and critique of *Letters on Natural Magic*. By invoking and ultimately subverting the well-trod trope of female magic panic, Gaskell exposes the patriarchal and colonial logic undergirding Brewster's account of virtual aesthetics. Instead of making fun of the women for their insufficiently rational response to the magic show or portraying their panic as a moral and intellectual failing, the novel suggests that disenchanted magic, with its ostensibly antidespotic and pedagogical design, is deployed as a means of perceptual and social control. In other words, the novel makes visible the ways that the pedagogy of disenchantment simultaneously claimed moral superiority over native magic for its supposedly modern, technological rationality and deployed Western magic as a disciplinary regime of civilizational acculturation.

I begin this chapter with the emergence of magic's pedagogy of disenchantment in the rise of optical conjuring and the spread of rational recreations from an elite practice to a mainstream discourse, showing how these trends come together in *Letters on Natural Magic*. I then turn to the ways that Brewster situates disenchantment in an ideological framework that presents the aesthetic appreciation of virtual images as a moral and epistemic virtue and trace the influence of his thinking on the rise of commercial museums of science and gendered and colonial discourses of magic spectatorship. Next, I introduce *Cranford* as an example of one of those discourses of magic spectatorship and argue that it shows the pedagogy of disenchantment at work in everyday life. I conclude with an analysis of how the novel responds to *Letters on Natural Magic* by challenging the authoritarian impulse lurking within the pedagogy of disenchantment's civilizational logic.

A Pedagogy of Disenchantment

By some counts, the single most important French campaign against anticolonial resistance in Algeria was a magic show. In 1856, the renowned French illusionist Jean-Eugène Robert-Houdin arrived in Algiers at the invitation of army colonel François-Edouard Neveu, political director of the Bureau of Arab Affairs, to perform two nights of magic shows for an audience of Arab elites.[7] Neveu believed that these elites were under the sway of the *marabouts*, Muslim mystics and miracle workers branded by the French as charlatans and accused of using their supernatural authority to foment revolt against colonial rule. Robert-Houdin's mission was to discredit the supernatural claims of the *marabouts* through a performance of the modern, technological magic he had already made famous in Europe. Or, as Robert-Houdin put it in his memoir *Confidences d'un prestidigitateur* (1858), "it was hoped, with reason, that my performances would lead the Arabs to understand that the marabouts' trickery is naught but simple child's play," a process that "naturally . . . entailed demonstrating our superiority in everything."[8] While there is no reliable evidence that the magic shows had their desired effect, most extant textual records laud its resounding success in quelling Indigenous resistance and, according to one French Algerian newspaper, "mov[ing] colonization forward twenty years."[9] Robert-Houdin himself crowed about his ability to deceive his audience with pretended miracles. His memoir justified colonial rule by presenting Algerians as childlike and primitive, "besought by an indescribable terror" that led them to jump out of their seats and frantically fight for the exit.[10]

Where did this remarkably strange idea of military-sponsored stage magic come from? Why did French colonial administrators believe that a magician could secure colonial rule in a violent period of anticolonial resistance? The answers to these questions can be found in the nineteenth-century cultural discourse that I call the pedagogy of disenchantment. Decades before Robert-Houdin appeared on stage in Algiers, he and other magicians, trick designers, showmen, and scientific popularizers were already working to legitimize magic as a bourgeois Western entertainment by presenting magic performance as an essentially pedagogical method of exposing charlatanism, imposture, and pretense to occult powers. Like Robert-Houdin, the British figures I discuss in this chapter routinely mobilized a construction of "magic panic," generally attributed to feminized and racialized audiences, against which they could articulate a mode of reasoned, pleasurable aesthetic appreciation of virtual images. The following pages turn to the emergence of nineteenth-century optical magic on stage and in popularizing texts to tell the story of how the pedagogy of disenchantment constructed virtual aesthetics in relation to patriarchal and colonial ideals of sovereignty.

In the mid-1850s, when Robert-Houdin traveled to Algeria at the invitation of colonial administrators, Western stage magic was in its golden age. Victorian magic shows were modern, sophisticated entertainments based on Enlightenment principles of rationality and skepticism; magicians were rebranded as "professors" and marketed as inventors of patented technology in a signal of their newly bourgeois respectability and professionalism.[11] Many early and mid-nineteenth-century magicians still specialized in sleight-of-hand tricks that used visual misdirection. The term "sleight of hand" as well as its nineteenth-century synonyms "legerdemain" and "prestidigitation" convey the origin of these illusions in manual skills of dexterity and manipulation—what Robert-Houdin called the art of calm yet agile hands.[12] During this same period, however, Victorian magic came increasingly to rely not only on nimble hands and quick fingers but also on optical apparatuses. Incorporating existing media like magic lanterns and bespoke devices composed of mirrors, glass, and projected light, mid-nineteenth-century magic rapidly became an optical art, one based in a deepening knowledge of human eyesight; optical principles of light, reflection, and refraction; and "how people react to what they see (or think they see)."[13] Historian of magic Jim Steinmeyer has termed this second kind of magic "optical conjuring" for its application of optical principles and media to magic performance.[14]

Victorian optical conjuring was a style of stage magic that sought not only to entertain the eye but also to cultivate the mind by teaching audiences the optical principles through which the eye was deceived. At the most basic level, optical conjurers harnessed the properties of light and glass to make things appear and disappear on stage. The most famous example is Pepper's Ghost, so-named for John Henry Pepper, showman at and later director of the Royal Polytechnic Institution in London where the illusion was first exhibited in 1861 and one of the trick's two inventors along with Henry Dircks. Pepper's Ghost not only made "ghosts" appear—materializing and dematerializing before the audience—but allowed them to interact with actors on the stage. To create lifelike ghosts, Pepper refined Dircks's original model for what he called his "Dircksian Phantasmagoria" by placing a large pane of glass in front of the stage and tilted 45 degrees toward the audience. The angle of the glass and its flawless transparency rendered it invisible to anyone in the seats. When an oxyhydrogen lantern was trained on an actor beneath the stage, the glass acted as a mirror by reflecting the actor to produce a remarkably lifelike spectral image of a human being (figure 1.1). The reflection was "transparent and ghostly and would appear at a distance behind the glass equal to the actor's distance from the front of the glass," meaning that the spectral image appeared to move around the stage alongside the flesh-and-blood actors.[15] When all the actors were synchronized, this image—a perfectly uncanny theatrical ghost—could interact with the characters on stage.

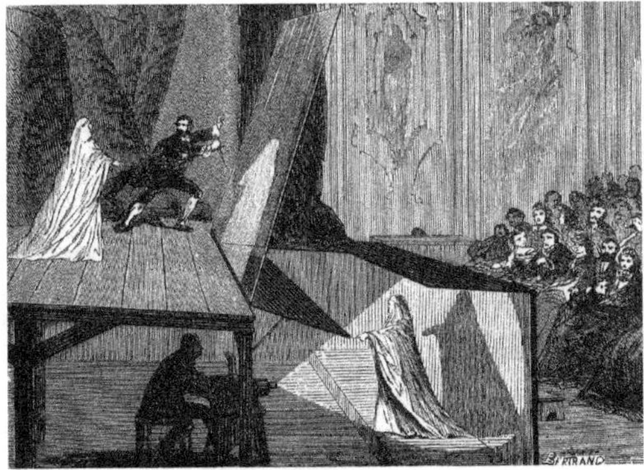

FIGURE 1.1. Pepper's Ghost. *Le Monde Illustré*, 1862.

Dircks' and Pepper's ghost illusion marks the beginning of a half century of spectral appearances and disappearances on the stage. The Ghost's appearance in an 1862 theatrical adaptation of Dickens's "The Haunted Man" at the Polytechnic included effects like a glowing skeleton materializing out of thin air, "hazy at first, then brighter and brighter, until it seemed to glow in a transparent, unearthly way"; a character leaving his chair only to "leave his own glowing, transparent soul behind"; and actors walking through walls.[16] While Pepper leased his patent for the Ghost across Britain and the United States, variations on his pane-of-glass technique proliferated and boasted improvements to the overall illusion. In the 1890s, the Cabaret du Néant in Montmartre, Paris, included an "x-ray illusion" based on the Pepper's Ghost technique in which a spectator, placed in an open coffin on the stage, is shown to transform into his own skeleton.[17] Shortly after the premier of Pepper's Ghost, the magician Colonel Stodare exhibited "The Sphinx," in which a head adorned with Egyptian headdress and detached from a body appeared on a small table and spoke to audiences at the Egyptian Hall. Invented by Thomas Tobin, this illusion used imperceptible mirrors beneath the table to reverse Pepper's Ghost by making the body of the actor playing the Sphinx disappear.[18] While these tricks are part of a long history of theatrical special effects, optical conjuring is distinct from the better-known tradition of trapdoors and hidden compartments used to make people appear and disappear on stage in that its effects rely on virtual images. Optical conjuring used virtual images to amuse spectators with things that are not really there.

Pepper's Ghost may be the clearest, best-known, and most influential example of optical conjuring, but the use of mirrors and glass to create virtual images has a long and vital history that stretches back to the sixteenth century. Reginald Scot's *The Discoverie of Witchcraft* (1584) first distinguished between two forms of magic, witchcraft and "juggling," an archaic term for conjuring. Unlike witchcraft, the existence of which Scot doubted, juggling was not supernatural or occult but an entertaining practice based on manual skill and ingenious devices performed "to the delight of the beholder."[19] Early modern conjurers like Giambattista Della Porta and Athanasius Kircher took on the identity of "natural magician," or the magician who reveals the wonders of nature, inventing in the process a new kind of optical magic that used lenses and mirrors to create fantastical virtual images.[20] In his treatise *Magia Naturalis* (1558), published in English as *Natural Magick* in 1658, the inventor and showman Della Porta described the way a polished glass window can reflect things into a room that are actually outside the room—the basis of Pepper's Ghost. If a spectator is standing outside and looking into the window, objects arranged out of his sightline behind or above him could appear to be inside. He called this magic trick "How we may see in a Chamber things that are not."[21]

Pepper's Ghost drew on a long tradition of optical entertainment that represented virtual images as ghosts in order to advance an antisupernatural pedagogy. Beginning in the late eighteenth century, optical magic shows like the phantasmagoria—a precursor to Pepper's Ghost that created spectral illusions using a hidden magic lantern—designed optical technological illusions that resembled ghosts, presenting effects that seemed supernatural while avowing their nonsupernatural origin. As the phantasmagoria showman Paul Philidor put it to his audiences, "I will not show you ghosts, because there are no such things; but I will produce before you enactments and images. . . . I do not wish to deceive you; but I will astonish you."[22] Shows like the phantasmagoria did not manufacture belief in the supernatural but rather generated what Gunning calls "entertaining confusion."[23] As one French spectator of the phantasmagoria wrote in 1800, "Reason has told you well that these things are mere phantoms, catoptric tricks devised with artistry . . . [yet] we believe ourselves to be transported into another world and another century."[24] I will discuss the phantasmagoria and its legacy in more detail in chapter 4. For now, I wish simply to highlight the way Victorian optical entertainers disavowed supernatural agency while capitalizing on the allure of visual illusion to help produce a disenchanted audience capable of understanding that the tricks are not real. Pepper's Ghost, for example, was advertised as "A Strange Lecture" with Professor Pepper, a showman known for his lecture-type demonstrations, performing alongside a magic lantern and other optical devices to emphasize the scientific and technological context for the Ghost illusion.[25] These shows played out as a hermeneutic game in which discerning spectators were encouraged to marshal their knowledge of technology, stagecraft, optics, and the human eye to wonder at how the tricks were achieved.

Letters on Natural Magic (1832)

We can see already see that Robert-Houdin's Algerian magic show participated in an evolving tradition of magic performance that considered the visual pleasures of optical technology and illusion to be means for demystification. But how did this tradition link visual pleasure and disenchanted spectatorship with the exercise of sovereignty? To answer this, I turn to what I consider the definitive formulation of optical magic's pedagogy of disenchantment in the early nineteenth-century writings of Sir David Brewster. An optical inventor and tireless scientific popularizer, Brewster will appear across the chapters of this book because, from the beginning of his career at the turn of the century until his death in 1868, he was involved with many of the most popular nineteenth-century optical toys, exhibitions, and entertainments. If his name is known today, it is as the inventor of what were arguably the two most beloved optical toys of the nineteenth century. His kaleidoscope, a coinage from Ancient Greek roots that literally means "observation of beautiful forms," was a tube that combined tilted mirrors with colorful pieces of glass to create ever-changing symmetrical views, while his lenticular stereoscope—a streamlined version of Charles Wheatstone's cumbersome tabletop device—transformed the way Victorians experienced photography by making it simple and accessible to view images in stereo.

Less well known is Brewster's copious body of writing that transformed the way people played with optical instruments and experienced optical shows. *Letters on Natural Magic* (1832) was the most influential of these volumes. First published in London by John Murray as part of Murray's Family Library, a collection of affordable and educational texts for the family reading market, *Letters on Natural Magic* introduced the scientific and technological origins of apparently magical phenomena to a mass audience. It was a treatise on illusions, including those caused by acoustics, hydrostatics, and mechanics, but its primary concern was with optical illusions. Of all the sciences, Brewster wrote, "Optics is the most fertile in marvelous expedients."[26] As a result, it is "the principal seat of the supernatural," proliferating visual phenomena that seem to be occult in nature.[27] What Brewster aimed to teach his readers was how to experience the beauty and wonder of such supernatural-seeming visual phenomena by correctly identifying their source in physiological or technological optics. Like his optical toys, which he promoted for their capacity for "rational amusement," *Letters on Natural Magic* views optical instruction and aesthetic pleasure as inextricable. I read this text as the nineteenth century's first theory of virtual aesthetics, which argues that optical literacy and antisupernaturalism are preconditions for the aesthetic enjoyment of virtual images.

Letters on Natural Magic united two strands of popular scientific writing. The first was a growing body of scientific literature that sought to explain the optical, physiological, and technological origins of what were called apparitions or spectral illusions, visual perceptions that cannot be empirically verified. The theory of apparitions was understood as a means of driving ghost belief out of Britain. John Ferriar's *An Essay Towards the Theory of Apparitions* (1813) and Samuel Hibbert's *Sketches of the Philosophy of Apparitions; or, an Attempt to Trace Such Illusions to Their Physical Causes* (1824) popularized scientific arguments against the existence of ghosts by arguing that apparitions were the result of ocular deceptions inherent to the human eye. Ferriar and Hibbert were both physicians, and they claimed that apparitions could be caused not only by overexcited imaginations and vivid memories but also by indigestion and diseases of the stomach, a theory that is probably best remembered today through Scrooge's retort to Marley's ghost in *A Christmas Carol* that he is nothing but "an undigested bit of beef, a blot of mustard, a crumb of cheese, a fragment of an undone potato."[28]

Letters on Natural Magic opens with a discussion of apparitions meant to train readers in how and why such illusions occur and to empower them to understand their own experiences of apparition through a demystifying scientific frame. Its pedagogical agenda was not to teach readers how not to see apparitions, which was considered an unavoidable condition of human vision, but rather to teach readers how to see apparitions without believing that they are ghosts.[29] In directing this antisupernatural pedagogy toward the working- and middle-class readership of Murray's Family Library, *Letters on Natural Magic* was a self-improvement tract invested in social change through the diffusion of scientific knowledge.

In addition to the scientific literature on apparitions, Brewster wrote as part of an Enlightenment tradition of magic demystification known as rational recreations. Inspired by John Locke's promotion of instructive scientific games for children's education, rational recreations were science experiments and conjuring tricks that children and their guardians could perform at home to learn about subjects like optics, chromatics, hydrostatics, and pyrotechnics through what Barbara Stafford calls the "participatory enactment" of scientific practice.[30] Families could purchase portable instruments like microscopes and magic lanterns along with affordable illustrated books of experiments that children could conduct with their new instruments and thus harness the playful allure of conjuring and the pleasures of visual illusion to make scientific knowledge easily comprehensible.[31] Rational recreations were imagined to protect individuals and, by extension, the nation, from despotism, imposture, and fraud by training them in practices of critical thinking and scientific rationality. For instance, William Hooper's four-volume set *Rational Recreations* promised to teach the reader "a knowledge of his own ignorance" through easy and fun experiments with sensational-sounding names like "the magician's mirrors," "the marvelous portrait," "the burning fountain," and "winter changed into spring."[32] Hooper's instructions on creating catoptric, anamorphic, and metamorphic virtual images and lessons on how to use invisible ink and perform card tricks were meant to show the reader "the fallacy of what he thought most certain, the evidence of the senses" and enable him to "divest himself of those prepossessions, from whence so many of the evils of life proceed."[33] Like *Rational Recreations*, *Letters on Natural Magic* is a collection of educational magic tricks that readers can perform at home. It advanced the mandate of defeating superstition by teaching readers about the tricky relationship between reality and the senses and empowering them to think and act self-reflexively.

What distinguishes Brewster's work within both these traditions of physiological optics and rational recreations is his commitment to theorizing and advocating for a kind of aesthetic experience distinct to the apprehension of virtual images. For example, an early chapter offers the medical case study of a "Mrs. A.," in fact the wife of the Edinburgh doctor John Abercrombie, whom Brewster treated when she was suffering from spectral illusions of dead and absent relatives. While some of the apparitions were acoustic only, most were visible and appeared to her with "all the vivid coloring and apparent reality of life."[34] Later, when laying out his design of a catoptrical phantasmagoria, Brewster encourages his readers to create similar apparitions technologically: a bright light-source trained on a bust or portrait of "an absent or dead friend" and placed before a concave mirror will create a virtual image very much like Mrs. Abercrombie's apparitions that can be projected on air or smoke. Her diseased visions become the model for an amusing and impressive technological entertainment: when "the instruments of illusion are themselves concealed," he writes, "even those who know the deception, and perfectly understand its principles, are not a little surprised as its effects."[35] Here, his project of explaining the theory of apparitions and encouraging readers to learn about vision through hands-on experiments transcends the purposes of education. He is clearly fascinated—even intoxicated—by the wonder of optics. We can see this aesthetic impulse from the beginning of Brewster's career. For instance, Stafford notes that Brewster's *Treatise on the Kaleidoscope* (1817) shows a "baroque penchant" for creating and exhibiting beautiful forms that Enlightenment visual education generally maligned.[36] More than a love of beauty, *Letters on Natural Magic* reveals Brewster's flair for showmanship.[37] He not only lays out experiments that teach optical principles, but he continually improves upon existing technological design with the aim of creating more entertaining virtual images and generating greater novelty ("surprise") among educated spectators, those who "know the deception."

For Brewster, virtual aesthetics is predicated on disenchantment and disbelief—on "know[ing] the deception" and "understand[ing] its principles." Disenchantment is what distinguishes an optical spectator from a scared person seeing a ghost. For a person who believes in the supernatural, an apparition is not an image—it is an occult presence, a visitation. Their experience is not aesthetic but an encounter with the living dead. Only a thorough disbelief in the supernatural frees the spectator to have an aesthetic experience of virtual images—to appreciate their beauty, to marvel at their lifelikeness, and to wonder at their uncanny appearance. In this sense, optical education serves a different function for Brewster than it did for Hooper. Hooper wanted to teach his readers to distrust the evidence of their senses and thus avoid succumbing to supernatural belief; Brewster additionally believes that these competencies are important because they make possible new kinds of visual pleasure. The basic optical literacy that he teaches in *Letters on Natural Magic* is meant to enable a new form of aesthetic playfulness that relies on an active and educated eye and a commitment to tracing visual phenomena to their material origins. Although his focus is on the appreciation of technologically produced virtual images, Brewster also believed that spectral illusions resulting from "bodily indisposition"—the digestive issues that his forebears Ferriar and Hibbert cited as the cause of apparitions—could be a source of aesthetic pleasure.[38] When one understands their physiological origins and correctly identifies them as symptoms of illness, he writes, "spectral apparitions are stripped of all their terror." It then becomes possible to "deriv[e] pleasure from the contemplation" even of the most "alarming" apparitions.[39] Like scientific education, diagnosis serves the purposes of entertainment.

Whether someone could be entertained by virtual images had inherently political stakes. For Brewster, the opposite of entertainment was not boredom or displeasure but submission to despotic power. This point of view did not originate with Brewster. In *Rational Recreations*, Hooper wrote that his book was an antidote for those who have indulged in "slavish submission to their own tyrannic passions." Both the fraudulence of the senses and the potential deceits that could be exercised on the senses by others are metaphorically depicted as forms of slavery from which one can be freed by the practice of rational recreations. Brewster's argument in *Letters on Natural Magic* is even more specific. He decries the use of optical illusions by those in power—governments, religious orders—in the service of supernatural imposture, while lauding the experience of being entertained by optical illusions as both the basis for and an expression of epistemic liberty. Writing about "the tyrants of antiquity" who "rule[d] with the delegated authority of heaven"—a charge that he also levels against the Catholic Church—Brewster describes "a dark conspiracy to deceive and enslave their species" exercised by princes, priests, and sages through the use of virtual images.[40] Because it requires practices of disenchantment and demystification, Brewster views the aesthetic experience of virtual images as a practice of sovereignty that can protect individuals from becoming epistemically and politically enslaved or, as he describes it elsewhere, from becoming "the dupe of preconcerted imposture—the slave of [their] own ignorance—the prostrate vassal of power and superstition."[41] Here, "dupe" is another word for "slave" or "vassal"; to be duped is to be made politically subordinate and stripped of legal rights. To be entertained by virtual images is to practice a form of self-government that thwarts and defies would-be tyrants and despots, turning their supernatural impostures into pleasing and amusing conjuring tricks. As an aesthetic experience, virtuality is an expression of political agency and discernment.

These oppositional constructions—the self-reflexive spectator and the dupe, the optical conjurer and the slave—have patriarchal and colonial connotations that are built into the popular scientific imaginary of the period. More than half a century before *Letters on Natural Magic*, Hooper had presented visual education as a protection against the feminized and racialized threat of sensory experience, a "passion" at once "slavish" and "tyrannic." Rational recreations were a masculinizing bulwark against the decadence of the senses, a patriarchal and colonial assertion of intellectual sovereignty over one's own primitive impulses. Brewster reproduces this logic in *Letters on Natural Magic* when he describes the superstitious person as a "slave" and "prostrate vassal." Brewster's fixation on forms of political and religious imposture exceeds Hooper's, however, and reveals distinct political ambitions and anxieties. *Letters on Natural Magic* was published the same year as the Reform Act of 1832, which extended citizenship rights to a new class of men including small landowners, householders, and shop owners and for the first time in written law formally barred women from the franchise. While his manifest concern is with ancient governments, Brewster's agenda of democratizing the rational recreation of optical play—what had been in the eighteenth century an elite set of practices and entertainments—comes at a time when a newly enfranchised male population were entrusted with stewardship of the nation and, by extension, the empire. Writing about the early American republic, Wendy Bellion argues that technologies of optical illusion cultivated citizenship by inaugurating "a cultural dialectic of deceit and discernment" that "challenged Americans to demonstrate their perceptual aptitude."[42] In this context, perceptual aptitude ensures political agency and "able citizenship."[43] During a period when liberal political theorists in Britain argued that "progress was a matter of increasing rationality and cognitive capacity," playing with optical technology and experiencing artful optical deceptions without being deceived was a kind of civilizational training that prepared Victorian men for the responsibility of the franchise.[44]

Brewster's concern with magic's use for the "dark conspiracy . . . to enslave" not only evokes the political reforms that were being debated and implemented in the early 1830s but also reflects their relationship to Britain's continued use of slavery in its colonies and violent practices of colonial conquest. The threat of being "enslaved" to despotic power simultaneously expresses British anxieties about the ambitions of neighboring European empires in the wake of the Napoleonic wars and the political philosophy that Jennifer Pitts calls imperial liberalism. Imperial liberalism combined a commitment to individual liberties with a belief in "civilizing despotism," or the selective use of despotism as a tool of colonial conquest.[45] The rationale of civilizing despotism, which was firmly entrenched in British politics by the 1830s, was that the peoples Britain marked for enslavement and colonization were "regarded as being at 'earlier' stages of development" than modern and enlightened Westerners, "cognitively limited," "mired in error and enslaved to superstition," and therefore "incapable of participation in their own government."[46] Brewster's discussion of ancient despotic conspiracies invokes the colonial stereotype of backward and barbaric nations. If his virtual aesthetics is characterized by the same practices of rationality and discernment necessary for citizenship, it also rehearses the epistemological justifications for empire.

The Boy Conjurer and the Foolish Woman

The civilizational agenda implicit in Brewster's optical pedagogy was made explicit by John Henry Pepper. Pepper was the optical entertainer and inventor who lent his name to the ghost illusion. Just as he put Brewster's pedagogy of disenchantment to work as lecturer at, and later director of, the Royal Polytechnic Institution, Pepper authored a children's book of scientific games and experiments in the tradition of *Letters on Natural Magic* and *Rational Recreations*. However, *The Boy's Playbook of Science* (1860) distinguished itself from the work of Brewster and Hooper in addressing itself specifically to a male readership that it metonymized as "Young England." Pepper thus focused explicitly on the moral and intellectual improvement of middle-class boys, a project that he viewed as integral to nation building and the future of Britain's empire.[47] "Young England" was exhorted to "nourish the desire for the acquisition of 'scientific knowledge'" as "a useful ally" in "the mental race he has to run with the educated of his own and of other nations," a race that Pepper further characterized as "'The Battle of Life.'" While Pepper's explicit gendering of scientific learning as a masculine endeavor seems to break from the gender agnosticism of Hooper and Brewster's work, which imagined both male and female readers, it also simply reveals what was implicit in these earlier works. Pepper strips away Brewster's meditations on scientific learning as a means to aesthetic pleasure to reveal what was always underneath: scientific learning as a "useful ally" in the deliberative masculine work of national and imperial governance. By presenting scientific education as a counterpart to "manly sports," Pepper defines science as a distinctly masculine recreation that is necessary for a boy's coming of age as a productive steward of empire. Cultivating the boy conjurer is tantamount to cultivating imperial progress.

The implicit gendering of Brewster's pedagogy of disenchantment was also made explicit in a subgenre of comic essays, stories, and cartoons that proliferated in the second half of the nineteenth century. These texts, which I call satires of superstition, sought to illustrate the importance of disenchanted spectatorship by the negative example of bad female spectators whose magic panic disrupts the respectable bourgeois space of the lecture hall. For example, in an essay called "A Shilling's Worth of Science" (1850), published in *Household Words* in its first year of circulation, the narrator tours the Royal Polytechnic Institution while bemoaning his "fate to sit next to two old ladies" at a lecture on "Magnetism and Electricity" who "seemed to be very incredulous about the whole business":

> "If heat and light are the same thing," asked one, "why don't a flame come out at the spout of a boiling tea kettle?"
>
> "The steam," answered the other, "may account for that."
>
> "Hush!" cried somebody behind them; and the ladies were silent; but it was plain they thought Voltaic Electricity had something to do with conjuring, and that the lecturer might be a professor of Magic.[48]

The trope of foolish women misinterpreting a scientific lecture-demonstration as a magic show had wide currency in the second half of the nineteenth century. In "Mrs. Brown Visits the Polytechnic" (1871), a story written by the English humorist George Rose under his pen name Arthur Sketchley, Mrs. Brown is invited to tag along to the Royal Polytechnic Institution when "young Trueman," a civil engineer set to marry her friend's daughter Mary-Ann, takes Mary-Ann to the Polytechnic "for to improve 'er mind."[49] But Mrs. Brown's mind, marked as inferior by her working-class accent, is not improved by any of the Polytechnic's many spectacular exhibitions. "There's too much in that Pollyntechnic for one human brain to stand," she complains, "as is downright bewilderin' to the understandin'." In reference to Pepper's Ghost, or the "ghosts 'as been showed in . . . [of] course they'd be real at the Pollyntechnic," Mrs. Brown reflects that "they're things as I don't think ought to be brought up for amusements, as is solemn things, and

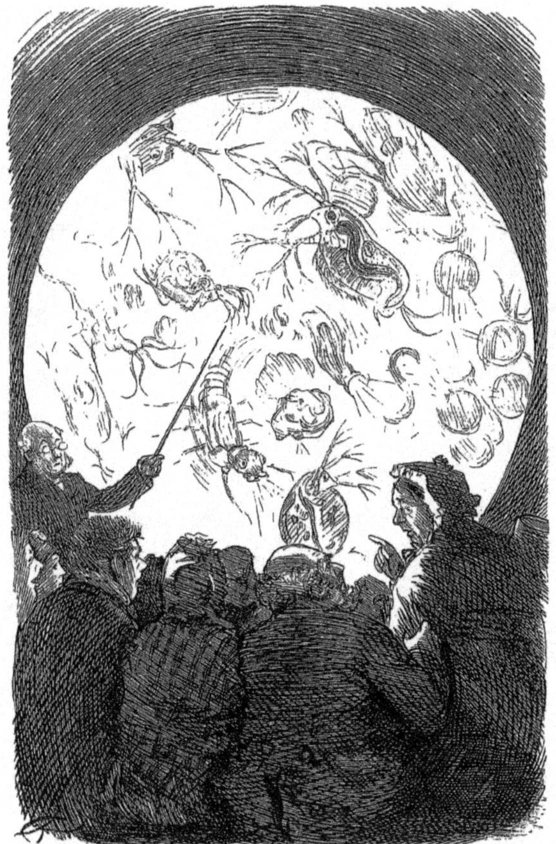

FIGURE 1.2. "Microscopy for the Million," cartoon by Charles Samuel Keene. *Punch, or the London Charivari*, 1878.

'as frightened parties to death."[50] In a *Punch* cartoon called "Microscopy for the Million" (1878), also set at the Polytechnic, a woman chastens her husband for his inability to understand the danger of a Polytechnic lecturer's demonstration of the projection microscope, which magnifies microscopic organisms on a screen: "What wad come o' us if thae awfu'-like brutes was to brek out of the watter!!" (figure 1.2). Confused and terrified, like Mrs. Brown, the woman in the *Punch* cartoon cannot improve or enjoy herself.

In these satires of bad female spectatorship, superstition is represented through a gender and class code that is implicit in *Letters on*

Natural Magic. The unruly women who disrupt the lecture-demonstration by whispering to one another or loudly complaining about "the larks played on you" by lecturers and entertainers are unable to distinguish scientific demonstrations from the occult magic that they were designed to debunk.[51] Inspired by Brewster's writing on natural magic and partly led by his disciple Pepper, the Polytechnic capitalized on the fashion for stage magic through a visually appealing brand of scientific entertainment that would demystify apparently supernatural phenomena and inculcate rational modes of visual spectatorship.[52] Advancing the pedagogy developed by Brewster in *Letters on Natural Magic*, the Polytechnic sublimated the appeal of the magic show to teach scientific principles, "pander[ing]," in Iwan Rhys Morus's words, "to their audiences' sense of their own superiority—their sense that they were the kind of people who could be depended upon to see through the smoke screen of effects."[53] Polytechnic shows were not meant to bewilder the understanding or play tricks, as Mrs. Brown charges, but rather to effect the opposite—to educate the understanding by subverting the logic of the magic trick through scientific demystification of spectacular illusions. The inability of these women to distinguish a lecturer from a conjurer and to recognize the artifice undergirding spectacles like Pepper's Ghost marks them as primitives in a temple of technological modernity. They are not only unable to participate in the hermeneutic game of deciphering the showman's spectacular illusions, but they are also unable to recognize that a game is taking place at all. All three texts cultivate that "sense of superiority" in its readers by mocking the confused "old ladies." Women are superstitious fools who offer a comic foil to the masculine spectator-detective; they are unable to experience the aesthetic pleasure of virtual images because they are too busy worrying about the "solemn" dangers of dark magic, ghosts, and monsters.

Like Robert-Houdin's memoir, with its representation of childish and frightened Algerian audiences, these satires of superstition model civilized spectatorship through negative example. Their focus on female spectatorship, often but not exclusively working class, extends Brewster's presentation of disenchanted spectatorship as a practice of self-sovereignty and a form of preparation for the responsibilities of citizenship and governance. While *Letters on Natural Magic* is concerned with the cognitive stance required to experience the aesthetic pleasure of virtual images, its political framework turns virtual aesthetics into an expression of civilizational progress. Without ever explicitly defining the ideal virtual spectator in gender, race, or class terms—and while even insisting on the democratic potential of the pedagogy of disenchantment to transform how all spectators experience virtual images—the book nevertheless implicitly associates the capacity for the aesthetic experience of virtual images with modernity, masculinity, class privilege, and whiteness. Drawing on the eighteenth-century tradition of rational recreations, Brewster characterizes the propensity for panic and superstition as atavistic, primitive, feminized, and working class and codes panic and superstition as expressions of racialized others whose inability to experience "rational amusement" justifies enslavement and colonial violence. In this sense, *Letters on Natural Magic* contributed to the growing association of the pedagogy of disenchantment with the patriarchal and imperial endeavors of "Young England" while defining the British and patriarchal will to power in terms of the capacity for the playful enjoyment of seeing things that are not there. In the second half of this chapter, I turn to a novel that responds to *Letters on Natural Magic*. By showing how the pedagogy of disenchantment breaks down when practiced by a group of women who attend a magic show, *Cranford* both participates in and challenges the satires of superstition that turned on the figure of the foolish woman.

The Great Cranford Panic

Halfway through Elizabeth Gaskell's 1853 novel *Cranford*, Miss Matilda Jenkyns pens a letter to the narrator, her friend Mary Smith, announcing that one Signor Brunoni is slated to exhibit "his wonderful magic" in the Cranford Assembly Rooms the following week.[54] An Englishman who styles himself as an Indian conjurer, "Magician to the King of Delhi, the Rajah of Oude, and the Great Lama of Thibet" (158), Signor Brunoni astonishes Miss Matty, Mary, and the other genteel ladies with his feats of prestidigitation. For these women, the magic show unleashes what the narrator calls "the great Cranford panic" (104), a period characterized by unfounded fears of despotism and ghosts connected to the mysterious conjurer and his inexplicable powers. As this brief summary suggests, *Cranford* simultaneously evokes and critiques the modern discourses and practices of optical magic spectatorship embodied in *Letters on Natural Magic*.[55] The narrative arc of "the great Cranford panic," comprising the magic show, the fears that it engenders, and the unmasking of the magician as the sick and impoverished English soldier Sam Brown, is a knowing subversion of the magic panic genre that makes explicit the patriarchal subtext of Brewster's work as well as the cartoons, essays, and stories that articulated the pedagogy of disenchantment through mockery of female magic spectators. Instead of making fun of the women for their insufficiently rational response to the magic show or portraying their panic as a moral and intellectual failing, *Cranford* challenges Brewster's presentation of magic as antidespotic by showing how it is deployed in the service of female submission to patriarchal control. Signor Brunoni's Cranford magic show and Robert-Houdin's Algiers magic show thus make a surprisingly apt pairing. In different ways, they both reveal how stage magic can function as an exercise of sovereignty authorized through its civilizing intent. I will make this case in two parts: first by showing how the novel mirrors *Letters on Natural Magic* by incorporating Brewster's optical pedagogy of disenchantment and then by concluding with an analysis of *Cranford* as critique.

Cranford's representation of magic spectatorship shows the discourse and procedures of the pedagogy of disenchantment in action in mid-century provincial social life. To make sense of Signor Brunoni's magic show, Gaskell's women characters—among them the narrator, Mary Smith; her close friend, Mathilda Jenkyns; a stubborn spinster named Miss Pole; and a superstitious widow, Mrs. Forrester—candidly discuss the science of apparitions, magic illusions, and physiological optics. This is all the more striking because Brunoni is not a modern optical magician but an itinerant sleight-of-hand conjurer of the old school who pulls handkerchiefs out of loaves of bread and makes canaries disappear. While the women view Signor Brunoni as a novelty, he is actually part of a class of traveling magicians who would be displaced by the rise of urban, site-specific, and technological magic entertainment beginning in the 1850s and 1860s. In other words, Brunoni represents a profession that is going extinct.

What makes the magic scenes modern then is not Signor Brunoni's magic but the way the women of Cranford behave as optical spectators by interpreting the magic show through optical frameworks. Consider Miss Pole and Mrs. Forrester's debate over the existence of ghosts and witchcraft, during which the former presents evidence against the supernatural drawn from work in physiological optics, citing "indigestion, spectral illusions, optical delusions, and a great deal out of Dr. Ferriar and Dr. Hibbert besides" (99). Like Scrooge, Miss Pole's reading of Ferriar and Hibbert marks her not only as a skeptic but also as a proponent of the theories of optical disenchantment underlying modern optical media culture, the same theories that animate Brewster's work.

In addition to invoking the propensity of human vision to seeing apparitions to argue that ghosts are not real, her belief that "there might be a scientific solution found for even the proceedings of the Witch of Endor" recalls Brewster's gambit of demystifying ancient magic and tales of the miraculous by attributing them to early experiments with optical technology (83). Miss Pole's sparring partner Mrs. Forrester, meanwhile, who "believed everything from ghosts to death-watches," exemplifies the belief in ghosts that Victorian optical pedagogy sought to drive out (83). When she calls upon her maid Jenny "to give evidence of having seen a ghost with her own eyes" (99), her trust in the testimony of the senses marks her as precisely the kind of reader Brewster hoped to reach with his cautioning remark that "the eye is the principal seat of the supernatural."

Gaskell even alludes to discourses of rational magic by including a stand-in for *Letters on Natural Magic*'s painstaking explanations of magic tricks. Miss Pole prepares to attend the magic show by transcribing diagrams for sleight-of-hand tricks from Matty's old encyclopedia, perusing "the nouns beginning with C" for conjuring:

> "Ah! I see; I comprehend perfectly," she remarks. "A represents the ball. Put A between B and D—no! between C and F, and turn the second joint of the third finger of your left hand over the wrist of your right H. Very clear indeed! My dear Mrs. Forrester, conjuring and witchcraft are a mere affair of the alphabet." (84)

This is a reference to the conjuring diagrams in books like *Letters on Natural Magic*, *Rational Recreations*, and *The Boy's Playbook of Science*. These diagrams are indeed "affair[s] of the alphabet": they label each component of the trick with a letter that has a corresponding explanation in the text, like the diagrams in a scientific treatise, in their quest to rationalize and democratize magic as a rational and instructive home activity. Although Miss Pole lacks the specialized equipment of a natural magic treatise like *Letters*, she is written as a parody of one of Brewster's earnest readers. Throughout the magic show, Miss Pole will read aloud from what she calls "receipts," or explanations of the tricks that she has copied from the encyclopedia onto scraps of paper, insisting that she could perform the magician's tricks herself "with two hours given to study the Encyclopedia and make her third finger flexible" (87).

However, just like the bad women spectators at the Royal Polytechnic Institution satirized in *Punch* and *Household Words*, Miss Pole's pedagogy of disenchantment fails to demystify the magic show, either for her companions or herself. "How he did his tricks I could not imagine," Mary reports, "no, not even when Miss Pole pulled out her pieces of paper and began reading aloud" (87). The other women share Mary's perspective: Miss Matty and Mrs. Forrester are "mystified to the highest degree" and even the urbane Lady Glenmore, "who had seen many curious sights in Edinburgh, was very much struck with the tricks" (87). Like the "two old ladies" in "A Shilling's Worth of Science," Miss Matty and Mrs. Forrester fear occult interference and ask Mary to see whether the rector is in attendance to ensure that "this wonderful man is sanctioned by the Church" (88). Although Miss Pole plays the role of the skeptic—she even shouts, "I don't believe him!" when Signor Brunoni appears on stage (86)—her use of the term "receipt" to describe conjuring diagrams prefigures her failure to make sense of the magic show and her ultimate succumbing to superstition and panic. An archaic version of the word "recipe," "receipt" here means a formula for a medicinal preparation or a dish; Miss Pole will later ask Mrs. Forrester for the "receipt" of her bread-jelly (103). Once again echoing the female spectators in "A Shilling's Worth of Science" whose only frame of reference for the lecture-demonstration on electricity is the experience of boiling water in a kettle, Miss Pole describes the masculine art of conjuring in terms drawn from the feminine arts of nursing and cooking. Thus, much like the satirical representations of female spectators at the Polytechnic, the Cranford women remain "astonished" even when the performance of magic is doubled by its own demystification (87).

The magic panic that seizes these women after Signor Brunoni's show—what the narrator refers to as "the great Cranford panic"—is not only consistent with the pedagogy of disenchantment's correlation between femininity and superstition but also reflects Brewster's concern about how optical illusions can solicit belief in their reality in audiences insufficiently knowledgeable about the science of visual perception. The "panic" is motivated by a series of strange episodes that "seemed at the time connected in our minds with" Signor Brunoni (89). At first, a series of robberies suggest "a trick fit for a conjurer" (91), while the death of Mrs. Jamieson's dog portends magical interference. "He had apparently killed a canary with only a word of command," the narrator muses in the free indirect discourse of the Cranford woman, "his will seemed of deadly force; who knew but what he might yet be lingering in the neighborhood willing all sorts of awful things!" (94).[56] The women's fears escalate until they light upon the possibility of ghosts, a turn that associates Brunoni's magic with that of optical ghost conjurers. Jenny's story about a ghost haunting the aptly named Darkness Lane alludes to this tradition of optical magic when it transposes the appearances and disappearances of sleight-of-hand magic into the conjuring of spectral apparitions and ghosts. In this context, Darkness Lane recalls not just the spooky locales of gothic fiction but also the use of what Noam Elcott calls "artificial darkness" for the technological projection of optical images.[57]

Even more explicitly optical is Mary's greatest fear. In the wake of the magic show, Mary is not afraid of ghosts but of ghostly virtual images produced with Brewster's favorite magical apparatus, the mirror. "If I dared to go up to my looking-glass when I was panic-stricken," she confesses, "I should certainly turn it round, with its back towards me, for fear of seeing eyes behind me looking out of the darkness" (97). Mary's fear of disembodied "eyes looking at me, and watching me" is realized in the previous chapter, when Signor Brunoni stares out at the audience before the show through the curtain "with two odd eyes, seen through holes" (86). Mary's "pet apprehension" thus reconfigures this old-fashioned conjurer and his run-down set as a menacing technological optical illusion. When Mrs. Jamieson inspects her spectacles during the magic show "as if she thought it was something defective in them which made the legerdemain," the gesture playfully references the capacity of glass to create illusions. By associating Signor Brunoni's old-school magic with mirrors and glass and with apparitions and ghosts, *Cranford* signals its investment in the modern technological and optical magic that Brewster promoted in *Letters on Natural Magic*. Brunoni's magic is not based in the creation of virtual images, but the response of the Cranford women makes it seem as if it were.

Cranford's representation of optical disenchantment and the demystification of magic extends to its construction of the magician himself. The character Samuel Brown is an Englishman who "learnt some tricks of an Indian juggler"—otherwise known as a conjurer or prestidigitator—during his military tour of India and now performs "Indian magic" for provincial English audiences under the moniker Signor Brunoni (109). The "great Cranford panic" subsides when the mysterious Signor Brunoni is revealed to be the impoverished Englishman Samuel Brown, who performs his tricks with the help of an improbable double: his twin brother. Thus, the demystification of the conjurer demystifies his magic. This narrative unfolding not only reproduces magic's pedagogy of disenchantment but also reflects the performativity of Victorian magic theater. Many British magicians performed as characters of their own invention, with foreign-sounding names and titles calculated to evoke cosmopolitan prestige; among them was Antonio van Zandt, a British sleight-of-hand magician and possible model for Signor Brunoni, who performed under the stage name Signor Blitz.[58] Signor Brunoni more specifically captures the nineteenth-century practice of magic as racial performance. Performing Indian magic while "magnificent[ly]" clad in a turban, a guise that earns him the nickname of "the Grand Turk" (86), Brunoni evokes two traditions of racial imposture in stage magic. The first is the phenomenon of nineteenth-century European and American magicians who masqueraded as Indian, Chinese, Egyptian, or ambiguously Oriental conjurers, such as the American magician William Ellsworth Robinson, who darkened his skin with greasepaint and dressed in traditional Chinese costume to become the magician Chung Ling Soo. The second and more widespread form of imposture was white magicians' claim to perform authentically Indian magic, from sleight-of-hand tricks popularized in England by Indian magicians such as Ramo Samee and Khia Khan Khruse to technological set pieces enhanced by trumped-up tales about the illusion's origin in India.

We can therefore see how *Cranford* narrativizes the optical pedagogy of disenchantment theorized by David Brewster. A group of credulous women are consumed by panic and fear when a foreigner performs supernatural acts. Thrown off by the patently weird and incoherent combination of his Turkish dress, Italian name, fake French-sounding accent, and Indian conjuring tricks, the women at once accuse him of being a practitioner of dark arts, a savage "Mussulman," and a "French spy" preparing to launch a fresh wave of the Anglo-French Wars. When the foreigner is revealed to be a white Englishman, the supernatural occurrences become comprehensible as illusions and tricks and "somehow, we all forgot to be afraid" (103). Brewster warned that belief in ghosts would make the British vulnerable to becoming "the dupe of preconcerted imposture—the slave of [their] own ignorance—the prostrate vassal of power and superstition."[59] *Cranford* seems to enact these consequences satirically by portraying Matty and her friends as "dupe[d]" and "[en]slave[d]" by ignorance; like the *Punch* cartoon of the angry woman spectator disrupting the projection microscope demonstration with her fear that the "brutes" will break out of water and attack, their superstition takes the form of unfounded fears of an assault on Britain by foreign enemies. Now that the panic engendered by Signor Brunoni's "first coming in his Turkish dress" has been replaced with sympathy upon "his second coming—pale and feeble," Miss Pole's "receipts" for

Signor Brunoni's performance give way to the actual medicinal receipts with which she and the other women nurse Sam Brown back to health. Disenchantment restores the boundaries of whiteness and Britishness, the sovereignty of nation and empire over the racial other, and traditional gender roles as the women return to their rightful place as caregivers of men.

A Trick Fit for a Conjurer

If we stay with *Cranford* a little longer, there is more to find. To say that it simply reproduces Brewster's pedagogy of disenchantment is to overlook the novel's subtler but no less important critique of disenchanted spectatorship. In a previous publication, I made the case that *Cranford*'s representation of magic is metafictional.[60] Rather than portraying magic panic as a symptom of undisciplined female minds, *Cranford* introduces stage magic among a set of tropes for how fiction can construct the real—tropes that include quixotic readers, trickster storytellers, and the serialized novels of Charles Dickens. I called my essay "In Defense of Credulous Women" because it pointed to the ways that the novel models a salutary phenomenology of reading through female credulity, including through the reflexive twinning of the narrator, Mary, with Signor Brunoni, as two slippery figures who construct perceptual experience through parallel forms of sleight of hand. To illustrate the case I made in my article, let me return momentarily to a scene we have already discussed: Miss Pole's study of conjuring diagrams in the encyclopedia. Miss Pole's claim that "conjuring is a mere affair of the alphabet" is undermined by her inability to keep the alphabet straight, a cognitive failure that is underscored when her transcriptions of the diagrams do not actually help her understand how Signor Brunoni's magic tricks work. However, the breakdown of Miss Pole's practices of skepticism—and their transformation into an excess of credulity—also constitutes a metafictional reflection on the novel. As Hilary Schor has noted, Miss Pole's remark on conjuring integrates magic into the novel's broader concern with "affair[s] of the alphabet" like reading, writing and storytelling.[61]

To understand what *Cranford* has to say about the relationship between conjuring and fiction as two alphabetic affairs, we must begin with the fact that Miss Pole's theory of conjuring does not hold up. Although it is technically explicable through diagrams, Gaskell refuses to validate her statement that it can be reduced to them—that it is "mere[ly]" alphabetic. Reading her receipts during the show does not actually rationalize Signor Brunoni's magic, neither for Miss Pole nor her friends. Even when the performance is doubled by its own demystification, simultaneously exhibited and explained, the women remain "astonished." One explanation for the women's astonishment is that they are simply too stupid to be educated. Another is that the perceptual power of the magic trick is greater than the sum of its parts in rules, apparatus, and manual dexterity, even when those component parts are shamelessly exposed. My article argued the latter. It proposed that *Cranford* views both magic and fiction as affairs of the alphabet only up to a point. Both are illusory media that ultimately transcend the alphabet by coming to feel and seem real, independent of the tools and techniques that create them.

Cranford thus takes aim at the culture of rational recreations and valorizes the novel in one fell swoop. Its portrayal of female magic spectatorship illustrates the aesthetic experience of wonder with which Brewster associated virtual images, in which "even those who know the deception . . . are not a little surprised at its effects," while challenging his claim that the scientific and technological analysis of magic has the meaningful pedagogical force that he insists on. At the same time, *Cranford* reflects on itself as a form of entertainment like magic by proposing that its illusory and mystifying effects on a reader's perception has its origin in, but is irreducible to, the rationalist atomization of dictionaries and encyclopedias. On the grounds of its metafictional exploration of literary aesthetics, I argued that *Cranford* can be read as a subversion of the pedagogy of disenchantment. The susceptibility of Gaskell's women characters to believing what they see and the states of confusion and panic that erupt as a result of that susceptibility express what Gaskell understands as the shared capacity of magic and fiction to produce new forms of aesthetic pleasure that emerge through rather than against a cultural logic of disenchantment. *Cranford*'s credulous women allow the novel to explore the pleasures of believing in the reality of an illusion that reading novels and spectating at magic shows both provide, pleasures for which diagrams, treatises on optics, and satires of superstition fail to account.

In the final pages of this chapter, I would like to turn to another way that the novel critiques magic's pedagogy of disenchantment. If the novel defends credulous women, it is also ambivalent about the figure of the magician and his capacity to inspire credulity. While "A Shilling's Worth of Science" and "Microscopy for the Million" view female magic panic as a punch line, *Cranford* reflects on how and why the patriarchal underpinning of the normative model of disenchanted spectatorship turns women into jokes. In doing so, it both affirms and challenges the political framework for Brewster's virtual aesthetics. "When knowledge was the property of only one caste," Brewster wrote in *Letters on Natural Magic*, "it was by no means difficult to employ it in the subjugation of a great mass of society."[62] Speaking of the use of optical illusions by elites as a demonstration of divine authority, Brewster offers a variation on the classic Enlightenment argument that the democratization of knowledge is a defense against despotism. *Cranford* replies that knowledge—in the form of the scientific principles and practices endorsed by Brewster—remains the property of only one caste: men. Like Mary Wollstonecraft in *A Vindication of the Rights of Woman*, who wrote that women were "rendered weak and wretched" by "a false system of education," Gaskell insists that female superstition is not a natural state but the artificial product of women's exclusion from the realms of intellectual advancement.[63]

This is vividly rendered through the return of Matty's long-lost brother Peter Jenkyns to Cranford. A storyteller and trickster, Peter is Sam Brown's double. Like the conjurer, Peter has lately arrived from India. His arrival is a result of the magic show; it is Mary's discovery of his whereabouts during a conversation with Mrs. Brown, the magician's wife, that leads to her tracking him down. Characterized by his disappearance and reappearance in Cranford, both equally sudden and mysterious, Peter is almost like an incarnate magic trick—one of optical conjuring's virtual images made flesh. At the same time, the novel marks Peter as a purveyor of oral magic tricks—"paradigm[s] of the imperial adventure tale" that exploit what Patrick Brantlinger has called the construction of India as "a realm of imaginative license . . . a place where the fantastic becomes possible."[64] He tells stories that are "more wonderful . . . than Sinbad the sailor" and "as good as an Arabian night any evening" (152). Matty's word for Peter's lifelong propensity for playing tricks, "hoaxing," derives etymologically from "hocus pocus" and positions Peter's stories about shooting cherubs in the Himalayas as verbal prestidigitation that takes in listeners by exploiting their gullibility.

Like Signor Brunoni, Peter is in the business of tricking women. Although Mary acknowledges that because "I had vibrated all my life between Drumble and Cranford, I thought it was quite possible that all Mr. Peter's stories might be true although wonderful" (152), she later confirms her suspicion that "he was making fun of me" (150). Peter's stories of shooting cherubs in the Himalayas succeed in impressing his female audience by taking advantage of the gender inequity between his knowledge and experience and that of his listeners. While Peter can move across continents, Mary and Matty are so immobile they cannot even read a globe let alone traverse one. Their ascription of "equators and tropics, and such mystical circles" as "very imaginary lines indeed" and "the signs of the Zodiac . . . [as] so many remnants of the Black Art" (129) collapses the masculine realm of science with feminized superstition, echoing Miss Pole's attempts to rationalize the magic show through her "receipts." The entire world beyond Cranford—the world beyond the direct experience of the women—is in the hands of men like Peter and Signor Brunoni to create.

Peter's tall tales extend the novel's theme of magic tricks and credulous women spectators while laying bare the epistemic violence of disenchanted magic culture. The similarity between Peter and Brunoni is admittedly more structural than it is temperamental. Unlike Sam Brown, a desperately poor man trying to make a living plying his trade, Peter enjoys tricking women for his own gratification and his stories are, in Wendy Carse's words, "at least partially motivated by a basic contempt for the others' supposed gullibility."[65] The conjurer does not design magic tricks that will cause harm to his female audience while appealing to men, even if that is the result of his performance: the narrator takes pains to note that the rector is all "broad smiles" at the magic show and his retinue of schoolboys are "in chinks of laughing" (88), able to enjoy the tricks with the kind of disenchanted pleasure for which Brewster advocated and which is not accessible to the women. Peter deliberately edits his stories when speaking to the rector, who would be more likely to see through his lies: "I don't think the ladies of Cranford would have considered him such a wonderful traveler," Mary observes, "if they had only heard him talk in the quiet way he did to him" (152). Even taking into consideration this difference in disposition and intent, however, Peter and Signor Brunoni wield epistemic power over women in similar ways. Consider that Mary's scrutiny of Peter's stories is prefigured in her response to the conjurer. Earlier in this discussion, I referenced Mary's fear of "eyes looking at me, and watching me" and proposed that this description reconfigures Signor Brunoni's hidden presence before the magic show, when he looks at the audience from behind the curtain "with two odd eyes, seen through holes." The fact that his eyes are visible to Mary is, on one hand, a sign of how ramshackle the magic show is, with a makeshift strung-up curtain in place of the posh, site-specific theatrical magic that was dominant in the 1850s, with stages designed for the conjurer's precise needs. On the other hand, Mary's description of the magician's disembodied eyes registers the spectatorial and relational dynamics underlying magic illusions: the way the magician controls what and how the viewer sees through visual manipulation, just as Peter controls what and how his listeners know.

In fact, Mary's fear—her own personal contribution to "the great Cranford panic"—is an astute recognition of the way visual magic subverts the apparent power dynamic implicit in the spectatorial situation. While the women believe they are the ones watching the spectacle of the conjurer's illusions, the illusions succeed based on the conjurer's ability to watch his audience covertly. In the magic show, to look is to risk an abdication of one's sovereignty over oneself, to be susceptible to the remotely controlling presence of the conjurer whose tricks and illusions signify the manipulation and distortion of one's perceptions.[66] Before the show, when Mary describes the curtain first as "obstinate" and then as "tantalizing," she takes it as a figure for the whole apparatus of the conjurer and his illusions: a dazzling surface that doubles as an occlusion. The curtain represents the epistemological boundary that splits off mysterious phenomena from their source. In Mary's formulation, it is the *curtain* that "would stare at me with two odd eyes"—the curtain that controls what she can and cannot see, simultaneously forcing her to look and making it impossible for her to know. The conjurer becomes a curtain with eyes, a concealment that watches. When Mary later accounts for her fear of being watched by someone she cannot see—of seeing only the fact that she is being watched—the novel subverts the trope of magic panic as foolish female behavior by taking seriously the potential for gender violence built into magic's visual art of perceptual manipulation.

Accounting for Mary's critical response to both Peter and the conjurer demands that we see the credulity of the Cranford women in a different light. Rather than reading their experience of the magic show as an attack on their town by unspecified foreigners and ghosts and thus as a sign of their lack of intellectual fitness and inability to participate in the rationalizing and civilizing work of disenchantment, we can understand it like Mary's fear of eyes, as a displaced anxiety about patriarchal domination—a fear that finds expression in, even if it far exceeds, the experience of magic spectatorship. If the women really are being watched by curtains, then their belief in spectral male eyes invading the privacy of their all-female domestic spaces and a spate of robberies in which "houses and shops were entered by holes made in the walls, the bricks being silently carried away in the dead of night" begins to seem less farfetched (90). When Miss Matty asserts that this "trick was fit for a conjurer" and laments that his magic can circumvent "locks and bolts, and bells to the windows," she, like Mary, reckons with the spectral despotism of patriarchal power, at once everywhere and nowhere, invading even the homes of single women living in a town where "all the holders of houses, above a certain rent, are women" (3).

Read in this way, the final chapter of *Cranford* becomes newly troubling. In "Peace to Cranford," the rift between the sisters-in-law Mrs. Jamieson and Lady Glenmire after the latter's marriage to a country doctor is repaired by Peter when he "bribe[s]" Mrs. Jamieson to join them in attending another magic show that he has organized to patronize "my poor conjurer" (158). "Peace to Cranford" is effected through a combination of Peter's "wonderful stories"—tricks that he plays on Mrs. Jamieson and that he considers integral to "propitiating her"—and Signor Brunoni's magic (158). If we understand storytelling and magic to be constitutive of the kind of reasoned, democratic, and civilizing aesthetic pleasure that Brewster promotes in *Letters on Natural Magic*, we might consider this a happy ending, one in which imaginative entertainment is critical to the maintenance of social bonds and to the integrity of the nation. If we take seriously Mary's objections to Peter's stories and Signor Brunoni's magic as expressions of covert surveillance, social discipline, and perceptual control, then the novel ends with a reintegration of patriarchy as a kind of occupying force in this community of women. An occupying force perhaps not so unlike the French in Algeria, who also turned to a series of two magic shows in the belief than perceptual tricks would encourage cognitive and political dependence on colonial rule. Signor Brunoni is no Robert-Houdin, the affable Peter's stories are not a form of violent colonial conquest, Mrs. Jamieson's cold shoulder toward her sister-in-law is not an anticolonial uprising, and the genteel and thriving women of Cranford are not stand-ins for colonized North Africans. Yet the gender and racial representations of magic panic that we find in *Cranford* and in Robert-Houdin's memoir both hinge on the idea of conjuring as a selective act of despotism in the service of Western civilizational gains—despotism that purports to promote scientific rationality while securing British imperial and patriarchal rule. In this regard, both the real case study of Robert-Houdin in Algeria and the fictional case study of Signor Brunoni in Cranford make apparent the role of disenchanted magic in conceptualizing sovereignty and civilization in the mid-nineteenth century.

Rather than reading *Cranford* as another representation of foolish spectators victimized by their own credulity, like those that we see in *Letters on Natural Magic*, Robert-Houdin's account of his Algerian audiences in *Confidences d'un prestidigitateur*, and the comic sketches in *Household Words* and *Punch*, I have asked us to consider this novel as a critical investigation of the pedagogy of disenchantment—one that employs the trope of foolish women in order to help us understand the racial, colonial, and gender implications of the movement for rational magic spectatorship. If *Cranford* offers a defense of credulous women, it also mounts a defense of magic panic. The women's magic panic is not the result of their failure to employ the demystifying scientific procedures that Brewster outlines in *Letters on Natural Magic* but an indictment of what the novel presents as rational magic's reinstantiation of an authoritarian relation between conjurer and spectators, even as it insists that it is eradicating the despotic uses of magic. *Cranford* presents magic panic not as superstition but as community resistance to patriarchal control.

The following two chapters of the book continue to explore how showmen, scientific popularizers, and novelists theorize virtual aesthetics through imperial frames. One way that we see this is in the imaginary of optical technology as a means of making remote times and places experientially proximate. In chapter 2, I show how the travel writer Edward William Lane popularized an Egyptian magic trick known as "the mirror of ink" and turned it into an imaginary virtual medium that enabled a new kind of imperial gaze that H. G. Wells called "real vision at a distance." Building on my reading of *Cranford*'s metafictional uses of magic, I turn to the work of George Eliot to argue that she theorizes the novel as a technology for producing virtual images and experiences.

CHAPTER 2

The Mirror of Ink

Realism, Orientalism, and Vision at a Distance

In 1853, a Sudanese sorcerer named Abderramen al-Masmudī sat down with the Victorian explorer Richard Francis Burton to tell a story from his life. "It is true that I suffered captivity in the fortress of Yakub the Afflicted," al-Masmudī confides, "the cruelest of the governors of Sudan." To survive his imprisonment, the sorcerer makes a promise: "that if he granted me my life I would show him forms and appearances more marvelous than those of the *fanusi jihal*, the magic lantern."[1] The governor agrees to al-Masmudī's terms. Drawing a magic square in the Afflicted One's right palm, the sorcerer pours a circle of ink into its center and proceeds to make any person or scene the governor wishes to see appear inside it. Like a Scheherazade of pictures, the sorcerer survives night after night by indulging the governor's insatiable desire to see "the appearances of this world" in this magic mirror of ink.[2] This is not a passage from Burton's diaries or one of his well-known works of travel writing. It is Jorge Luis Borges's "The Mirror of Ink" (1944), a story that he attributes to Burton's *The Lake Regions of Equatorial Africa* in a characteristic metafictional flourish. Borges's mirror of ink is also metafictional. A multilayered figure for the relationship between reading and seeing, stories and pictures, the mirror of ink is at once a stand-in for storytelling and an imaginary optical technology "more marvelous than . . . the magic lantern"—that is, an optical technology like cinema. In the words of the film theorist Raymond Bellour, literature and cinema seem in this tale to "exchange their properties," the literary text acting as a virtual screen and the process of reading as a form of virtual spectatorship.[3]

We can understand Borges's story as a parable of reading in which reading is a practice of seeing things that are not there. This is not, however, an account of the Romantic visionary, "affected more than other men by absent things as if they were present," as William Wordsworth puts it in *Lyrical Ballads*.[4] The mirror of ink makes such visualization possible whether you are a man of sensibility or a murderous tyrant. It is an image machine, one that technologizes perception itself. The imaginary of the literary text as a machine that makes you see pictures may sound familiar because it is still present in the ways that we talk about reading novels today. When a novel absorbs us, Peter Mendelsund writes in *What We See When We Read: A Phenomenology* (2014), we describe it as "a continuous unfolding of images . . . We imagine that the experience of reading is like that of watching a film."[5] Mendelsund's central argument is that we make this claim against the evidence of our senses. Reading a novel is nothing like watching a film and at best an obliquely visual experience. The purpose of this chapter is not to challenge or amend this "false memory" of reading with a more precise account of the imaginative practices involved in reading fiction.[6] Instead, I ask where this false memory came from in the first place. When did we begin to tell the story that reading is optical and virtual? Why did the materiality of the text, its ink and paper, become a magic mirror? What cultural needs were met by imagining fiction as a technological extension of vision?

This chapter offers answers to these questions by tracing the longer history of the mirror of ink. For while the story of the mirror of ink does not come from Burton, neither is it Borges's invention. Instead, it originates in the travelogue of an Egyptologist named Edward William Lane, who described it in his best-selling book *The Manners and Customs of Modern Egyptians* (1836). Borges's attribution of the tale to a different British imperial explorer and travel writer is a displacement that reveals more than it conceals, a strategic choice that turns the mirror of ink as a technology for revealing "the appearances of this world . . . all that dead men have seen and all that living men see" into a figure for colonial travel writing that makes foreign lands visible as objects of control.[7] Borges suggests that the Sudanese governor's insatiable appetite for images of the world is an imperial appetite and encourages us to understand the image stories of the mirror of ink—that magic lantern of words—as the product of such an appetite. In other words, if Borges's mirror of ink offers us a model of nineteenth-century virtual aesthetics as the meeting point of fictional narrative and technological optics, it also insists that such a virtual aesthetic is inextricable from the British imperial context from which it emerged.

The premise of this chapter is that Borges is basically correct. The true history of the mirror of ink as an imaginary medium was constructed by nineteenth-century travel writing, sciences of mind, and fiction. Building on Susan Zieger's assertion that "ink is a crucial, undertheorized element of media history," this chapter excavates a nineteenth-century imaginary of ink as an imaginary medium for technologically enabled virtual sight long before the invention of cinema.[8] Zieger reads the trope of the mirror of ink in the work of writers like Lane, Harriet Martineau, and Wilkie Collins to argue that nineteenth-century ink gazing was a precursor to the Rorschach tests of the twentieth century, materializing a depth model of the unconscious as "a storehouse of information."[9] I return to some of these same sources to reconceive the mirror of ink not as psychoanalytic depth but as shimmering and intoxicating virtual surface. Rather than viewing it as a means of visualizing the spectator's interiority, I propose that the mirror of ink visualized the world outside the spectator, extending the range of their vision. By tracing discourses of ink as a projection medium—a kind of "magic lantern," in Borges's terms, that makes the sights of the world appear close at hand—the chapter argues that the literary text was similarly imagined as a technological extension of vision. The chapter also makes the case that this construction was often developed in relation to and as a solution for the literary question of how to make the far reaches of empire perceptually proximate for British people at home. The imaginary of virtual sight was deployed as a way of thinking about reading that developed in relation to the mid-century British desire for imperial conquest and control. To put it plainly, the trope of reading-as-seeing that Borges invokes in his short story and Mendelsund decries as a "false memory" comes to us via the imperial aesthetics of virtuality.

The chapter is organized around two case studies. The first is Lane's *The Manners and Customs of Modern Egyptians*, the work that popularized the mirror of ink. In spite of his own research, which told him that Egyptian natural magic affected the senses through the burning of narcotics, Lane took the metaphor of the ink as a mirror literally and insisted that it was a kind of optical illusion. In doing so, Lane fashioned the mirror of ink for the Victorian public as a Western optical technology that resisted the rationalizing impulse of Western optics. In chapter 1, I defined this rationalizing impulse as a pedagogy of disenchantment that sought to popularize optical technology as a means of training the British public in the principles of physiological optics and, by extension, civilizing practices of self-governance that marked them as epistemically superior to those living under British imperial control. Breaking from the orthodox view that Victorian optical spectatorship was fundamentally disenchanted, I presented the pedagogy of disenchantment as a discourse that obscures the ways in which magic belief and disbelief can and did coexist among audiences for optical illusions. *The Manners and Customs of Modern Egyptians* offers us one such example of a text simultaneously governed by notions of British epistemic mastery over the culture it describes and by an Orientalism that portrays the epistemic nonmastery of the author in the face of Egyptian magic as evidence of Egypt's irreducible mystery. While Lane's insistence that the mirror of ink cannot be explained by Western science offers an example of disenchantment and enchantment coexisting in a single act of media spectatorship, it is also a strategy that turns the mirror of ink into an analogy for and counterimperial challenge to Lane's imperialist travel writing. In this context, Lane presents the exhaustive descriptions of *The Manners and Customs of Modern Egyptians* as a print technology that, like the magic trick, will make you see things in ink.

I turn next to *Adam Bede* (1859), George Eliot's novel of everyday life in rural England on the cusp of the industrial revolution. Eliot is generally read as the most literary of the canonical novelists, a philosopher of language and admirer of Dutch painting devoted to realism's visual codes as an ethics of sympathy and observation as well as a mode of representation.[10] She is not, in other words, a common object of study for scholars of technology and popular visual culture. I revisit Eliot as theorist of virtual aesthetics, arguing that she turns to the figure of the mirror of ink in order to define novel reading as a form of technological virtual experience. Drawing not only on *The Manners and Customs of Modern Egyptians* but also from a growing body of literature that sought to explain the mirror of ink through the popular science of mesmerism, *Adam Bede* reflexively offers a media theory of itself as the reader's visualization in a "mirror of ink." Along with *The Lifted Veil*, the gothic novella she wrote just after completion of the novel, *Adam Bede* reveals that we have imagined reading as a "continuous unfolding of images" long before we have been going to the movies and that the novel was an optical technology long before it was cinema. With its striking invocation of "Egyptian sorcery" in a novel of provincial England, it also offers us a way of understanding the emerging framework of technological perception that found its expression in the mirror of ink as a response to the new imperial world order. Eliot's theory of the novel as a mirror of ink ultimately provides us with a model of reading as what H. G. Wells called "real vision at a distance" in a story written just months after the invention of cinema.[11]

The Magic Mirror of Ink

The authoritative Western account of the magic mirror of ink was written by Edward William Lane, who saw the magician Sheik Abd al-Qadir al-Maghrabi perform it in Cairo in 1834. Lane's narrative of the experiment formed the centerpiece of a chapter on magic in *The Manners and Customs of Modern Egyptians* (1836), published in two volumes by Charles Knight, and it was almost immediately singled out by reviewers and readers as a significant point of interest in the text. In a review of *The Manners and Customs of Modern Egyptians* for *Quarterly Review*, Sir John Barrow devoted several pages just to discussing the mirror of ink, calling it "one of the most extraordinary feats of magic that have been recorded since the days of the Pharaohs."[12] The mirror of ink quickly became an attraction to readers on its own merits. The narrative of Sheik Abd al-Qadir's trick was excerpted for publication in newspapers and magazines, mentioned in the Cairo edition of John Murray's guidebooks, and discussed openly as an example of a potentially supernatural phenomenon. It may have helped fuel the appetite for the three revised editions that kept *The Manners and Customs of Modern Egyptians* in print into the twentieth century—editions in which Lane added updated footnotes to his discussion of the mirror of ink to register his views on the growing public debate surrounding the trick.

Lane was a pioneering scholar of Egypt and, for Edward Said, among a handful of writers responsible for developing a British Orientalist scholarly tradition.[13] An engraver's apprentice working in London, Lane was swept up by Egyptomania in the decades following Napoleon Bonaparte's Egyptian campaign (1798–1801) and the West's discovery of Egyptian history, art, and culture.[14] After studying Arabic and Egyptian history in London, Lane embarked on the first of three research trips to Egypt in 1825, fired up with the ambition to "throw myself entirely among strangers—to adopt their language, their customs, and their dress—and . . . to prosecute the study of their literature." He settled in Cairo, took on the name of Mansur Effendi, and adopted the manners, customs, and dress of a Muslim, even praying alongside his Egyptian friends at the mosque.[15] The fruits of this first trip, a historical manuscript called *Description of Egypt*, failed to find a publisher, but he managed to secure a contract for a different book that would focus on modern Egypt. Lane used his advance to return to Cairo in 1833 for additional research toward what would become *The Manners and Customs of Modern Egyptians*. Within weeks of his arrival, he followed up on a lead he had received years before from Henry Salt. Salt was Britain's consul-general to Egypt and an avid collector of Egyptian artifacts, and during Lane's first trip to Egypt he confided that he had met a "magician of great power" who made images appear in a mirror of ink.[16] Lane was keen to see this for himself, but Salt was unable to supply the magician's name or address. Between his two Egyptian sojourns, Lane conferred with fellow travelers in London who supplied this missing piece of information, and in February 1834, he secured an introduction to Sheik Abd al-Qadir. Within a few years, the sales of *The Manners and Customs of Modern Egyptians* would turn him into the famous "Cairo magician" sought after by European travelers.

"Description of Egypt" could be imagined as a sort of spiritual subtitle for *The Manners and Customs of Modern Egyptians*, or an account of its literary method. In *Orientalism*, Said focuses on its exhaustive—and, quite frankly, exhausting—use of description, its ambition to "make Egypt and Egyptians totally visible . . . in swollen detail."[17] For Lane's readers, this was an asset. Lord Brougham, founder of the Society for the Diffusion of Useful Knowledge, praised Lane for his descriptive powers; *The Manners and Customs of Modern Egyptians* was meant to showcase this strength.[18] The visuality of Lane's descriptive prose was enhanced by his use of a camera lucida, a pocket-sized optical technological drawing aid that superimposes an image of an object or scene onto the page so that it can be quickly sketched.[19] In addition to allowing him to capture visual information efficiently for later analysis, his rough sketches served as the basis of the illustrations that Lane created for *The Manners and Customs of Modern Egyptians*. Visualization is therefore more than a metaphor for Lane's ethnographic approach—it is both a practice and a process, one that yielded images as well as words. Lane's multimedia approach to "describing" Egypt—and the role of pictures in both mediating and supplementing his descriptions—is important context for understanding how Lane represented the mirror of ink as itself a synthesis of image and text.

The Manners and Customs of Modern Egyptians described the mirror of ink in characteristically minute detail. First, a boy of eight or nine years old was procured from the streets to act as a clairvoyant medium. (According to the Abd al-Qadir, "boy[s] not yet arrived at puberty" were among the select class of people capable of seeing in the magic mirror; the others were "a virgin, a black female slave, and a pregnant woman.")[20] Lane chose the boy himself from the street and was confident there was no collusion between him and the magician. The magician requested of his host a reed-pen, ink, paper, and scissors, which he used to inscribe invocations to the genii Tarshun and Taryooshun. A charm "to open the boy's eyes in a supernatural manner" was also written out by Abd al-Qadir; the passage from the Koran—"And we have removed from thee thy veil; and thy sight to-day is piercing"—was placed inside the boy's skullcap (269). Throughout the ritual, the invocations were burned in a chafing dish prepared with frankincense, coriander seed, and benzoin. The final preparation was the titular mirror of ink. In the boy's outstretched hand, Abd al-Qadir drew a "magic square" consisting of Arabic numerals and, in the center, "poured a little ink, and desired the boy to look into it, and tell him if he could see his face reflected in it." When the boy confirmed that he could see his face clearly, Abd al-Qadir kept hold of his hand and instructed him "to continue looking intently into the ink; and not to raise his head" (270).

The ritual proceeded in the form of a dialogue between the magician and the boy. As perfumed smoke from the chafing dish filled the air, Abd al-Qadir asked the boy if he saw anything in the mirror of ink. "Trembling, and seeming much frightened," the boy reported that he saw "a man sweeping the ground." When the man was done sweeping, the boy was instructed to ask him to bring a flag.

> The boy did so; and soon said, "He has brought a flag." "What color is it?" asked the magician; the boy replied, "Red." He was told to call for another flag; which he did; and soon after he said that he saw another brought; and that it was black. In like manner, he was told to call for a third, fourth, fifth, sixth, and seventh; which he described as being successively brought before him; specifying their colors, as white, green, black, red, and blue. (271)

After this procession of flags came preparations for the sultan. The boy was told to ask the man in the ink to pitch the Sultan's tent and order the soldiers to come and set up camp around it. Once the soldiers slaughtered, cooked, and ate a bull; brought coffee to the sultan;

and formed a court, the centerpiece of the illusion could begin. Abd al-Qadir "now addressed himself to me; and asked me if I wished the boy to see any person who was absent or dead" (272). Lane made a series of requests to the magician—first for Admiral Horatio Nelson, the British naval officer and national hero for his victories during the Napoleonic War; and then an acquaintance with a common Egyptian name—and Abd al-Qadir then instructed the boy to request of the sultan that the absent person be brought "before my eyes, that I may see him" (272). For Lane, this was the most exciting as well as most inscrutable part of the trick because it seemed to work. Unlike the case of the flags and the soldiers, which the boy might simply pretend to see, the boy was able to accurately describe the people Lane asked for as if they had truly appeared in the ink.

While Lane insisted that he could not explain the trick, his eyewitness description is itself a kind of interpretation. Earlier in the same chapter of *The Manners and Customs of Modern Egyptians*, Lane categorized the mirror of ink as Islamic natural magic that uses perfumes and narcotics to induce hallucinations (263). Because Abd al-Qadir burned strong-smelling spices and benzoin in his chafing dish, it would make sense for Lane to consider that they played a role in the trick. Lane insisted, however, that the trick was not somatic but something else entirely: a form of optical illusion. In his account, "I named Lord Nelson; of whom the boy had evidently never heard," but whom the boy describes seeing in the ink as "a man, dressed in a black suit of European clothes: the man has lost his left arm." The boy equivocates, however: "Looking more intently, and more closely, into the ink, [he] said, 'No, he has not lost his left arm; but it is placed to his breast.'" Nelson did lose his arm in battle and was frequently depicted in paintings with the sleeve of his jacket pinned to his breast; Lane felt the boy's self-correction "made his description more striking," even if less accurate, presumably because it implied he was looking closely at an image visible only to him and trying to interpret faithfully what he saw (272). Lane was also intrigued that the boy incorrectly identified Lord Nelson's left arm, rather than his right, as the missing limb. "Without saying that I suspected the boy had made a mistake," he writes, "I asked the magician whether the objects appeared in the ink as if actually before the eyes, or as if in a glass, which makes the right appear left. He answered, that they appeared as in a mirror. This rendered the boy's description faultless" (273). Lane submits the boy's mistakes as evidence that the mirror of ink functioned like an optical medium that creates optical illusions through reflection. He literalizes the metaphor implicit in the name "mirror of ink": the boy does not see visions of absent persons "as if" in a mirror, he sees them in a mirror that can reflect persons and things that are not really there.

Susan Zieger has argued that the nineteenth-century trope and practice of ink gazing fueled by *The Manners and Customs of Modern Egyptians* turned the materiality of ink into "a screen practice and a visual technology similar to photography and cinema" and a parlor game akin to optical toys like the thaumatrope.[21] This dynamic transformation of ink into a medium of the virtual image is not only the result of its subsequent popularization in literary culture. When Lane disregards the evidence of his own research into narcotic magic to fixate on the reflective properties of the ink, turning ink into a mirror and optics into a property of ink, he is already conscripting the Western frameworks of optical technology and virtual spectatorship into his analysis. It is likely that his perspective is shaped by David Brewster's *Letters on Natural Magic*, the treatise on scientific and technological magic that I discussed at length in chapter 1. Published four years before *The Manners and Customs of Modern Egyptians*, *Letters on Natural Magic* would have offered Lane a framework for how lens- or mirror-based technologies could produce images of dead or absent persons, as in the hidden magic lanterns used to "conjure" apparitions in phantasmagoria shows. Like Abd al-Qadir's mirror of ink, the phantasmagoria also claimed to conjure apparitions of the dead or absent by request. Its production of spectral virtuality through what Noam Elcott calls "artificial darkness," achieved through a dark room, invisible screen, and slides painted with lampblack, meant that the images of the dead appeared against a black ground. When Lane applies the concept of the mirror that produces virtual images, he also brings into view the ways that the hallucinatory darkness of the ink acts as a screen. While the registers of mirrors, projection, and darkness evoke the theatricality of technological optical magic, the drop of ink is a handheld medium that seems to technologize the body itself. When the boy gazes into his own hand to see visions, he reconfigures the media practice that Tom Gunning calls the manipulation of visual perception through the coordination of hand and eye.[22] The thaumatrope, an optical toy invented by British physician John Ayrton Paris about a decade before *The Manners and Customs of Modern Egyptians* was published, was a printed disk with two pieces of string on either side that the user spins between the thumb and forefinger; the effect known today as flicker fusion results in the user seeing both sides of the disk at once in a virtual composite image. As the Egyptian boy looks "intently" and "closely" into his own hand to distinguish the finer details of the image of Lord Nelson, he recalls the fashionable men and women in British parlors whose hands and eyes worked in concert to create pleasurable visual illusions.

In other words, what Lane presented to the readers of *The Manners and Customs of Modern Egyptians* as an Oriental magic trick was in fact a repackaging and reimagining of Western rational recreation and popular visual entertainment. This was not lost on his readers. In his review of *The Manners and Customs of Modern Egyptians* for the *Quarterly Review*, Barrow believed that he could solve the mystery of the mirror of ink using the Western frameworks of optical technology and stage magic. He compared Abd al-Qadir's performance with a method for creating the technological apparition of "an absent or deceased friend" that Brewster presented in *Letters on Natural Magic*.[23] In this scheme, which I referred to in chapter 1 as an instance of Brewster's aesthetic imagination, a picture of the person is placed upside down and reflected by a concave mirror (figure 2.1).[24] The spectator sees neither the mirror nor the picture, but a spectral apparition in the opening in the wall, which Brewster represents in his illustration with an ornate frame. Brewster even suggests filling the frame with smoke "from a chafing dish, in which incense is burned," so that the image appears reflected onto the

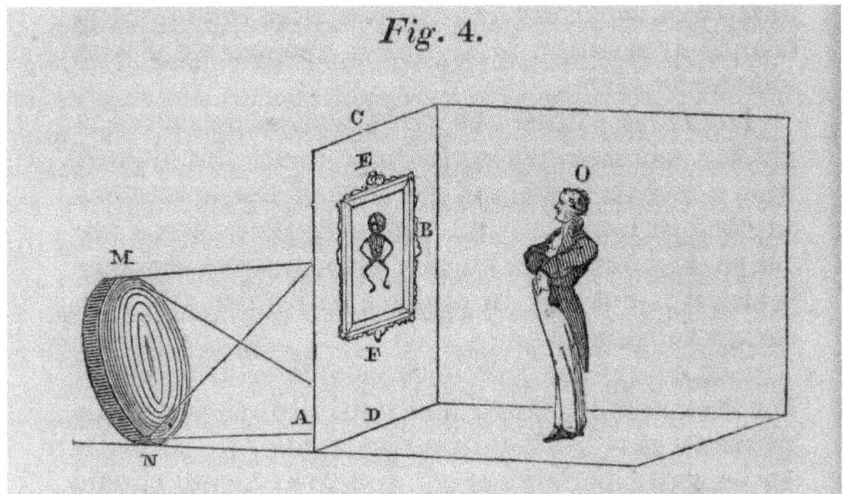

FIGURE 2.1. A spectator sees an apparition in a picture frame produced by a concave mirror hidden behind the wall. David Brewster, *Letters on Natural Magic*, John Murray, 1832.

smoke "in the same manner as a beam of light is rendered more visible by passing through an apartment filled with dust or smoke."[25] Probably inspired by the similarities between the two tricks, both involving chafing dishes and incense, Barrow believed that Abd al-Qadir was performing a version of Brewster's illusion. It was most likely that the boy was not seeing the images in the ink, Barrow argued, but the reflections from a series of pictures "thrown from the surface of a concave mirror," with the smoke from the chafing dish creating "a cloud of smoke . . . on which those images were received."[26] This would explain why the boy saw a reversed image of Lord Nelson, with the wrong arm held to his breast.

Yet Lane himself insisted that "the boy [had not seen] images produced by some reflection in the ink." In a footnote added in the revised third edition published in 1842, he rejected Barrow's theory that the images were produced through the use of optical technology.[27] He maintained instead that the performance was unexplainable, at least to him: "If the reader be alike unable to give the solution, I hope that he will not allow the above account to induce in his mind any degree of skepticism with respect to the other portions of this work."[28] The mirror of ink was thus presented as an irreducible mystery at the center of a grand work of demystification. After all, *The Manners and Customs of Modern Egyptians* was considered a deeply informed Orientalist travelogue that sought to make Egypt comprehensible and knowable to British readers and to provide, through words, an imaginative tour of landscapes, cities, customs, and people. Lane's broader discussion of Egyptian magic, which involves a scrupulous taxonomic description and account of the use of narcotics to induce hallucinatory experience, is exemplary of this method. Lane's refusal to rationalize the mirror of ink even within the taxonomic framework he himself had created speaks to the modern British appetite for a mystical Orient in a text that otherwise eschews popular sensationalism. His "hope" that the trick not "induce . . . skepticism" toward the rest of the work insulates the mirror of ink episode as a singular event within the narrative, charged with supernatural potential that repels the author's ethnographic rationalism.

Why does Lane, the sober scholar, present the mirror of ink this way? Jason Thompson, Lane's biographer, describes Lane's attitude toward Egyptian magic as "ambivalent . . . yielding to the persistent human desire to believe something real lies behind the veil of the occult."[29] This ambivalence is a powerful example of what Jason Ananda Joseph Storm,

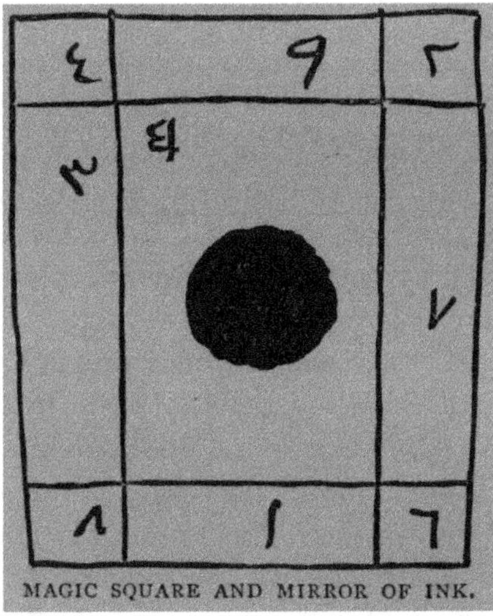

MAGIC SQUARE AND MIRROR OF INK.

FIGURE 2.2. The mirror of ink, as drawn by Edward William Lane. *The Manners and Customs of the Modern Egyptians*, Charles Knight, 1846.

in *The Myth of Disenchantment*, calls "the haunting presence of magic in the very instances when disenchantment [is] itself being theorized."[30] Lane collapses the binary of rationalism and superstition on which the pedagogy of disenchantment depends by applying its scientific and technological account of apparitions in the service of identifying an example of genuine supernatural magic. Instead of speculating about Lane's belief system, I want to propose that the decision to present the mirror of ink as a mystery allows it to play an important structural role in *The Manners and Customs of Modern Egyptians* as a double for the book itself. This doubling is evident on a very basic level of mediation and materiality. A printed story about ink as a magical medium cannot help but have reflexive affordances. This reflexivity becomes explicit in Lane's reproduction of Abd al-Qadir's magic square with the circular disk of ink at the center, lightly grained like a thumbprint and intoxicatingly illegible (figure 2.2). A copy of what Lane saw Abd al-Qadir draw in the boy's hand, the image is at once ethnographic document, illustration, and metatext, grounding the mirror of ink in the materiality of paper and ink and linking it to the processes of writing and printing. It is quite literally "made" of the same materials as the book and reflects the function of the book as something to read, look at, and hold in the hand.

Even as it foregrounds the materiality of the book, the mirror of ink also performs what Leah Price describes as the bourgeois disarticulation of book from text in Victorian letters. Price argues that, for Victorian novelists, "to take in a book is to tune out its raw materials," so much so that absorption in the literary text is valorized as a forgetting of its physical medium, a construction that finds paradigmatic form in George Eliot's reflection on the book's "transfiguration" through the act of reading: "We no longer hold heavily in our hands an octavo of some hundred pages . . . but we seem to be in companionship with a spirit, who is transfusing himself into our souls."[31] The mirror of ink is structured by a similar kind of "transfiguration" of physical object into spiritual transfusion. Grounded in the physicality of ink in the palm, just as Eliot imagines the printed pages "held heavily in our hands," the mirror of ink paradoxically effects a kind of mediation without materiality because the ink turns into a communication technology that "transfuses" dematerialized, virtual images into the mind (or soul). In Lane's illustration, the circle of ink at the center of the square simultaneously forecloses signification and figures the way ink marks on a page come to signify, through the act of reading, a process that turns words made out of ink into a sequence of mental images. It represents mediation itself.

The mirror of ink also has strong resonances with Lane's imperial literary project. The magician's unveiling of a hidden reality is strikingly similar to Lane's own personal vocabulary for his romance with Egypt. The verse from the Koran that Abd al-Qadir writes out as part of the ceremony—"and we have removed from thee thy veil; and thy sight to-day is piercing"—echoes the words that Lane himself wrote upon first arriving in Egypt in his initial unpublished manuscript. "As I approached the shore," he wrote, "I felt like an Eastern bridegroom, about to *lift up the veil* of his bride, and *to see*, for the first time, the features which were to charm, or disappoint, or disgust him" (emphasis added).[32] Lane's description of lifting Egypt's veil illustrates what Anne McClintock calls "male travel as an erotics of ravishment" that depicts knowledge as "male penetration and exposure of a veiled, female exterior."[33] In the mirror of ink, the boy's "veil" is removed so that his vision can "pierc[e]" through reality into the supernatural realm; as a traveler, Lane removes Egypt's "veil" so that it will reveal itself to him fully, even carnally. The erotics of ravishment are not only epistemological, presenting the country as a mystery to be probed and rationalized through print, but also clearly imperial; a bride is, after all, the property of the bridegroom. In this sense, the mirror of ink may have reminded Lane of his camera lucida, the handheld optical instrument that allowed him to trace sights in his sketchbook. The camera lucida allowed Lane to hold Egypt in his hand and turn it into print, rendering a country and its people as media to be consumed by the Western gaze. In all these ways, the mirror of ink functions within the text as a figure for Lane's sojourn to Egypt and a metatextual representation of the reading experience that *The Manners and Customs of Modern Egyptians* seeks to create. After all, Lane also promised to "unveil" Egypt for the reader through a combination of words and pictures.

The inexplicable power of the mirror of ink—its status as optical magic that was somehow also occult—served to construct the mirror of ink as a hybrid figure for text and image, reading and seeing. In the 1840s and 1850s, commentators would turn to the mirror of ink as an explanatory framework for the "magic" of reading and of fiction. An 1842 essay in London's *Mirror of Literature, Amusement, and Instruction* advocating for the value of reading and writing proposed that "that strange illusion, the mirror of ink, of which travelers in Egypt speak with so much wonder . . . is no longer a juggle, as shewn in that most common and yet most amazing of all arts, reading. There truly is the ink as magic mirror." To "look" into the inked words on the page is to "behold . . . those whom the wizard writer would conjure to our view," a construction that is already implicit in *The Manners and Customs of Modern Egyptians*.[34] While the mirror of ink is a "juggle," or a trick, reading is a "true" conjuring of images through ink. In other cases, the mirror of ink was conceived as an inexhaustible well of stories. "The boy evidently saw just such scenes as are depicted in the wildest stories in the Thousand Nights," wrote the American evangelical William MacLure Thomson, "and I suspect that this very art was in greater perfection then than now, and that the gorgeous creations of that work were, in many cases, mere verbal pictures taken from the magic mirror of ink."[35] In this construction, the boy "reads" the pictures he sees in the ink, which are then transcribed in ink as the text of the *Thousand and One Nights*. These figurative instantiations of writing as conjuring, reading as seeing, and fiction as magical apparition take their energy from the mirror of ink's apparent refusal to be explained.

Thus, the Borges story with which we began does not invent but simply makes explicit the imaginary surrounding the mirror of ink from the moment of its emergence in Victorian literary culture. By taking the optical potential of the ink to generate images as a figure for the travelogue as a descriptive literary mode, *The Manners and Customs of*

Modern Egyptians offers the mirror of ink as an optical technology and infinite text, a figure for reading as a transcendence of the materiality of the codex that reconfigures it as pure perception. What is lost in Borges's story, however, is the account in *The Manners and Customs of Modern Egyptians* of descriptive writing as a distinctly Orientalist and imperialist mode that is not only analogized in but also troubled by the mirror of ink. Borges purports to quote a tale printed in Burton's *The Lake Regions of Equatorial Africa*, one in which Burton himself reproduces the story of the Sudanese magician in his own voice. Burton is therefore not a witness to the mirror of ink; he simply records the story reported by the magician. In *The Manners and Customs of Modern Egyptians*, the mirror of ink is something that happens *to* the Orientalist and is held at a remove from him through the mediating role of the boy. Lane sees the trick happen, but he does not see the images appear.

In this way, the apparent kinship of the mirror of ink with the imperialist literary project of describing Egypt is also a source of disturbance because it threatens the specular logic that positions Egypt and Egyptians as the objects of the imperialist gaze. Lane the "bridegroom," who "throw[s]" himself "among strangers" so that he can see and experience what other Europeans cannot, is startlingly disempowered by the magician's trick, stripped of his epistemological privilege to see and record. The mirror of ink turns on the boy seeing pictures where Lane only sees the hypnotic black circle. Here, it is the Egyptian child who has the power to see and to narrate, making the imperialist dependent on native knowledge that, in spite of his privileged status as "bridegroom," he himself cannot unveil. While it serves as a figure for Lane's representational project, the mirror of ink also subverts what Mary-Louise Pratt calls the "imperial eyes" of nineteenth-century travel writing by creating a virtual scene foreclosed to all but the native subject.[36]

Given this context, it is even more provocative that Lane's account of the trick centers on the boy's accurate description of Admiral Nelson. The naval commander responsible for bringing the Mediterranean under British control during the Napoleonic era, Nelson made Egypt accessible to Lane and to other British travelers and Orientalists. In a work that represents Lane's objectifying gaze on Egypt and Egyptians, what does it mean that an Egyptian boy can peer into what to Lane looks like a black void and see a British imperial hero? Lane looks at the boy, but through the mediation of the mirror of ink, the boy seems to look back. When he looks at Nelson, describing his costume and scrutinizing his war injury, he effectively meets Lane's imperial gaze.

The mirror of ink allows the boy to claim what Nicholas Mirzoeff calls "the right to look"—a right that Mirzoeff reads as a claim to political subjectivity and a means of contesting the authority of imperial visualizations like Lane's.[37] *The Manners and Customs of Modern Egyptians* thus gives birth to a deeply ambivalent figure for the literary and visual culture of nineteenth-century British Empire, one that stands simultaneously for the Orient as the product of British representations and for its unrepresentability, for the Orient as object of British inquiry and for its inscrutability to British knowledge. If the infinite representations of the inkblot double the exhaustive visual descriptions of *The Manners and Customs of Modern Egyptians*, they also threaten to supersede Lane's account and therefore to challenge his rhetorical and scopic enactment of Western hegemony.

Perhaps this is why Lane would disavow the mirror of ink so forcefully a decade later. In the pages of his sister Sophia Lane-Poole's *The Englishwoman in Egypt* (1845), he reported on a repeat visit to see the mirror of ink and declared the performances "ridiculous for their complete want of success," accusing Abd al-Qadir of fraudulence and imposture.[38] As we will see in the following section, British discourse on the mirror of ink was in no way diminished by his disavowal. From Harriet Martineau to George Eliot, Victorian writers seemingly responded to the counterimperial rebelliousness of the mirror of ink, its refusal to be brought under British control, by rewriting it as a product of Western scientific knowledge and figure for realism in the novel.

Put Your Face to the Glass

What could the magic mirror of ink possibly have to do with the novels of George Eliot? A painstaking work of realist world building, Eliot's first novel *Adam Bede* (1959) relates the lives of a handful of characters in the fictional town of Hayslope at the turn of the nineteenth century. Among them are a Methodist woman preacher, an honest and hardworking carpenter, a careless young squire, and a coy dairymaid whose romantic entanglements and spiritual striving are the basis of the narrative. The novel's first setting, a carpentry workshop, reveals its preoccupation with the sturdy, the solid, and the well built, and its subsequent guided tour of farm, dairy, and woods with the provincialism of preindustrial English life. Its claim to being the first realist novel in the nineteenth-century British tradition rests, in the eyes of many scholars, on what the narrator calls "the faithful representation of commonplace things," an aesthetic that the novel compares to the "pictures of a monotonous homely existence" in seventeenth-century Dutch painting.[39] Scholars generally draw on the aesthetics of realist painting to define Eliot's representational philosophy as a deliberate avoidance of sensationalism or the exotic—Cairo, say, and its magicians.[40] But those who know the novel well recall its famous opening lines, which unexpectedly conjure this narrative world into being through reference to Egyptian sorcery. The novel begins:

> With a single drop of ink for a mirror, the Egyptian sorcerer undertakes to reveal to any chance-comer far-reaching visions of the past. This is what I undertake to do for you, reader. With this drop of ink at the end of my pen, I will show you the roomy workshop of Mr. Jonathan Burge, carpenter and builder in the village of Hayslope, as it appeared on the eighteenth of June, in the year of our Lord 1799. (5)

The humble world of *Adam Bede*, beginning with the "roomy workshop" of a carpenter and builder faithfully represented in all its regional and historical specificity, comes into being through the Egyptian magic act that we have heard so much about. The lines announce, of all things, Lane's *The Manners and Customs of Modern Egyptians* as an intertext for this classic novel of English life.

Eliot follows Lane's lead in *The Manners and Customs of Modern Egyptians* by invoking the mirror of ink as part of a metaphor for the relationship between writers and their readers, one that figures the literary text in visual terms. The narrator, who presents himself as the author and is gendered throughout as masculine, is an "Egyptian sorcerer" who uses "the drop of ink at the end of my pen" in the same way that Abd al-Qadir uses the mirror of ink in the boy's palm: to reveal visions of the past, but in the novel, it is in the form of settings and characters. One imagines the ink pooling at the end of the pen and dropping onto the page, so shiny in its black opacity that it becomes paradoxically lucid with reflections. The reader is the "chance-comer," a role that collapses the positions of the boy who witnesses the images in the ink and the Western traveler who witnesses the boy's magical visions. The identification of the reader as a traveler is a convention of realist fiction that Alison Byerly calls "virtual travel," or the inscription of the reader's physical presence and mobility in a fictional world, a set of techniques that she links to the forms of direct address in guidebooks and other travel media.[41] Yet Eliot's "chance-comer" is initially defined by their immobility. They do not physically travel but stand still to gaze into the mirror of ink, a process that seemingly transports them to other times and places. Eliot is comparing the novel's creation of a diegesis to the construction of virtual sight that we find in the imaginary of the mirror of ink. She conceives of the book as a virtual medium that uses the material technology of ink on paper—the printed word—to make images appear to the reader, an experience that itself stands for a fully embodied and multisensory immersion in a simulated world. After all, the carpentry workshop comes into being not only as a picture to be "shown" but also one that is smelled, heard, and felt on the skin as the scent of pinewood filters through the door, a worker sings in his strong baritone, and the afternoon sun falls hot on the workers.

Although the opening of *Adam Bede* is frequently discussed in scholarship on the Victorian novel, often in the context of the novel's metafictional use of mirrors as figures for literary representation, its articulation of fictional aesthetics remains insufficiently theorized.[42] This is because, instead of the opening lines, critics have primarily focused on the novel's famous chapter 17, "In Which the Story Pauses a Little," for Eliot to deliver a theory and a defense of literary realism. In this chapter, the novel-as-mirror is conceived as a means for truthful representation as the narrator strives to "give a faithful account of men and things as they have mirrored themselves in my mind . . . as if I were in the witness-box narrating my experience on oath" (157). As Meegan Kennedy has shown, this construction is not of the novel as a simple reflection of nature but rather of the novel as legal transcription of the mind's optical mediation of everyday experience.[43] This "faithful account" of the ordinary Eliot further compares to the deidealized aesthetics of Dutch paintings, with their old women bending over flower pots and vulgar village weddings.[44] Both the mirror and Dutch painting are linked to practices of observation that are precise, humble, faithful, and hardworking, expressions of a scrupulous humanism deeply inflected with Protestant values of simplicity and self-abnegation. Without denying the importance of painting as among the novel's varied visual metaphors for literary representation, it is worth asking why *Adam Bede* begins not with a painted image but rather a virtual image—not with a mirror that reflects the real but one that creates it—not with what Rachel Teukolsky calls Eliot's realism of "authentic truth-telling" but instead a realism of exotic Oriental fabulation.[45] This is a different model of visuality than the one Eliot develops in chapter 17 of her novel and cannot simply be subsumed into it.

When critics do discuss the opening of the novel at length, they tend to provide, at best, only cursory treatment of the origins of the mirror of ink metaphor in Lane's *The Manners and Customs of Modern Egyptians*, overlooking the larger context of its circulation as a figure for optical magic, perceptual illusion, and the imperial gaze. Yet this context is of critical importance to an analysis of *Adam Bede* as a theory of representation in novel form. Without understanding what exactly the mirror of ink was, how can we fully appreciate what Eliot imagines the novel to do? For example, when J. Hillis Miller analyzes the mirror of ink metaphor as a reflexive figure for mimesis, he argues that "the ink drop is a mirror that is no mirror" but "a transformation of the material world into another realm, the realm of performative writing that creates what it seemingly only describes. In that realm one encounters something outside the optic laws of reflection . . . that is, some of the problematic aspects of language."[46] This analysis relies on a misunderstanding of both the conjurer's mirror and the mirror of ink as figures in Victorian literary culture. First, Miller assumes that the mirror's "optic laws" are mimetic, drawing on an equivalence between a mirror image and verisimilitude that elides the mirror's relationship to optical magic and virtual images in nineteenth-century culture. Second, he assumes that Eliot is turning the Egyptian mirror of ink into a figure for literary technique and the phenomenological operations of a literary text in producing or creating reality for the reader, overlooking the fact that Eliot draws on a longer history of the mirror of ink as a trope for that "transformation of the material world into another realm," reconfiguring it for her own purposes. We know that these opening lines are more than a pithy play on words—they are part of a tradition of figuring the act of reading as seeing immaterial images. If the mirror of ink serves as a metaphor for *Adam Bede*'s narrator "creating" what he "seemingly only describes"—the workshop of Jonathan Burge, the world of the novel—then it is in a precise echo of the optical technological properties and imaginary virtual capacities that the mirror of ink had come to stand for: not the optic law of reflection as one-to-one reproduction of the external world as image, but the use of lenses and mirrors to create, through images, something that was not there before.

We can understand *Adam Bede*'s reflexivity more fully if we consider its place in responding to and shaping the imaginary of the literary text as a machine for virtual perception—an imaginary that unfolded, among other places, in writing on the mirror of ink. By the 1850s, the mirror of ink had a life of its own in British letters and belonged to

Victorian popular and scientific culture as much as it did to Lane's travelogue. Eliot's mirror of ink is not exactly Lane's mirror of ink, but a trope reconfigured by two decades of writing that associated it with scientific and technological explanations for how people see things that are not really there. This included work on optics, as we saw in the preceding section, but also on sciences of mind, especially the highly popular and much debated science of mesmerism. *Adam Bede*'s mirror of ink thus registers a variety of techniques for enabling ordinary people to see things that are not there. By unpacking these contexts, I will demonstrate that *Adam Bede* imagines the writer as part optical showman and part mesmerist, the reader at once as spectator at an optical show and clairvoyant medium. What this shows us is that Eliot turns to the mirror of ink as part of her theorization of a virtual literary aesthetics: an account of the aesthetic experience of reading the novel as seeing things that are not there.

The mirror of ink does not appear again in *Adam Bede*, but neither does it exactly disappear. It haunts the novel's other strange mirrors, all of them strangely flawed, from the burnished dining room table "turned up like a screen" in which the vain milkmaid likes to admire her reflection (67) to the narrator's famous assertion that he will "give a faithful account of men and things as they have mirrored themselves in my mind," even though "the mirror is doubtless defective; the outlines . . . disturbed, the reflection faint or confused" (159). The opening lines of the novel establish a metaleptic motif associated with readerly visualization that weaves its way through the novel. Metalepsis is the literary device through which a text acknowledges and draws attention to its own artifice. The opening lines of the novel are examples of what Monika Fludernik calls the "metaleptic metaphor" because metalepsis is folded into the extended metaphor of the mirror of ink.[47] When the narrator says, "This is what I undertake to do for you, reader," he breaks the illusion of the fictional world, addressing the reader directly and reminding them that it has been manufactured for them by the writer. As Fludernik notes, however, the effect of this metaleptic metaphor is not to "[disrupt] immersion" but instead to "deepen the reader's involvement in the fiction."[48] This is an effect that Eliot employs repeatedly in book I of *Adam Bede*, a volume that takes the form of a virtual tour of the town of Hayslope and what will become its narratively significant locations: the carpentry shop, the hall farm, the dairy, the woods. For example, the narrator says invitingly, "Let me take you into that dining-room, and show you the Rev. Alolphus Irwine, Rector of Broxton, Vicar of Hayslope, and Vicar of Blythe." He invites us to "enter softly" and "stand in the open doorway" so we do not awaken "the glossy-brown setter who is stretched across the hearth" (50). Later, we are enjoined to "[put] our eyes close to the rusty bars of the gate" of the Hall Farm and to "peep at the windows," trying to see inside the house (64–65). The narrator instructs: "Put your face to the glass panes in the right-hand window: what do you see?" (65) These are all examples of metalepsis that intensify the diegesis rather than rupturing it and that instantiate the act of reading as virtual visual perception. To read is to be taken into rooms and to have characters shown to us, to look and see—acts that are all performed in relation to, and under the direction of, the narrator.

Adam Bede's mirror of ink is thus not an opening gimmick that is quickly discarded nor is it simply part of a broader motif of mirrors, reflections, and optical visuality. It is an instantiation of the novel's metafictional exploration of narration as a representational technique. In his analysis of the mirror of ink metaphor in *Adam Bede*, Neil Hertz argues that, "after the opening paragraph, Eliot does not so explicitly or elaborately thematize her text's relation to its readers."[49] What I am endeavoring to show here is just the opposite: Eliot sustains the reflexivity of the mirror of ink motif through these instances of metalepsis, which figure the relationship between narrator and reader as shared spectatorship of a virtual scene, one that is created by the narrator but only enacted through the process of reading. Jacob Romanow has argued that metafiction is a representational technology intrinsic to Victorian realism—an "essential means of rendering realism realistic."[50] Eliot's metafictional practice exposes the reader to the novel as a representational technology for making us see things. By insisting that the novel's scenes are made visible to us through a magic mirror, Eliot codes *Adam Bede* as a feat of optical conjuring in which the showman astonishes his audience by making images appear through the use of hidden mirrors and lenses. She makes explicit the role of writer as optical showman and magician who "show[s]" us and makes us "see." Eliot's metafiction thus opens into a theory of literary mediation that makes the reader's imaginative visualization central to producing realism's realness. She asks us to see ourselves seeing, to visualize the reading experience as itself an act of visualization.

Eliot's commitment to narrative world building as a kind of show-and-tell also points us to the political significance of her allusion to *The Manners and Customs of Modern Egyptians*. Although an Orientalist travelogue may seem an unlikely intertext for a novelistic retrospective on British national origins, Eliot's guided tour of Hayslope recalls the very genre that Lane is working in as well as his addiction to descriptive excess. Rachel Teukolsky and Alison Byerly have compared *Adam Bede* to forms of travel literature like the travelogue and war journalism, both focusing on how the second chapter is focalized through the perspective of an anonymous traveler.[51] While Byerly rightly argues that this device grounds the novel in "a *traveler*'s perspective, the view of someone who stops briefly, makes judgments, and then moves on," I wish to draw attention to the ways that this choice of focalization participates in the novel's broader conceptualization of what Teukolsky calls ethnographic witnessing. For Teukolsky, the figure of the traveler stands for someone like the Crimean War journalist tasked with "sending back visual evidence of foreign customs taken on the spot."[52] As we have seen, this is also the task of an ethnographer like Lane, albeit at a slower and more deliberative pace, and it is equally the task that Eliot's narrator describes himself as undertaking through an allusion to *The Manners and Customs of Modern Egyptians*. Like Lane in Cairo, unveiling Egypt for the common reader, Eliot's narrator wants to "show you" a particular time and place; while Lane takes us into the mosque and public bath, down streets and past fountains, Eliot takes us into the hall farm, the dairy, and the woods. The writer is sometimes the tour guide, making things visible by inviting us to notice them. Sometimes he instructs in the imperative tense, the scene unfolding through the language of command: "See them in the bright sunlight, interrupted every now and then by rolling masses of cloud" (64). By coding the diegesis as a mirror of ink, Eliot makes explicit what is only implicit in *The Manners and Customs of Modern Egyptians*: the conceptual similarity between the writer's world-building ambitions and the conjuring of images. At the same time, the reference to *The Manners and Customs of Modern Egyptians* makes explicit what is otherwise only implicit in *Adam Bede*: provincial realism's adoption of the imperial gaze to reenchant the sights and scenes of English life. If the narrator is "like the Egyptian sorcerer," he is also something like the British Orientalist ethnographer. Eliot adapts the techniques of the Orientalist travelogue to conjure English history as an apparition and make it alive in the present.

So far, my reading of Eliot's mirror of ink has emphasized the relationship between her philosophy of realism and practices of optical showmanship that produce virtual images. I turn now to how *Adam Bede*'s metafictional exploration of the narrator's perceptual control over the reader's vision engages with mesmerism. Mesmerism was a science of mind believed to allow one person to transfer their energy, or "vital force," to another person by inducing a trancelike state.[53] Although I have argued that Lane's account of the mirror of ink was influenced by Western frameworks of optical technology and the creation of virtual images, by the late 1840s, mesmerism replaced optics as the prevailing explanation for the mirror of ink in British discourse. The connection had already crossed Lane's mind when he was writing *The Manners and Customs of Modern Egyptians*. Noting that Abd al-Qadir maintained physical contact with the boy throughout the performance, he remarked in a footnote that "this reminds us of animal magnetism," using another term for mesmerism.[54] But it was another Cairo travelogue, Harriet Martineau's *Eastern Life, Past and Present* (1848), that definitively changed the way Victorians understood the mirror of ink. Martineau was a chronic invalid and the author of *Letters on Mesmerism* (1845), which detailed her experience treating her illness with mesmerism. Shortly after the success of her mesmeric cure, she undertook a vigorous tour of Egypt and the Near East, stopping in Cairo to see the magician that *The Manners and Customs of Modern Egyptians* had made so much of.[55] "I have brought away a very clear and strong impression of the whole case," she wrote in *Eastern Life, Past and Present*.[56] The mirror of ink was mesmerism: Sheik Abd al-Qadir made his assistants see images in the ink by mesmerizing them. When the trick worked—which, in her opinion, it rarely did—it was not because of the magician's mesmeric skill but because his assistants were clairvoyant.

Clairvoyants were those capable of "see[ing] events, people, and places at a geographical or chronological distance" while mesmerized.[57] Their powers included predicting the future and seeing into the past, and they were even known to diagnose illnesses by looking beneath the skin and to travel to overseas colonies from their own homes.[58] Although it strained the credulity of even many proponents of mesmerism, clairvoyance was not considered to be a supernatural power. As Martineau explained, "human beings have, under certain conditions, a power of Prevision and Insight, altering with ordinary states of mind."[59] For believers, clairvoyant vision was as natural and rationally explicable as ordinary vision, but it was only accessible when mesmerized. Martineau's insistence that she had returned from Cairo with a "clear and strong impression" of the mirror of ink as mesmerism was racialized, contrasting her presence of mind with what she characterized as the "susceptibil[ity]" of "the Hindoos and the negroes," but it was also clearly intended as a riposte to

Lane's inability to explain the trick in *The Manners and Customs of Modern Egyptians.*[60] As a careful student of mesmerism, she was, like Lane, struck by the physical contact between the magician and the boy and its resemblance to the "mesmeric passes" used to induce a trance state. The boy's quivering eyelids, meanwhile, signaled to her "the presence of mesmeric action."[61] To prove her theory, Martineau insisted on taking the boy's place in the experiment. She reported seeing "such odd things in the pool of ink,—it grew so large before my aching eyes, and showed such strange moving shadows and clear symmetrical figures and moving lines."[62] Ironically, Martineau's "clear and strong impression" is authenticated by her weak and fuzzy vision.

Martineau's explanation of the mirror of ink was widely accepted in the second half of the nineteenth century. Proponents included Richard Francis Burton, the explorer to whom Borges credits the mirror of ink tale. In his own Cairo travelogue, published less than a decade after Martineau's, Burton scoffed at Lane's sensationalized version of the mirror of ink as well as his claim that the trick had "excited considerable curiosity and interest throughout the civilized world." How could the "civilized world" be so fascinated when "in London, Paris, and New York, [they] might have found dozens studying the science"?[63] What Burton meant was that Lane's supposed discovery of the mirror of ink was really just a rediscovery of mesmerism, repackaged as Egyptian magic. Burton elaborated on this point more than twenty years later in a talk on "Spiritualism in Eastern Lands" (1878) by emphasizing the similarities between the mirror of ink and hypnotism.[64] Hypnotism was a technique developed by Scottish surgeon James Braid, who argued that what others called mesmerism was a voluntary state created when the patient chose to focus their mind on an external sensory stimulus. Burton cited an account of a hypnotic variation on the mirror of ink that used a white earthenware plate covered with geometric figures and cabalistic words in an echo of Ab al-Qadir's magic square. The subject would focus their sight on a particular point until they began to see "a black spot in the middle of the plate [that] grows larger, changes in shape, and transforms itself into different apparitions, which float (or rather pass in procession) before the subject."[65]

Martineau's reframing of the mirror of ink as mesmerism also influenced mesmeric demonstrations themselves. Mesmerism and hypnotism were popularized through public demonstrations that recalled sorcery, with mesmerists directing insensible subjects to stand, sit, or swing their arms "as if by the wand of a magician."[66] As early as the

1850s, these performances began incorporating references to the mirror of ink. In a demonstration reported on by novelist Wilkie Collins in a series of essays for *The Leader* titled "Magnetic Evenings at Home," a "black mirror"—a piece of wood shaped like a hand mirror with polished coal in place of a looking glass—was used as a surface or screen on which the mesmeric clairvoyant visualized the sights and scenes directed by the guests.[67] While the mesmerist claimed that this object was the "wishing-stone" of astronomer John Dee, the performance clearly reimagined the mirror of ink by substituting for the ink drop another black substance posing as a mirror. It is certainly clear that Collins took it this way. His report not only inspired a short story, "My Black Mirror," that portrayed John Dee's mirror as a virtual technology that visualizes "the image of my former travels" on "the surface of the cannel coal," it may also have influenced his famous portrayal of the mirror of ink in *The Moonstone* (1868).[68] As we will see in chapter 3, which discusses *The Moonstone* at some length, the novel's mystery turns on a trio of Brahmins who perform the mirror of ink on a young English boy, using him as a medium to predict future events. Collins's representation of the trick breaks its association with Egypt and Islam but shows that he, like Martineau and Burton, understood it as mesmerism: details like "the Indian . . . touching the boy's head" and the boy standing "like a statue" reflected the physical contact required to induce a trance state, while the use of the trick to see the future puts Martineau's theory of clairvoyance into practice.

Adam Bede participates in this genealogy of the mirror of ink as mesmerism. Its account of the novel as a mirror of ink, and the narrator as an "Egyptian sorcerer," presents it as an apparition that is at once optical and mental—a "black spot" that "transforms itself" into pictures through the mediation of the text. Eliot would have learned about mesmerism from her partner George Henry Lewes, a student of physiology and psychology who believed in mesmerism's more modest claims but scorned the existence of clairvoyance, a point he made in a scathing response to Collins's "Magnetic Evenings at Home."[69] It is reasonable to assume that she, like Lewes, would have read Collins's articles on clairvoyance and made the same set of connections between the black mirror, the mirror of ink, and mesmerism that Collins did in his own literary work. However, Eliot also had direct experience of mesmerism. In the summer of 1844, she was mesmerized by a dinner companion; as her friend Cara Bray described it, "she could not open her eyes, and begged [the mesmerist] most piteously to do it for her."[70] It is not clear whether Eliot was asking to awaken from the mental images that some mesmeric patients describe or simply to regain control over her own body. Either way, *Adam Bede*'s reflexive commentary on the relationship between the writer and the reader mimics this relationship between the mesmerist and the mesmerized by placing the reader's vision under the author's control. When the narrator instructs the reader to "put your face to the glass panes in the right-hand window" and asks "what do you see," he makes the power to look and see dependent on his narration, on what he directs her to see through the images he makes appear: "A large open fireplace, with rusty dogs in it, and a bare boarded floor" (65). To say, as the narrator does in the opening lines, that "I will show you the roomy workshop of Mr. Jonathan Burge" is also to say that your vision is in my power.

The narrator's metaleptic directions evoke even more specifically a clairvoyant practice that blended the practices of ethnographic travel writing with mesmerism. Sometimes called "traveling somnambulism," this kind of clairvoyance involved people under mesmerism "travel[ing] . . . to distant places, where they could stroll around, see local sights, and enter houses."[71] Traveling somnambulism was as locomotive as it was visual in that mesmerized subjects "experienced actual movement to a destination," where they would then verify their clairvoyant travel through visual descriptions of architecture, interior decoration, and people.[72] It was also deeply narrative, a kind of travel literature executed collaboratively by the mesmerist and the mesmerized person. As Emily Ogden explains, "Somnambulists could transport themselves in imagination to other cities only if those in rapport with them first convinced them, through narrative, that they were really traveling," a process of interactive storytelling that involved "regularly following the somnambulist's suggestions and negotiating with her sense of the plausible."[73] The narrator's injunction to "put your face to the glass"—to "look" and "see"—reflects actual narrative techniques used by mesmerists to send clairvoyants on journeys of the mind.

Through the metaleptic metaphor of the mirror of ink and its discursive connections to mesmerism and optical technology, *Adam Bede* imagines the literary text as a medium by which human vision can be extended. My use of the term "medium" here is meant to capture both of its meanings as an image-producing technology and a spiritualist practitioner. The novel presents itself as a kind of optical mesmerism on the reader, managing and even controlling their perception like a mesmerist while making them see a series of images like an optical showman. In this imaginative synthesis, Eliot's variation on the mirror of ink most closely resembles an obscure science called psychography, or the writing of thoughts, that brought mesmerism and optics together to posit the existence of telepathic communication. In the early 1840s, an American physician and mesmerist named Robert Collyer published a pamphlet in which he argued that Lane's description of the mirror of ink in *The Manners and Customs of Modern Egyptians* proved that human beings could transfer their thoughts to one another. Ink itself was not required—"any dark fluid will answer to the same purpose"—and Collyer advocated using a bowl of molasses placed between the two subjects. The "recipient" and "operator" both look into the molasses. "When the angle of the incidence from my brain was equal to the angle of reflection from her brain," Collyer explains, "[the recipient] distinctly saw *the image* of my thoughts at their point of coincidence."[74] Collyer illustrated this explanation with a diagram that broke down how the optic laws of reflection applied to the transference of thoughts, portraying two men with broken lines representing the angle of incidence flowing from their brows (figure 2.3). With their matching mutton chops and the same head of hair brushed into slightly different shapes, operator and recipient are themselves mirror images, as if the psychographic process has turned them into twins.

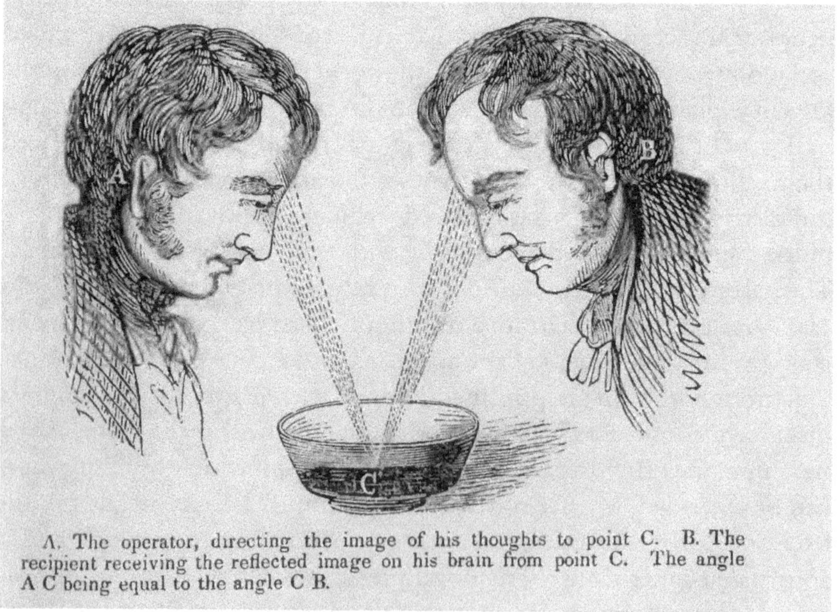

FIGURE 2.3. Psychography in action: the bowl of molasses experiment. Robert H. Collyer, *Psychography, or, the Embodiment of Thought*, Redding, 1843.

The nearly identical men in Collyer's illustration also recall photographic doubles. This is not a coincidence: Collyer described psychography as "a mental photographic process" that is "nearly identical with the daguerreotype process," which had just been invented. In 1836, Lane described the mirror of ink as similar both to optical technological magic and mesmerism. In Collyer's version of the mirror of ink, any distinction between optical technology and mesmerism collapses. Images are thoughts and thoughts are images. Like light, thought image is a physical property that can be reflected and refracted, mediated and manipulated. While light writing, or photography, produces light images, psychography, or thought writing, produces thought images. *Adam Bede* conceives of the relationship between writer and reader in remarkably similar terms. The novel is a mirror of ink that allows the reader to "see" the images that have "mirrored themselves" in the writer's mind—a technology of thought transference that expresses itself in images. This is not a mimetic realism that aspires to duplicate the world in images but a psychographic realism that transforms the world into mental images that can be communicated between reader and writer.

Scholars frequently turn to *Adam Bede*'s metaphorics of mirroring to understand what the novel has to say about fictional representation, guided by the assumption that mirrors are simple reflecting devices that create a one-to-one equivalence between image and representation. Yet as I have endeavored to show, mirrors were so much more than this in the Victorian imagination, from spectral technologies and conjuring surfaces to mesmeric and telepathic media to imaginary portals to other times and places. A mirror need not be a looking glass; it could also be the concave mirror favored by magicians. It might even be a drop of ink or bowl of molasses or, as in *Adam Bede*, a burnished oak dining table. *Adam Bede* uses multiple visual metaphors for the novel, both painterly and optical, and my aim here is not to offer the mirror of ink as a master key to Eliot's theory of representation that cancels out the others. Rather, I wish to demonstrate that when Eliot compares her novel to images in a mirror of ink, she is not engaging with the mirror's verisimilitude but rather the mirror's virtuality. When we read the novel through its imperial and technological metaphorics, it becomes clear that *Adam Bede* envisions the realist novel as a kind of optical-perceptual machine that aspires to the condition of the virtual image.

Eliot spelled out this aspiration even more clearly in *The Lifted Veil*, the novella she wrote just after finishing *Adam Bede*. *The Lifted Veil* is often read as an outlier in Eliot's oeuvre because of its explicit investments in Victorian "new media" and sciences of mind.[75] A work of gothic horror narrated by Latimer, a man gifted (or cursed) with clairvoyant powers, its fantastical account of the prophetic visions that flood his sight "like the new images in a dissolving view" certainly breaks stylistically with the scrupulous realism with which Eliot is most associated. As a result, it has become common to read *The Lifted Veil* as an experimental riposte to Eliot's realist novels. For instance, Richard Menke argues that the novella constitutes an "alternative model of visual realism" that "challenges or inverts" what he conceives of as Eliot's painterly theory and practice of realism in *Adam Bede*.[76] While Menke compares this model of realism to photography, Eliot's use of optical technological figures like that of the dissolving view to describe the psychic and visual mechanics of Latimer's clairvoyance suggests an altogether different set of media references. A dissolving view is a magic lantern projection effect created with two or more lenses so that one projected image dissolves into another on the screen. Latimer's visions are like the "new image" that slowly supplants the first, "canceling out and replacing his consciousness of his surroundings" in what Jules Law calls "the mode of virtual or alternate reality."[77]

Given the case I have made for Eliot's realism as part of the mid-century imaginary of virtual sight, I wish to challenge the assumption that *The Lifted Veil* operates according to an alternative model of visual realism to that of *Adam Bede*. Latimer's visions are simply a rethinking of Eliot's mirror of ink, and *Adam Bede* and *The Lifted Veil* are both media theories of the novel as a technology for producing the real as virtual visuality. The similarities are evident in Latimer's first clairvoyant vision, which he experiences when his father describes to him an upcoming trip and leaves "my mind resting on the word *Prague*, with a strange sense that a new and wondrous scene was breaking upon me." He sees "a city under the broad sunshine," "the time-eaten grandeur of a people doomed to live on in the stale repetition of memories," and "a patch of rainbow light on the pavement, transmitted through a colored lamp in the shape of a star." This last he recalls with "special intensity" and will recognize when touring a synagogue in Prague's Jewish quarter as a projection in the shape of a Star of David, an image that mirrors Latimer's comparison of the vision itself to the dissolving projections of the magic lantern.[78] The spoken word, the clairvoyant vision, and the optical technological illusion are closely linked, just as the written word, mesmeric experience, and optical technology are closely linked in

Adam Bede. The prominent place of Jewish iconography both in Latimer's vision and his later verification of the vision is not a random detail but a reinscription of the Orientalism that undergirds Eliot's account of realism's virtuality in *Adam Bede*. The symmetry between the "dissolving view" of Latimer's vision and the "colored lamp in the shape of a star"—two technologies for light-based projections—grounds the capacity for virtual sight in the exotic otherness of European Jewry, just as *Adam Bede* associates virtual sight with Egyptian Muslims.

The title of *The Lifted Veil* draws us back to *The Manners and Customs of Modern Egyptians*. The title is usually sourced to Percy Bysshe Shelley's sonnet that begins "Lift not the painted veil that those who live / Call life," and it seems to describe both Latimer's condition and the highly dramatic scene in which a scientist lifts the "dark veil" of a woman's death through a blood transfusion that temporarily brings her back to life."[79] While I do not contest this reference, I agree with Neil Hertz that Eliot may also be thinking of another lifted veil, that of the Koranic verse recited and transcribed by the magician in Lane's description of the mirror of ink trick: "And we have removed from thee thy veil; and thy sight today is piercing."[80] Latimer is like the reader of *Adam Bede* whose sight has been unveiled by the optical-mesmeric narrator and can "pierc[e]" into other places and times. In his suffering at these involuntary visions, we can hear echoes both of Eliot plaintively crying out to her mesmerist to regain control of her eyes and her narrator's mesmeric control over the reader's sight when he directs them to "put your face to the glass." Rather than reading *The Lifted Veil* as a deliberate breach of *Adam Bede*'s realism, I propose that the tale's gothic conceit simply allows Eliot to extend her phenomenological inquiry into the novel as media technology that creates in the reader's mind what Peter Mendelsund calls "a continuous unfolding of images."[81]

Real Vision at a Distance

This chapter has endeavored to show how the fantasy of reading as "watching a film," in Peter Mendelsund's words, actually predates the invention of cinema. From Lane to Eliot to Borges, writers have turned to the changing landscape of virtual image media to imagine the literary text as a technology for transmitting images into the reader's mind. My object in making this case is not to lay claim to the mirror of ink as a protocinematic figure, as if cinema were the fulfillment of the nineteenth century's dreams of new technology, or to say that novelists imagined the cinema before its invention. The version of virtuality that we find in the mirror of ink is significantly different from the one we find in cinematic spectatorship, and I do not mean to conflate them. Instead, I have endeavored to reveal certain striking continuities between cinema and the virtual aesthetics of the mirror of ink. These continuities are not an invitation to read the mirror of ink as protocinematic but instead to read the cinematic as a post–mirror of ink formation.

We see the legacy of the mirror of ink, for example, in one of the best-known and most frequently cited accounts of early film spectatorship. In 1896, playwright Maxim Gorky saw cinema for the first time at the Nizhny-Novgorod All-Russia Exhibition in Moscow. "If only you knew how strange it is to be here," he wrote. "Here" is not the Théâtre Concerto Parisienne, the notorious theater and brothel where the cinematograph was on display, but the dominion of cinema itself, what he called a "Kingdom of Shadows" that existed within the films of the Lumière brothers. Cinema is a place that opens a phantasmal world within the world that Gorky describes as a trance: "You are forgetting where you are. Strange imaginings invade your mind and your consciousness begins to wane and grow dim."[82] Your body is in the theater, but your eyes are in the far-off places framed by the screen—an external world that also becomes an inner vision that "invade[s] your mind." *Adam Bede*'s reading-as-seeing-moving-pictures becomes, in early film spectatorship, seeing-moving-pictures-as-reading-*Adam Bede*. Like Eliot's narrator, who tells the reader to "put your face to the glass panes of the right-hand window," the images on the screen direct the spectator in what and how to see, a process that Gorky renders in the free indirect discourse of the Kingdom of Shadows itself: "You are forgetting where you are." Cinema has a voice, and it is the voice of a hypnotist—a voice like the narrator of *Adam Bede*.

The Victorian origins of this conception of reading as a technological extension of vision also make it clear that the fantasy of seeing at a distance of time and space is inextricable from the project of empire. The mirror of ink is, in *The Manners and Customs of Modern Egyptians*, a figure for the literary project of making visible and knowable to British readers a nation that they had formally occupied thirty years earlier and in which they had ongoing geopolitical interest. This is why it is no accident that Lane's telling of the trick hinges on the appearance of Admiral Nelson, a visualization of the imperial history that made this encounter between Lane and Abd al-Qadir possible in the first place. The ongoing fascination with the use of ink as a mirror, seen not only in *Adam Bede* but also in its re-creation by British and American mesmerists as black mirror and molasses, testifies not only to its reflexive potential as metaphor for writing or its conceptual link to the dark screens onto which magic lanterns throw their spectral images but also its racializing of darkness as a source of mystery and occult knowledge. The colonial resonances of the trick are only heightened when the American Collyer proposes switching one colonial commodity for another: black ink—called in Britain "Indian ink" for its source in the colonial trade with India—for molasses, derived from sugar and historically sourced by the United States from West Indian sugar plantations.[83] These dark portals to other minds, times, and places are haunting figures for the colonial scene and its absent presence in Western life.

Seen in this way, the mirror of ink can be read as a figure for the dislocations of nineteenth-century empire, the way it demands that we live in one place while governing or being governed by another. The same year that Gorky first saw the Lumière films, H. G. Wells published a short story called "The Remarkable Case of Mr. Davidson's Eyes" about a London man whose eyes are on "a little rock to the south of the Antipodes Island."[84] While he walks around his home, he sees a beach, penguins, and a ship in the distance—"an altogether phantasmal world."[85] This is not an imaginary scene but a real place that Davidson sees in real time, "his sight mov[ing] hither and thither . . . about this distant island" as he moves "hither and thither in London." Davidson's eyes "are the best authenticated case in existence of real vision at a distance."[86] "It may be possible," the story concludes, "to live visually in one part of the world, while one lives bodily in the other."[87] "The Remarkable Case of Mr. Davidson's Eyes" takes the imperial virtual aesthetics of the mirror of ink to its logical extension, removing the medium of the magic mirror and embedding the visual prosthetic in the eyes themselves.[88] At the same time, "real vision at a distance" names the conceit of a work of Orientalism like *The Manners and Customs of Modern Egyptians* or a realist novel like *Adam Bede* that purport to "show" us a time and place that is real but simply exists at an otherwise insurmountable remove, a way of seeing that the global reach of the British Empire seemed to demand of Victorians.[89] In chapter 3, I consider how the display of plundered Indian jewels at London's Great Exhibition in 1851 gave rise to new desires for vision at a distance—specifically, for diamonds that, not unlike the mirror of ink, would visualize through their fantastical glow the pleasures and dangers of colonial India.

CHAPTER 3

Mountains of Light

The Koh-i-Noor at the Great Exhibition

On July 1, 1850, the *HMS Medea* docked in Portsmouth, England, after a long and tumultuous journey from Bombay, India. On board was a small iron safe inside a red dispatch box marked with a wax seal. Inside the safe was the Koh-i-noor diamond. The most famous diamond in the world and arguably the single most valuable object in the entire Indian subcontinent, the Koh-i-noor, or Mountain of Light, made its way to England as a spoil of the Second Anglo-Sikh War.[1] Two days after its arrival, on July 3, the British East India Company would celebrate its 250th anniversary by presenting the diamond to Queen Victoria at Buckingham Palace. British newspapers announced the Koh-i-noor's arrival as the triumph of the British Empire in India. "After symbolizing the revolutions of ten generations by its passage from one conqueror to another," the *Times* of London wrote, "the celebrated Koh-i-noor, the great diamond of the East, comes now, in the third centenary of its discovery, as the forfeit of oriental faithlessness and the prize of Saxon valor, to the distant shores of England."[2] As the newest of the crown jewels, "we may look upon its acquisition as a fitting symbol of that supremacy that we have so fairly won."[3]

This characterization of the Koh-i-noor diamond captures the shared agenda of the British East India Company and colonial government, who used the diamond's history to cast the conquest of

India in a positive and progressive light.[4] In the eighteenth and early nineteenth centuries, Indian diamonds that circulated in Britain were both symptoms and symbols of the plunder imperialism that turned ordinary men into nabobs and revealed the greed and exploitation at the heart of the colonial project in India.[5] The Koh-i-noor was meant to rebrand British India as a moral endeavor: as "the forfeit of oriental faithlessness . . . fairly won." This was effective colonial propaganda, and perhaps it would have worked if the Koh-i-noor had not been displayed at London's Great Exhibition of 1851. This chapter tells the story of how the public exhibition of the Koh-i-noor diamond and the conditions of mass spectatorship subverted and undermined its state-authorized function as a prize of Saxon valor. When the Victorian public flocked to the East Nave of the Crystal Palace on May 1, 1851, and peered through the iron bars of the giant birdcage that held the Koh-i-noor, they did not see a "fitting symbol" of empire at all but a smallish, dull-looking, glassy nub of a stone. *Punch* satirized the Koh-i-noor as a "Mountain of Darkness" wearing "a gloom which nothing could dispel."[6] The Koh-i-noor was, in a word, unimpressive. Even the *Illustrated Exhibitor*, the official guide to the Great Exhibition, warned that, "although the Koh-i-noor is a great source of attraction for those who visit the Crystal Palace for the first time, it is at least doubtful whether it obtains such admiration afterwards."[7]

What the reception history of the Koh-i-noor exhibit shows is that spectators perceived the diamond through the framework of virtual aesthetics. They were not responding to it as a spoil of war or a material artifact of historical value but rather as an optical technological medium that they expected would be visually pleasing when it sparkled in the light. What the court and colonial government overlooked when the decision was made to place the Koh-i-noor on display was that Victorian diamonds not only signified what John Plotz calls "portable property," metonymic of the transfer of wealth from colony to metropole, but they also operated in Victorian culture as an optical technology that created mesmerizing visual effects through the refraction and reflection of light.[8] Understood through this framework, a diamond is only appealing insofar as it makes light perform. Audiences were disappointed when the diamond failed to live up to its name, Mountain of Light; that is, they were disappointed that the name failed to capture what they had come to expect would be this historic large diamond's medium-specific optical effects.

This chapter excavates a counternarrative of the Koh-i-noor diamond's significance for British perceptions of colonial India that emerges when we consider the history of its reception through the framework of virtual aesthetics. Drawing on essays, reviews, cartoons, and fictional narratives about the Koh-i-noor, I argue that the public responded to the diamond not as an imperial *symbol* but instead as an imperial *medium* by imagining that its optical virtuality could offer them virtual contact with India.[9] Like the mirror of ink, the magic trick we saw in chapter 2 that purported to "unveil" the vision of an ordinary boy so that he could see people and places otherwise unknown to him, the Koh-i-noor was constructed in the Victorian imagination as a crystal ball—another technology, to borrow H. G. Wells's phrase, for "vision at a distance." Thus, this chapter contributes to scholarship on nineteenth-century exhibitions and world's fairs that consider how the Great Exhibition's displays produced multiple, sometimes contradictory narratives of empire.[10] Against the British East India Company and colonial government's construction of the Koh-i-noor as "a fitting symbol of supremacy," I excavate an imaginary of the Koh-i-noor diamond that only comes into focus when we take seriously audience disappointment as an articulation of a competing set of attitudes and assumptions about the intersections between empire and spectacle. Audience response, understood expansively here to include novels and stories that fictionalized the Koh-i-noor's display at the Great Exhibition, reveals that Victorians drew on the context of optical culture to Orientalize the virtuality of the Koh-i-noor diamond. In this view, the optical effects of diamonds—sparkling, magnifying, and glowing in the dark—were imagined as staging a form of colonial encounter.

The chapter begins by contrasting two views of Indian diamonds in the mid-nineteenth century: as optical media and as symbols of empire. By telling the story of the Koh-i-noor as plunder of the Second Anglo-Sikh War, tribute to Queen Victoria, and exhibition at the Crystal Palace, I argue that the fraught reception of the Koh-i-noor at the Great Exhibition reveals competing ideas about how Victorians should experience Britain's Indian empire from their insulated perch in England. The disappointment of spectators at seeing a famous Indian diamond that did not sparkle is a symptom of an emergent desire for an optical empire: an empire that would express itself through virtual aesthetics.

I turn next to two literary works that fictionalize the Koh-i-noor in order to animate the discourse of diamonds as optical media that offer spectators a virtual encounter with empire. The first is "The Diamond

Lens" (1859), a little-known short story by the Irish-American writer Fitz-James O'Brien. O'Brien lived in London in the early 1850s, when he edited a short-lived magazine devoted to the Great Exhibition. "The Diamond Lens" is the tale of a large Brazilian diamond with the "Oriental" name Eye of Morning that the protagonist, Linley, grinds into a lens for his microscope. Through his diamond lens, he discovers a world inside a drop of water—a thinly veiled rendering of a tropical colony ripe for resource extraction. The second literary work, Wilkie Collins's novel *The Moonstone* (1868), is well known for taking the Koh-i-noor as its inspiration. The story of a plundered Indian diamond that "invades" an English country home before it mysteriously disappears, *The Moonstone* portrays its fictional Koh-i-noor as an optical medium that pervades the minds of its English spectators, creating new sensations that are frightening yet pleasurable. While "The Diamond Lens" imagines the diamond as a scopic technology of empire, facilitating "vision at a distance" to render the colonial scene as virtual image, *The Moonstone* imagines a diamond that penetrates the English body and deranges English perception through its optical effects. By presenting these two models of virtual encounter with a colonial scene, I argue that virtual aesthetics offered Victorians a framework for making sense of the presence of empire in everyday life.

Mountains of Light

We are accustomed to thinking of diamonds as rare and valuable objects, not as optical media. Most cultural and literary histories of nineteenth-century diamonds adopt the frameworks of material and economic history to consider diamond as "portable property" that originated in imperial extraction and circulated through systems of inheritance, courtship rituals, and property laws.[11] I follow this line of inquiry by reading diamonds as colonial commodities that symbolized India's status as British possession. India was firmly imprinted in the British imagination as the source of diamonds. This link was not purely imaginary: until the discovery of diamond mines in Brazil in 1725, and with the exception of black diamond crystals found in the mountains of Borneo, all the world's diamonds came from India.[12] Yet even after the late nineteenth-century South African diamond rush, the profound and historic connection between diamonds and Indian wealth, power, and prestige remained a fixity of British culture.[13] This can be explained at least in part by the British East India Company's notorious plundering of diamonds for personal wealth in the late eighteenth and early nineteenth centuries. For Shashi Tharoor, "it was Indian diamonds, which the nabobs brought back to Britain with them, that made the Empire real to the British public."[14] Diamonds are therefore metonymic of Indian empire itself; to possess a diamond is not just to possess a piece of India, forged in the depths of the Earth and therefore of the land itself, but to possess India in miniature.

Yet diamonds are not just property or material culture or things. They are also visually spectacular; as Adrienne Munich puts it, diamonds have "the power to addict the eye."[15] I adopt a phenomenological approach to material culture that recognizes diamonds as optical media that create virtual effects through their unique reflection and refraction of light. To borrow Isobel Armstrong's formulation in *Victorian Glassworlds: Glass Culture and the Imagination*, her cultural history of glass, diamonds are both material and medium.[16] As we will see, Victorians described the materiality and medium specificity of diamonds in relation to glass, focusing not only on diamonds' hardness and supposed imperviousness to shattering, but also their greater luminosity and capacity for magnification. Especially after 1851, when the Koh-i-noor, Daria-i-noor, and Hope diamonds were all exhibited in London at the Great Exhibition and seen up close by over six million people, diamonds "made the Empire real to the British public" not only through their circulation on British soil but equally through their strangely compelling visuality.

Nineteenth-century British consumers, spectators, and scientists recognized diamonds as aesthetic objects with medium-specific visual effects. Three effects in particular dominated the discourse. The first is that diamonds sparkle. They look like containers for light that are always overflowing, shimmering and glittering with excess luminosity that streams outward and engulfs them. This effect is the result of both the material properties of diamonds and the way they are cut. Diamonds naturally have a high refractive index and strong dispersion, allowing them to bend and break up light so that they sparkle brightly and give off a colorful glow. The shape into which a diamond is cut and the number, shape, size, and angle of facets determine how bright and fiery it will be. As Marcia Pointon explains, a diamond does not reveal its full beauty until it is modified by the human hand, the process of cutting and polishing transforming it from "precious raw material" to "acculturated artefact."[17]

I propose that we think of a diamond's sparkle as a technological media effect. The introduction of steam-powered and motorized diamond-polishing machines in the nineteenth century meant that diamonds were funneled to Europe as raw materials mined in colonial territories like India, South Africa, and Brazil and then fashioned into commodities through modern industrial technology. Compared with the manual cutting and polishing of gemstones, these methods allowed for the creation of rounder and more brilliant diamonds—diamonds technologically designed to sparkle brightly.

The fascination with sparkling suggests that a diamond was not just something beautiful to see, it was also something to see with. Put more plainly, a diamond could be an instrument for seeing light that delights the eye by making light perform. It is not only a technological artifact—it is also an optical technological medium, akin to the magic lanterns, mirrors, and panes of glass used to throw pictures onto a wall or make specters appear on a stage. Diamonds worn as jewelry can act as lenses without images. What they make visible is light itself: light that sparkles, shimmers, glows. This quality leads me to a second medium-specific quality of diamonds in the Victorian imagination: their phosphorescence. Phosphorescence names the phenomenon whereby a material that has been exposed to light continues to emit light even after the source disappears. The Hope Diamond—a large Indian diamond that was displayed next to the Koh-i-noor at the Great Exhibition—famously glows a deep orange-red for up to a minute after the lights go out. As Adrienne Munich shows, Victorian lapidaries incorrectly believed that all diamonds were phosphorescent.[18] Although we now know that only a small fraction of diamonds have this quality, the outsized status of phosphorescence in the nineteenth-century diamond imaginary underlines the construction of the diamond as a sort of machine for visual effects. Diamonds not only disperse light—they also store light, feasting on it like vampires to produce an uncanny afterglow.

Diamonds sparkle; diamonds phosphoresce; and finally, diamonds magnify. This third characteristic requires us to shift our context for diamonds from the ornamental to the scientific. At a moment when the laboratory study of optics was taking off, nineteenth-century opticians and physicists were fascinated by what the optical structure of diamond could offer to the creation of scientific instruments. Among them was David Brewster, the inventor of the kaleidoscope and stereoscope, whose popularization of optical technology and theory of virtual spectatorship was the subject of chapter 1. Early in his career, Brewster undertook an optical analysis of diamonds and other gemstones. In *A Treatise on New Philosophical Instruments* (1813), he wrote that the high refractive index of diamonds made them an ideal material for magnifying lenses, arguing that diamond lenses could improve the microscope by increasing its resolution. Brewster's plan was impractical—diamonds are, of course, very expensive—but it nevertheless inspired two men of science, C. R. Goring and Andrew Pritchard, to make and sell microscopes containing diamond and sapphire lenses.[19] In *The Microscopic Cabinet* (1832), which includes a lengthy account of Pritchard's construction of the jewel microscope with illustrations by Goring, Pritchard argues that diamond's superiority to glass as a magnifier "must enable us to penetrate farther into [an object's] real texture than we can hope to do by any artificial arrangement whatever."[20]

By "must," what Pritchard really meant was "should." His theory of the diamond lens was not entirely supported by his experiments, which revealed that diamonds were finicky to work with and often flawed in a way that introduced new aberrations into the microscopic image. Nevertheless, the jewel microscope expanded the nineteenth-century diamond imaginary by making diamonds into functional optical technologies for scientific investigation. Pritchard's belief in what the diamond lens "must" make visible, in spite of evidence to the contrary, made the diamond's existing status as technological medium explicit by constructing it as a miraculous visual prosthetic.

Meanwhile, Brewster continued to fantasize about how to blend the ornamental use of diamonds in jewelry with their scientific use as magnifiers. In 1864, he again raised the possibility of replacing the magnifying glass with the magnifying diamond, this time in a report on the stanhope viewer, or *bijou microscopique*. The stanhope viewer is an optical technology that places microphotographs inside novelty souvenirs and pieces of jewelry. The photographs could be peeped at through a simple microscope made of a glass cylinder and embedded in the bijou ("jewel").[21] If a diamond was a readymade magnifying lens, Brewster thought, why not simply pair a diamond ring with a microphotograph so that a man may gaze at a private image of his beloved that adorns his own hand?

The organizers of the Great Exhibition failed to recognize that the Koh-i-noor diamond was not only a material artifact and a deeply significant piece of British property but also an optical medium. Nor did they consider that the spectators they lured to the Crystal Palace on the promise of seeing this famous diamond with their own eyes might expect to witness some of the rather spectacular visual effects they had been taught to expect from a diamond named "mountain of light." Instead, the Koh-i-noor as a symbol of British imperial sovereignty was what was advertised for the Great Exhibition. Given pride of place as the third item listed in the *Official Descriptive and Illustrated Catalogue*

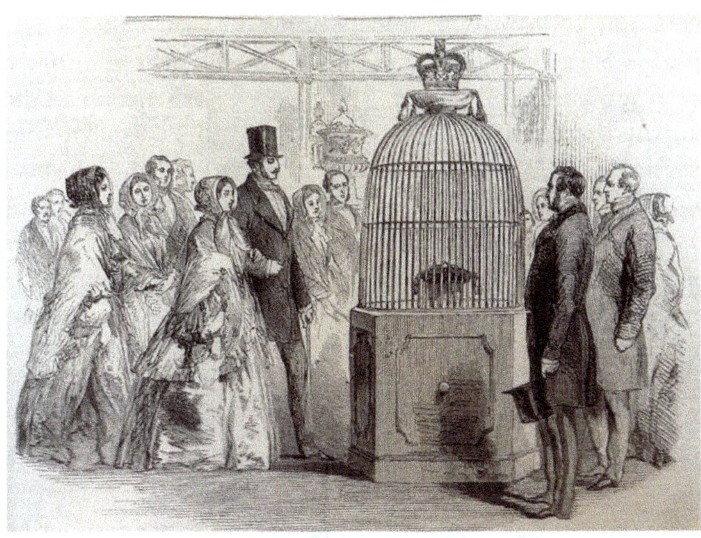

FIGURE 3.1. The Koh-i-noor diamond in its original display at London's Great Exhibition of 1851. *Illustrated London News*, May 31, 1851.

of the Great Exhibition, and classified under "Articles Exhibited by her Majesty the Queen,"[22] it was centrally located in the Crystal Palace's East Nave inside what one exhibition reviewer described as "a great parrot cage" topped with a British royal crown (figure 3.1).[23] There, the Koh-i-noor sat, resting luxuriantly on a red velvet cushion, between the Daria-i-noor (or Sea of Light), and the Hope diamonds.

The rhetoric of the display was heavy-handed in its imperial symbolism. "The Koh-i-noor was a miniature crystallization of the [Indian] subcontinent enclosed in a cage," Lara Kriegel writes, "a material reminder of Britain's hold" over India.[24] The cage was not only a metonym for Britain's empire but also for the diamond's new owner, Queen Victoria. As Danielle Kinsey points out, the arc of the diamond's cage evokes the hoopskirts worn by female spectators to the Great Exhibition. Seen this way, the cage is a representation of the queen: a golden hoopskirt in a crown.[25] The exhibit's location within the Crystal Palace was also significant. While its central location made it unmissable, its close proximity to the Indian Court—just across the hall from the East Nave—strategically linked this British treasure to its historic roots.[26] The *Catalogue of the Great Exhibition*'s description of the Koh-i-noor as "The Great Diamond of Runjeet Singh, called 'Koh-i-noor,' or Mountain of Light," identified the diamond not as Queen Victoria's property but as belonging to its prior owner, from whose treasury it was seized after the annexation of Punjab. Priti Joshi notes the conflicting language of the *Catalogue of the Great Exhibition*, which describes the diamond as "of" Runjeet Singh but "exhibited by" the queen.[27] Rather than an inconsistency in the presentation of the Koh-i-noor, this language reinforces the historical and geopolitical significance of the diamond's transition from Indian to British ownership. What is important is not that Queen Victoria possesses the "Great Diamond" but that she possesses "The Great Diamond of Runjeet Singh" and along with it his kingdom. The diamond's physical proximity to the Indian Court and identification as at once "of" India and belonging to Britain served to position India, like the Koh-i-noor, as Britain's most precious jewel. The message of the display was clear: the Koh-i-noor was not only a material embodiment of imperial history but also the star of the Great Exhibition's providential narrative of British supremacy over South Asia and, by extension, the globe. John Forbes Royle, the Anglo-Indian botanist who superintended the Indian exhibit at the Crystal Palace, summarized this position succinctly when he remarked that India was not just the jewel in the crown of the British Empire but "the Koh-i-noor of the British crown."[28]

As we saw in the opening paragraphs of the chapter, this narrative of the Koh-i-noor as "prize of Saxon valor" predated the exhibition by at least two years. Foremost among its architects was James Broun-Ramsay, better known as the Marquess of Dalhousie, who earned that title from Queen Victoria in appreciation for his personal efforts to acquire the Koh-i-noor for the British Crown. Dalhousie served as governor-general of India between 1848 and 1856, an interstitial but politically critical moment before the establishment of the British Raj. At this stage, India was a formal colony of Britain, but it was still under the administration of the British East India Company, a trading company acting as a trustee of the British Crown. Under Dalhousie's rule, the British East India Company generated revenue and consolidated British power in India through the ruthless expropriation of Indian land. Dalhousie's annexation of Punjab not only incorporated into British India a vast territory previously ruled by the Sikh Empire; it also placed the British East India Company in possession of the contents of the Lahore Treasury, including the infamous Koh-i-noor. As Dalhousie himself wrote of his success: "It is not every day that an officer of [the British] Government adds four millions of subjects to the British Empire, and places the historical jewel of the Mogul Emperors in the Crown of his own Sovereign."[29]

Dalhousie's description of his victory as "plac[ing]" the Koh-i-noor "in the Crown" reflects what turned out to be a controversial act. The

Second Anglo-Sikh War ended when Duleep Singh, the ten-year-old ruler of the independent Sikh kingdom of Punjab, was forced by the British to sign a treaty explicitly demanding that "the gem called the Koh-i-noor . . . shall be surrendered by the Maharajah to the Queen of England."[30] All at once, Punjab and Koh-i-noor became British property. This decision was criticized by the Court of Directors of the British East India Company. Some officials considered the Lahore Treasury as "prize-property," war booty or loot seized in battle and traditionally sold at public auction and redistributed to the troops as bonuses according to their rank. The gifting of the Koh-i-noor to the queen denied the company its usual practice of enriching itself and its soldiers with spoils of war.[31] Other British East India Company officials looked upon Duleep Singh's "surrender" of the Koh-i-noor to Queen Victoria as a performance orchestrated by Dalhousie to satisfy his own vanity or as an repugnant instance of plunder imperialism.[32] In contrast, Dalhousie saw his overreach as strategic, not only for his own professional advancement but for nation and empire. "The Koh-i-noor had become in the lapse of ages a sort of historical emblem of conquest in India," he explained. He was right: the Koh-i-noor has a sensational biography that includes tenure in the court of the Mughal emperor Shah Jahan; its theft by Nader Shah, the Persian emperor who invaded Mughal Delhi in 1739; its gifting to Ahmad Shah Durrani, founder of the Afghan Empire, in 1751; and its extortion from an exiled Afghan ruler by Sikh emperor Ranjit Singh in 1813.[33] Ranjit, who wore the Koh-i-noor on the front of his turban or in an armlet, went to great lengths to acquire the famous diamond for the Sikh Empire and transformed it into a symbol of Sikh sovereignty.[34] Dalhousie wanted the Koh-i-noor diamond to sit in Queen Victoria's crown as a sign of British sovereignty not only in Punjab but over the entire Indian subcontinent. The British crown would be "its final and fitting resting-place," he wrote, where it would "shine, and shine, too, with purest ray serene."[35] Although some press reports were openly critical of Duleep Singh's forced surrender of the diamond, most embraced the jingoism of this gesture. The *Times* account that I quoted at the beginning of the chapter, which calls the diamond a symbol of "the revolutions of ten generations" and "a fitting symbol of that supremacy that we have so fairly won," shows the success of Dalhousie's narrative of the Koh-i-noor as "historical emblem of conquest" in the popular imagination.

Dalhousie was not an aesthete. He did not choose the most beautiful stone in the Lahore Treasury, nor the most brilliant; he chose the piece that had the greatest symbolic power.[36] Whether the diamond's rays were truly "pure" and "serene" was not his concern; the important thing was that the Koh-i-noor shone metaphorically as an emblem of British racial, imperial, and cultural supremacy. On May 1, 1851, the patrons of the Great Exhibition who strolled, rushed, even raced to the gold birdcage in East Nave to see the Koh-i-noor did not share Dalhousie's priorities. By the end of the first day, it was already clear that there was a problem: The diamond did not shine in a literal sense.[37] "The 'Koh-i-noor' is a great source of attraction to those who visit the Crystal Palace for the first time," wrote the *Illustrated Exhibitor*, the illustrated guide to the Great Exhibition, "but it is at least doubtful whether it obtains such admiration afterwards. More than one spectator turns away disappointed from the sight of the precious jewel; and many more seem to think that a vast deal of pains has been taken to secure what is, after all, only a *very fine specimen of charcoal*."[38] This reception of "precious jewel" as "charcoal" disenchants it through the logic of industrial capitalism. Precious jewels are the province of India, where Oriental despots sit in gemstone-crusted thrones—not commodities but treasures. In contrast, charcoal is the base fuel of the British industrial economy. The emphasis on the gross materiality of the diamond, its stubborn refusal to be anything more than a mere object, was common. Writers debased the Koh-i-noor by comparing it to "a thick piece" or an "egg-shaped lump" of glass, or in one memorable phrase, "a glasslike knob, about the size of a prolonged nutmeg."[39] This comparison was validated by the presence of an actual glass replica of the Koh-i-noor at the Great Exhibition, manufactured by the British glassware maker Apsley Pellat and displayed in the North Gallery of the Crystal Palace, that "quite rival[ed] in brilliancy the two-million original downstairs."[40]

The stone that spectators saw in the gilded cage was not what they had imagined based on the feverish descriptions of the "Mountain of Light" they read in the press. However, their disappointment was not simply the result of the high expectations created by the media. The frequent comparisons between the Koh-i-noor and glass indicates that audiences thought the diamond was not sufficiently diamond-like and that it resembled a quotidian material, not the incalculably rare artifact Dalhousie and others swore it was. In other words, audiences evaluated the Koh-i-noor through the framework of medium specificity that defined diamonds by their not-glass-ness and valued them for their distinct optical effects. A diamond should be more than a "lump" or "knob," more, that is, than its physical form or shape because the performance of light that it creates should overflow its material frame. Audiences did not expect to see a "thick piece" of anything; they expected that the physicality of the diamond would be lost in its glow. They did not come for a "specimen" but for a miniature light show.

We can intuit what audiences expected to see in that gilded cage from descriptions of the Crystal Palace, Joseph Paxton's glass and iron structure inside of which "the works of industry of all nations" were exhibited. The *Times* reported that "with the bright sun shining on its ribs and sides," the Crystal Palace "shone like the Koh-i-noor itself"—a merely speculative comparison because at this point no one but a small handful of imperial officials, exhibition organizers, and the queen had seen the diamond with their own eyes.[41] The *Times* went on to characterize the Crystal Palace as "an Arabian Night structure, full of light, and with a certain airy unsubstantial character about it which belongs more to enchanted land than to this grossly material world of ours . . . the whole looks like a splendid phantasm."[42] The Crystal Palace was Koh-i-noor-like not only because it shone brightly but because it seemed to transcend matter to become light itself—immaterial, enchanted, phantasmal.

The diamond's failure to sparkle was more than a disappointment; it was a minor scandal. Exhibition organizers had assumed that displaying the diamond in a museum—the British answer to Ranjit Singh displaying it on his arm—would be sufficient demonstration of imperial sovereignty and authority in and of itself. Instead, subject to an aesthetic judgment that saw it woefully lacking, the Koh-i-noor became a mockery of Britain's imperial ambitions. As the *Leader* put it, "Destroy the diamond, and who would be inconsolable?"[43] Throughout May and June 1851, exhibition organizers attempted to salvage the reputation of Queen Victoria's diamond, the British East India Company, and the territorial project of empire building by resetting the diamond. Two chief problems emerged from these discussions: the diamond's cut and its setting. The Koh-i-noor had last been polished in the sixteenth century as a rose cut with a rounded oval top and flat bottom (figure 3.2). In their history of the Koh-i-noor, William Dalrymple and Anita Anand suggest that its unusual shape may have inspired its name: "it resembled a large hill or perhaps a huge iceberg rising steeply to a high, domed peak" with "short but irregular crystal trails or azimuths sloping off, like saddles or declivities falling from a Himalayan snow-peak."[44] Its 169 facets, tiny gradations along the surface of the gem, were designed to emit a soft prismatic light that differed from the kaleidoscopic radiance

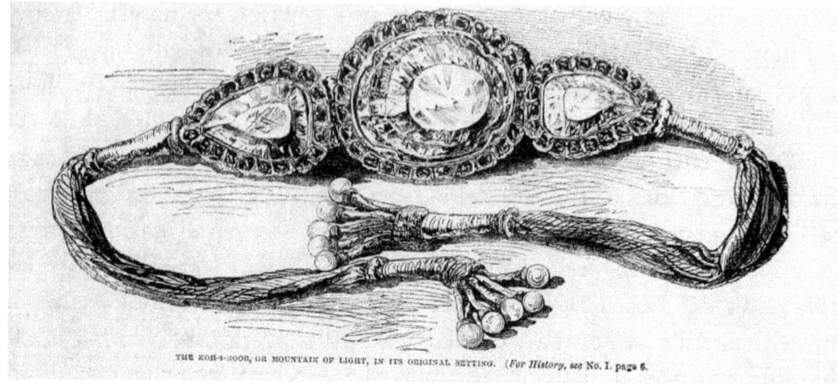

FIGURE 3.2. The Koh-i-noor diamond, center, as it was presented to Queen Victoria of England. *The Crystal Palace, and Its Contents: Being an Illustrated Cyclopedia of the Great Exhibition of the Industry of all Nations, 1851*, 1851.

of Victorian brilliant cut diamonds. The diamond's archaic shape was unfamiliar and disappointing to viewers because it refracted light in a manner they considered unspectacular. The problem was not the shape itself but its optical affordances; the large rose cut failed to produce the expected aesthetic effects. The *Illustrated London News* put this diplomatically: "The Koh-i-noor is not cut in the best form for exhibiting its purity and lustre, and will therefore disappoint many, if not all, of those who so anxiously press forward to see it."[45] Others were less circumspect. "It is not set 'à jour,' & badly cut, which spoils the effect," Queen Victoria wrote in her diary after the Koh-i-noor was presented to her by members of the British East India Company.[46] Gemologist Charles King called it "ugly and unskillful."[47] Perhaps to justify the displeasure of British spectators, a rumor emerged that the Indian lapidary who cut the Koh-i-noor was executed for his incompetence.[48]

The second obstacle to the diamond sparkling was the conditions of its display in the East Nave of the Crystal Palace. This, too, was an optical problem. "In the spectra produced by broad luminous spaces [like the Crystal Palace]," David Brewster explained in the *North British Review*, "all the colours are recombined into white light, and hence the disappointment which every person has experienced at the sight of [the Koh-i-noor, Daria-i-noor, and Hope diamonds]. Were the same gems to be worn by a lady in a drawing-room, with numerous bright lights, their effect would astonish the company."[49] At the Crystal Palace, the Koh-i-noor was as washed out as a daytime magic lantern show, bleached dull by the very luminosity that made Joseph Paxton's glass structure "shine like the Koh-i-noor."[50] Brewster was frequently on site as a juror at the Great Exhibition, and he put his optical expertise to work by building a wooden cabinet that would house the Koh-i-noor and block out light streaming through the glass roof and windows of the Crystal Palace. Six gas lamps and twelve angled mirrors were positioned to light the diamond most advantageously. The results were inconclusive. Margaret Maria Gordon, Brewster's daughter and biographer, recalled that under these new conditions, the diamond "threw out a radiance of colored light which delighted all who saw," a sentiment echoed by the *London Daily Standard*, which remarked on the Koh-i-noor's "extraordinary metamorphosis."[51] According to the *Illustrated Exhibitor*, on the other hand, "Whether the gaslight suits this Eastern gem better than sunlight is yet considered very problematical."[52] In spite of the positive press the new setting received, the Mountain of Light could not escape its reputation as, in *Punch*'s memorable phrase, a "Mountain of Darkness."[53]

The Diamond Lens

To rehabilitate the Koh-i-noor as an imperial symbol, it was necessary to fulfill the popular imagination of Indian diamond as optical medium. Only one solution remained. When the Great Exhibition closed in December 1851, Prince Albert sought the consent of Parliament to have the Koh-i-noor diamond recut in the Victorian style. Expert Dutch diamond cutters were hired and a steam engine specially commissioned. "It seems since to have struck the parties interested," *Punch* quipped, "that a precious stone which can't shine and won't shine, ought to be made to shine, even though a painful operation should be requisite."[54] "Ma[king]" the diamond "shine" according to British tastes and expectations would require its technological transformation, a process that served as a kind of imperial theater. The recutting allegorized what Britain saw as a not only extractive but modernizing imperial project in India by depicting the Koh-i-noor as simply another Indian "raw material" that could be made profitable when fed into British industrial machinery.[55] Without Britain, India is obsolete—a "precious stone" that "won't shine." *Punch* developed this theme through a cartoon representing the Koh-i-noor as an enfeebled maharajah led paternalistically to the grindstone by the Duke of Wellington, whom Prince Albert invited to make the symbolic first cut (figure 3.3). In the cartoon in figure 3.3, the Koh-i-noor is drawn to resemble raw diamond, uncut and unpolished. By personifying the diamond as a maharajah held

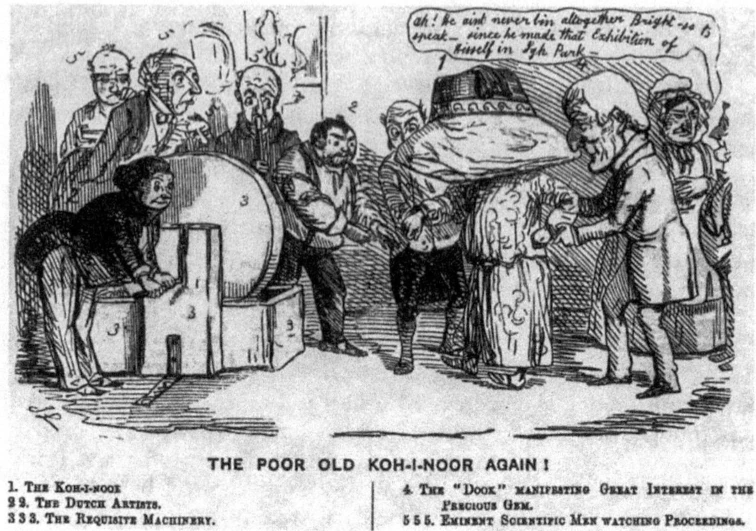

FIGURE 3.3. "The Poor Old Koh-i-Noor Again!" Cartoon from *Punch*, 1852.

up by the former prime minister and current commander in chief of the British Army, *Punch* further depicted the Koh-i-noor as a puppet ruler installed by the British. The Koh-i-noor "aint never bin altogether Bright," a woman commentates, a pun that correlates the diamond's failure to sparkle with the supposed intellectual inferiority and political dependency of Indians themselves. *Punch* draws attention to how the spectacle of the recutting sought to reclaim the Koh-i-noor's sparkle not as an exotic Oriental attribute but the result of Britain's modernizing and rationalizing imperial project, what *Punch* satirizes as British "surgery"—a term that captures all at once colonialism's biopolitical, civilizational, and technological ambitions. The Koh-i-noor's dullness, like India's backwardness, now justifies British possession and control. Only the British can make India sparkle.

Once again, Britain's political theater of the Koh-i-noor had unexpected results in the cultural imagination. In their attempt to popularize the Koh-i-noor diamond as a historical symbol of empire and then to redeem their failure by making the diamond's sparkle contingent on British technological intervention, Dalhousie, Prince Albert, and other Great Exhibition organizers ironically popularized diamonds as "Oriental" optical media. The very public drama of the Koh-i-noor's refusal to sparkle in ways that Victorians expected was a primer in diamonds as light-based toys that produce visual effects only under particular optical conditions. At the same time, the drama made clear that the British East India Company and the British Crown were promoting brands of empire that were not speaking to the tastes and appetites of the British public. Rather than plunder empire or moral empire, the British public expressed a desire for an optical empire that would express itself through the diamond's virtual aesthetics. Spectators wanted to experience empire through the Koh-i-noor's medium specificity, as if the fiery shimmering of an Indian diamond or its phosphorescence could transmit or mediate the subcontinent for those in London. A diamond's sparkle remained, in the popular imagination, uniquely Indian.

The Koh-i-noor's display at the Great Exhibition thus unleashed literary imaginings of large colonial diamonds as technologies for "vision at a distance"—diamonds that made empire perceptible through their optical properties. Put another way, reception discourse produced the Koh-i-noor as an imaginary medium for the virtual perception of empire, one that seemed to combine the virtual effects of diamonds with the representational capacities of optical media like the magic lantern, diorama, and stereoscope. In the second half of the chapter, I will discuss two works of fiction that unfold this reception fantasy through stories about plundered colonial diamonds that not only sparkle brilliantly but make the far reaches of empire virtually proximate precisely through their optical effects. The first of these is a story called "The Diamond Lens" by the Irish-American writer and editor Fitz-James O'Brien. O'Brien was a curious and chaotic figure. Born in 1828 into a well-to-do landowning family in Cork, Ireland, he grew up in Limerick, where he had a firsthand view of the devastation caused by the Irish Famine of 1845. He published political verse in an Irish nationalist weekly but left for London as soon as he came of age, blowing through his considerable inheritance over four years before the end of a love affair with a married woman drove him out of the country. Emigrating to the United States in 1852, O'Brien mingled with men like Walt Whitman in the avant-garde literary scene and Bohemian drinking circles of Pfaff's Beer Cellar in New York, where he was as well known for his drunken brawls as his supernatural tales inspired by the work of E. T. A. Hoffman and Edgar Allan Poe. He exchanged his Irish patriotism for antislavery and pro-Union politics, even enlisting in the Union Army as a volunteer. He died in 1862 from complications from a gunshot wound at the Battle of Bloomery Gap in West Virginia.

Although written in the United States, "The Diamond Lens" was inspired by O'Brien's sojourn in London and bears the imprint of O'Brien's experience seeing the Koh-i-noor at the Crystal Palace.

O'Brien was no stranger to the Great Exhibition. In 1851, he served as editor and contributor for a periodical called the *Parlour Magazine of the Literature of All Nations*. A two-volume publication that anthologized international short stories, poems, and serialized novels translated into English, the *Parlor Magazine of the Literature of All Nations* presented itself as the Great Exhibition's literary counterpart, capitalizing on the public's enthusiasm for "the works of all nations." In the words of the editors, the *Parlour Magazine* "pin[ned]" itself "to the skirts" of the Great Exhibition to drum up subscribers and make a profit.[56] Seven years later, in January 1858, O'Brien would publish a story in *The Atlantic* that unmistakably referenced the Great Exhibition's star exhibit.

"The Diamond Lens" is a scientific romance about the colonial theft of a large, spectacular diamond that is ground into a lens for the world's most powerful microscope. Admired by H. P. Lovecraft as a "masterful [tale] of strangeness and terror," the story is told in the first person by a man named Linley, a Victor Frankenstein figure whose obsession with microscopy leads him first to a shattering scientific discovery, then to personal ruin.[57] Dissatisfied with the microscopes available to him, "those imperfect mediums," Linley's object is to discover "the secret of some perfect lens" capable of "pierc[ing] through all the envelopes of matter down to its original atom."[58] A spirit medium, Madame Vulpes, allows Linley to ask the ghost of Antonie van Leeuwenhoek, the seventeenth-century Dutch pioneer of microscopy, how to perfect the microscope. Van Leeuwenhoek's advice: "a diamond of one hundred and forty carats . . . will form the universal lens" (15). With his diamond lens trained on a single drop of water, Linley becomes the first person to see inside an atom and discovers within it a whole world in luminous, ethereal shades of purple, opal, and gold. A "Form" dwells in this landscape which Linley, following van Leeuwenhoek, calls an "animalcule" or single-cell organism; deciding it possesses "a female human shape," he names it Animula and falls desperately in love (26). Forced to watch Animula "dying" as her waterdrop evaporates on its slide, Linley collapses and awakes "lying amidst the wreck of my instrument" (32). In the final lines of the story, Linley is a poor lecturer on optics known as "the mad microscopist" (33).

I read "The Diamond Lens" as a piece of Koh-i-noor fiction, one that speaks to the desire of Great Exhibition patrons for a diamond that would live up to its potential as an optical technology. There are many clues that Linley's diamond is meant to make readers think of the Koh-i-noor. Linley agonizes that the kind of diamond he is after can only be found "in the regalia of Eastern or European monarchs," referring to famous gems like the Koh-i-noor that were expropriated from India by Western empires. The 140-carat diamond he finds is not Indian but is stolen from the mines of Brazil, the only other source of diamonds outside India and Borneo during this period. O'Brien was a staunch abolitionist and a subplot involving an enslaved miner in Brazil allowed him to embed into the story a critique of the Atlantic slave trade.[59] However, the diamond is named "The Eye of Morning" according to what Linley calls "Oriental practice," a name that is calculated to remind readers of the Mountain of Light. Like the Koh-i-noor, it is described as "a vast rose cut." Even if its provenance is a Brazilian mine, the diamond is ultimately stolen from the miner by his French overseer, an antisemitic caricature of a Jewish peddler, in an example of colonial plunder that recalls the Koh-i-noor's acquisition by the British.

Linley's diamond does everything that spectators dreamed the Koh-i-noor would. As a medium for light, it is visually spectacular: light "seemed to pulsate in its crystalline chambers" as it "shivered" the "mild lamplight . . . into a thousand prismatic arrows." The diamond's ability to sparkle turns it, as its name suggests, into a kind of eye—a prosthetic that extends human vision. Just as mesmerism and optical technology are united in George Eliot's *Adam Bede* and *The Lifted Veil*, here the spirit medium and optical technological medium collide, both instruments for the perception of hidden or absent realms. Even before Linley grinds it into a lens, the Eye of Morning is described as something to see *with*, a medium that makes light "pulsate" and "shiver." O'Brien draws on optical discourses of diamonds that were popularized by media reports of the Koh-i-noor's display at the Great Exhibition, but the story also betrays his deep knowledge of the history of the diamond microscope. Linley's desire for "some perfect lens whose magnifying power . . . should be free from spherical and chromatic aberrations" (9)—defects in the microscopic image that make the edges of the object indistinct and create a distracting rainbow effect—reflects the precise issues that beset the compound microscope in the early decades of the nineteenth century and that led Andrew Pritchard and C. R. Goring to experiment with creating magnifying lenses out of diamond. The "vast rose cut" that Linley ultimately acquires not only references the style of the Koh-i-noor before its recutting but reflects Pritchard's own choice of a rose cut for his diamond lens in *The Microscopic Cabinet*.[60]

By fusing the history of the Koh-i-noor with that of the jewel microscope, "The Diamond Lens" constructs the Eye of Morning as an optical-imperial technology. Throughout the story, the diamond's technological use as a lens analogizes ocular discovery as territorial conquest, transforming the colonial diamond into a tool of colonization. Linley imagines himself as an "Alexander" who stands "trembling on the threshold of new worlds," a metaphor that codes microscopy as empire building. Although Linley refers to the ancient empire of Alexander the Great, at the time one of the largest empires in world history, the resonances with modern imperial projects—especially that of Great Britain—are clear. It is therefore no coincidence that what Linley discovers inside the diamond is an impossibly lush territory fertile with natural resources ripe for extraction. Linley literalizes his own metaphor of new worlds when he describes the glowing orb within the atom as a natural environment characterized by "brilliant ether." He sees an "illimitable distance" of "prismatic forests" and "vast auroral copses" filled with "leaves and fruits and flowers gleaming with unknown fires." Linley's vision of the atomic particle is an allusion to the creation of the world in the Book of Genesis, "an illuminated chaos, a vast luminous abyss" that slowly resolves, with his "depress[ion] of the lens," into the Garden of Eden, complete with a tree that, snake-like, hands Animula a piece of fruit. At the same time, this sublime terra nullius made visible by a colonial diamond recalls nineteenth-century constructions of the tropics as a new world characterized by its "luxuriant, dense, and fecund" landscapes.[61] The forest's "cloud foliage" is not only dense with fruit, but with "many-colored drooping silken pennons" that evoke the military or naval flags of Euro-American imperial conquest from South America to South Asia. The construction of the waterdrop world as a prelapsarian garden further codes it as an unspoiled landscape to be colonized. Linley's melancholy exile from Eden—his inability to enter this forest of light except through his gaze—is itself represented as a form of resource extraction, as the drop of water slowly evaporates under the heat from his lamp. Linley's technological-imperial gaze uses up the waterdrop, feasting on it until Animula dies a withering death and her world disappears into nothing.

O'Brien breaks with mid-nineteenth-century expectations of the microscope when he describes this waterdrop world as "a beautiful chromatic desert"—a landscape. During this same period, at museums like the Royal Polytechnic Institution, the oxyhydrogen microscope made a popular spectacle of projecting onto a screen the myriad living animalcules inside a drop of water.[62] Recall the cartoon "Microscopy for the Million" in figure 1.2 in chapter 1, in which the woman spectator at the Polytechnic fears that the microscopic monsters writhing and squirming in spectral and magnified form will break loose and attack. Linley reflects the popularity of such views while drawing attention to the story's deliberate withholding of them when he expects to see "some living organism" and when he compares the world's only "inhabitant," Animula, favorably to the animalcules that readers would be familiar with—"the coarser creatures" seen in "the more easily resolvable portions of the water-drop." Instead of the circular white projections of the oxy-hydrogen microscope, signifying a kind of empty nothingness within which animalcules move, O'Brien imagines the microscope as a technology for virtual contact with a habitable environment. Although the story turns on Linley's scopophilic desire for this nonhuman organism, her inaccessibility is represented less as a function of her biological organization than it is of her confinement in the *place* that the microscope reveals, a place as far away as "the planet Neptune."

A product of colonial resource extraction and plunder imperialism, the diamond lens is thus more than a microscope: it is an imaginary technology for virtual travel to the colonies that enables a form of scopic plunder. In this regard, it recalls another optical device that, like the Koh-i-noor, made its public debut at the Great Exhibition: the lenticular stereoscope. Invented by David Brewster, the man responsible for helping design a new display case for the Koh-i-noor, this simple handheld stereoscope transformed what was initially a cumbersome scientific instrument into a marketable commodity and launched what would become by the 1850s "a mass global visual culture."[63] A stereoscope is an optical technology that allows a spectator to see a two-dimensional picture in three dimensions. Brewster's stereoscope is, at its most basic, a wooden box with two lenses. Against the back "wall" of the box, like a screen, is a slot where users can insert a stereograph, a card with two nearly identical photographs pasted side by side. When the spectator looks through the lenses and focuses their eyes, they see the scene represented in the photographs as a single virtual image endowed with an illusion of depth and relief. Queen Victoria's admiration of the new optical toy at the Crystal Palace set off a craze for the stereoscope that led to the sale of 250,000 copies in three months. Like Linley's microscope, which extends his gaze so that he can apprehend an otherwise invisible world, the handheld stereoscope was a visual prosthetic that enabled embodied and haptic visual experience of places around the world. Referencing the popularity of tourist views of Britain, Europe, and the United States in the late 1850s, *The Athenaeum* hailed the stereoscope as "travel made easy."[64] At the turn of the century, Elmer Underwood and Bert Underwood's *Travel Through the Stereoscope* series would offer travel and around-the-world stereocard boxes accompanied by books that offered topographical, demographic, historical, and cultural context for each image—a virtual guided tour in a box.[65] O'Brien's diamond microscope is a kind of fantasy stereoscope for real-time visual access to the colonial scene.

Although O'Brien's story predates the stereoscopic tours that promised to take spectators "around the world in 60 minutes," the context in which the stereoscope was introduced to the public immediately coded it as an imperial technology. Not only was it exhibited at the Crystal Palace, but the Crystal Palace and its myriad exhibits were the subject of some of the first stereoscopic photographs, linking what Tiago de Luca describes as the "encyclopedic" capacity of the stereoscope to the global and imperial aims of the Great Exhibition to catalog and display the works of all nations.[66] A stereograph from a mid-1860s world's fair makes this imperial and encyclopedic ambition explicit. At the center of the composition is Atlas's globe, its mirrored surface reflecting spectators, exhibits, the cascading arches of the ceiling, and the photographer himself as if in a fish-eye lens (figure 3.4).[67] The globe is a sign of the totalizing representation of the world in things exemplified in both the fair and the stereoscope. Both the Great Exhibition and the stereoscope offered, in Anne McClintock's terms, "new form[s] of commodity spectacle . . . a progressive accumulation of panoramas and scenes arranged, ordered and catalogued according to the logic of imperial capital."[68] Both made possible virtual travel to places around the globe in order to authorize

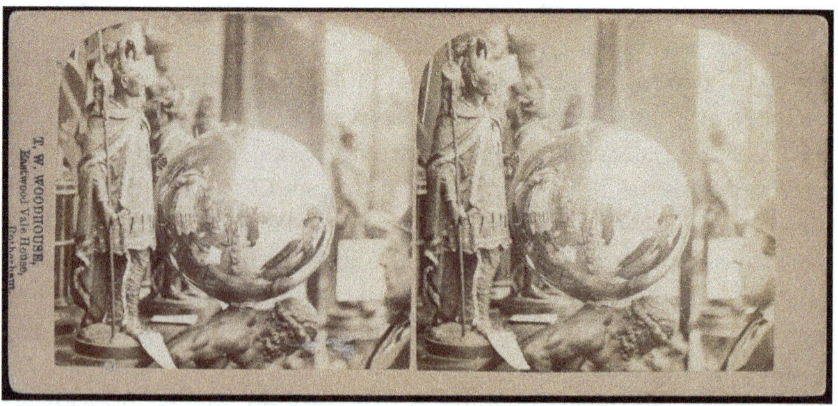

FIGURE 3.4. Stereograph of an international exhibition, 1865 or 1867, T. W. Woodhouse. © Victoria and Albert Museum, London.

and articulate what Louise Purbrick calls "specular dominance" over other lands, cultures, and peoples.[69] "The Diamond Lens" not only draws on the Koh-i-noor, producing a science fiction version of the Indian diamond that makes explicit the colonial fantasies it generated, but it also draws on the broader context of the Great Exhibition's construction of Britain as a scopic empire. What is seen through the diamond lens is a virtual image of the colonial scene, a category of visual culture reminiscent of colonial and travel stereoviews. The vast fertile landscape inside a waterdrop made visible by an "Oriental" rose-cut diamond recalls Victorian constructions of India as, in Lara Kriegel's words, "the closest approximation of infinity on earth" because its "endless valleys and fields" could potentially supply the Western world's natural resources.[70]

Linley's microscope is thus an imaginary medium: a diamond that is also a microscope, telescope, and stereoscope and that functions as a technology for imperial possession. Although the story seems to be about the impossibility of possession, as Animula cannot be claimed from her waterdrop world, it actually demonstrates that to see *is* to possess. Linley cannot be a colonial settler—he cannot inhabit the waterdrop world—but he can still extract sexual and affective value from that world from a remote distance. In this way, "The Diamond Lens" is a specular allegory of resource extraction economies. The diamond microscope facilitates a form of imperial technological gaze in which to see is to take ownership over and ultimately to exhaust a resource that is simultaneously finite and infinitely renewable—every waterdrop will have its own "prismatic forests," its own Animula. With its abolitionist subtext, the story occupies an uncomfortable middle ground between colonial fantasy and anticolonial parable. O'Brien speaks to the widespread disenchantment with the Koh-i-noor by fictionalizing the colonial diamond both as a medium for a virtual aesthetic experience that makes the colony visible as pleasure dome and as a medium of colonization in and of itself.

A Moony Gleam in the Dark

Ten years after "The Diamond Lens" was published in *The Atlantic*, *All the Year Round* and *Harper's Magazine* serialized an imperial romance by Wilkie Collins called *The Moonstone* that once again imagined the Koh-i-noor as a virtual technology of empire. The novel tells the tale of a plundered Indian diamond, one that Collins claimed in the preface to have "founded" on the Koh-i-noor.[71] This diamond narrative is a mystery that begins with a series of strange events that occur when the

Moonstone falls into the hands of Rachel Verinder, the young heroine, on her eighteenth birthday. Three Indian men appear at the front door posing as traveling magicians. The diamond disappears. A maidservant, a formerly convicted jewel thief, starts to behave oddly and then drowns herself in quicksand. Was the diamond stolen by the Indians, Brahmin guards tasked with restoring the Moonstone to its rightful place in the Temple of Somnauth? Did the ex-thief strike again? Or did Rachel steal her own diamond, as Detective Cuff of Scotland Yard supposes, to pay off secret debts? The solution to the mystery turns out to be something else entirely, and instead of the detective, it is a half-Indian, half-English medical assistant named Ezra Jennings who uncovers the truth. Franklin Blake, Rachel's beau, was unknowingly given laudanum by another guest at Rachel's birthday party, causing Franklin to sleepwalk into Rachel's room and take the diamond for safekeeping out of fear that the Brahmins would attack her in the night. In an unconscious state, Franklin hands the Moonstone to Godfrey Ablewhite, his rival for Rachel's affections, who keeps it for his own and plans to have it cut into smaller gems and resold to pay off his gambling debts. The climax of the novel sees the Indians murder Ablewhite and repatriate the Moonstone to Somnauth, where it forms the third eye in an idol.

The Moonstone's status as third eye is our first clue that, like the Eye of Morning, this diamond has something to do with vision. Lavish descriptions bear this out by positioning the Moonstone as a medium for optical virtuality and identifies the capacity of optical technology to make visible what is beyond the ordinary range of human perception with Indian "magic." This racialization of the virtual, and in particular its construction as "Oriental," recalls the mirror of ink in chapter 2, and, as we will see, the mirror of ink actually makes an appearance in *The Moonstone* as another form of Indian magic. More specifically, Collins's quasi-mystical description of the Moonstone's phosphorescence—its ability not only to shine with the borrowed light of the sun but also to feed on the life force of those with whom it comes into contact—redeems the Koh-i-noor's poor reception at the Crystal Palace by animating the fantasy that its optical effects could offer spectators virtual contact with India.

Although Collins claims in his preface to have based the Moonstone on the Koh-i-noor, we do not have to take his word for it. Allusions to the Koh-i-noor are made quite explicitly throughout the novel. The Moonstone is described as a "Yellow Diamond" sacred to the Hindus and "set in the forehead of the four-handed Indian god who typifies the Moon"

(3), a variation on the legend that the Koh-i-noor originated in the forehead of an Indian god.[72] The Moonstone also comes with the "superstition" that it "feel[s] the influence of the deity whom it adorned" (4). These include a curse "predict[ing] certain disaster to the presumptuous mortals who laid hands on the sacred gem, and to all of his house and name who received it after him" (4), implying that the "disaster[s]" that occur to a range of characters may be the work of the diamond itself. This also came directly from a rumor that flourished in the British press that the Koh-i-noor was cursed to bring ruin upon the emperors and rulers who possessed it. The Moonstone transfers its curse to the British when the rapacious John Herncastle, a soldier in the British Army, steals it during the Storming of Seringapatam (1799), the climactic final battle in the Anglo-Mysore Wars that secured British control over the last remaining Indian territory in the hands of Mughal rulers. This scene of violent bloodshed and plunder displaces Dalhousie's theft of the Koh-i-noor at the culmination of the Second Anglo-Sikh War onto an earlier colonial war. Like Dalhousie, who bestowed his plundered Indian diamond on Queen Victoria, Herncastle wills the Moonstone to his niece Rachel on her eighteenth birthday. In case the historical parallels are not clear enough on their own, Rachel is literally described as a "queen" and pins the diamond to "the bosom of her white dress" as a brooch, just as Queen Victoria was known to wear the Koh-i-noor (70).

Collins clearly does more than model his fictional Moonstone diamond on the Koh-i-noor. He bases the plot on the history of the Koh-i-noor's possession by Britain, thinly veiling the plunder by Dalhousie in the prefatory story of Herncastle in Seringapatam and analogizing imperial conquest as a "curse" that backfires upon the conquerors. The idea may have come to Collins from his research on the Koh-i-noor. Among his gemology sources was Charles King's *Antique Gems* (1860), which describes the Koh-i-noor as a "fatal gift" that caused the "degenerat[ion]" not only of the Mughal Empire and the subsequent Eastern empires that possessed it, but also the British Empire. The presentation of the Koh-i-noor to Queen Victoria, King wrote, led to "the Sepoy revolt, and the all but total loss of India to the British crown," a reference to the Indian Uprising of 1857–1858.[73] Collins follows King by telling the story of the Indian Uprising as a moral and geopolitical consequence of Dalhousie's plunder of the Koh-i-noor for Queen Victoria. If Rachel represents Queen Victoria, the rapacious Indians who seek the Moonstone, three unnamed men who "care just as much about killing a man, as you care about emptying the ashes out of your pipe" (78), clearly stand in for the Indians rebels who revolted against British rule. When Rachel stands on the terrace of the country house, "innocent[ly] . . . showing the Indians the Diamond in the bosom of her dress," the racialized threat of sexual violence against her—and, by extension, the threat to the integrity of the British Empire—references the sensational accounts of the Indian Uprising in the British press as the systematic rape of white women by Brown men.[74] As Gabriel Betteredge, the country house steward who narrates this portion of the novel, puts it: "our quiet English country house" is "suddenly invaded by a devilish Indian Diamond."

Because it portrays Indian violence toward English people as a direct response to the violence of empire, many scholars read *The Moonstone* as a critique of colonialism. Among the most sophisticated and compelling of these readings is Ian Duncan's analysis of "imperialist panic," or the novel's tendency to generate suspense through the threat of thinly veiled anticolonial violence. Duncan argues that the novel attributes to the imperial project a kind of reverse colonial effect in which Britain takes on an Asian, rather than English, cultural identity. The diamond inheritance plot opens England to the empire, in the process diminishing its power: "When a conventional English domestic order is finally restored it appears reduced, artificial, bright but fragile, while the horizons of the world around it . . . are sublime and alarming."[75] I follow Duncan in reading the novel as a fantasy of England taken over—"invaded"—by Indianness, but I offer a different interpretation of the affective conditions and political stakes of this fantasy. The Indian "invasion" of the English country home—an invasion represented through the gift of an Indian diamond—is certainly tinged with the threat of violence, but it is also figured as drawing room entertainment and associated with the media aesthetics of optical toys, magic, and opium. The diamond's hold over the British characters—a state of tension and suspense not unlike that which the novel creates for its readers—is not a death sentence. It is a temporary state of thrill characterized by pleasurable fears but devoid of real danger; a recreational experience, in other words, made possible by colonialism. Rather than reading *The Moonstone* solely as an expression of "panic" over the loss of English identity, I read it as a positive statement of the transformation of English identity in the age of empire—Englishness enhanced and enriched by its ability to take on, at will, what it has constructed as Indian affects and perceptual states. *The Moonstone* celebrates colonial media and their pleasures.

To understand this, let us look at how the Moonstone diamond is presented to the reader. The scene of the diamond's first appearance in England responds to the fantasies about Indian diamonds that attended the Koh-i-noor's display at the Great Exhibition. In 1851, David Brewster had written that, although the Koh-i-noor disappointed at the Crystal Palace, it would "astonish the company" if "worn by a lady in a drawing-room, with numerous bright lights." This is just how Collins presents the Moonstone to the reader in a counterfactual scene that reenchants the diamond's British display. In effect, Collins rewrites the unveiling of the Koh-i-noor to the British public as a triumph that fulfills the desire for a diamond that would act as a virtual portal to India. This scene is narrated by Gabriel Betteredge, steward to the Verinder country house, and takes place in "the small drawing-room," where dinner party guests gaze reverently and desirously upon the diamond (66). Two women kneel before the Moonstone, "[screaming] with ecstasy," while Ablewhite "clap[s] his hands like a large child" (66)—reactions of awe and amazement that were expected from Great Exhibition patrons but that the Koh-i-noor apparently failed to deliver.

The Moonstone unites all three optical characteristics that Victorians expected from a large and rare Indian diamond like the Koh-i-noor: it sparkles, magnifies, and phosphoresces. Betteredge's description of the diamond as "about the size of a plover's egg" paraphrases common descriptions of the Koh-i-noor at the Great Exhibition as "the size of a pigeon's egg."[76] While the Koh-i-noor was satirized as an egglike lump of glass or, in the *Punch* cartoon, a raw piece of unpolished diamond, the Moonstone transcends its own materiality through its interaction with light. It "flashed . . . in a ray of sunlight that poured through the window" and "stream[ed] with the light of the harvest moon": a true mountain of light. In addition to sparkling, the Moonstone phosphoresces. After being exposed to sunlight, it "shone awfully out of the depths of its own brightness, with a moony gleam, in the dark." This turns the diamond into a "yellow deep" that "[draws] your eyes" inward: Betteredge reflects that "this jewel, that you could hold between your finger and thumb, seemed unfathomable as the heavens themselves" (67). These "unfathomable" depths are another optical illusion because the diamond creates a virtual effect of endless interior space when light refracts through its facets. Like "The Dimond Lens," Collins reflects the discourses surrounding the Koh-i-noor's display at the Great Exhibition when he presents the diamond as an optical toy. Like many parlor room optical toys, the Moonstone is structured by visual paradox. Just as the thaumatrope makes two pictures on either side of a card appear simultaneously, a phenakistoscope makes static pictures move, and a stereoscope makes a flat picture three-dimensional, the diamond makes substance insubstantial. It is a small hard object that, when held up to the window, becomes an infinite visual field of pure light. While Latimer turns his large rose-cut diamond into the lens of a microscope, Rachel, Betteredge, and the other members of the party conduct their own kind of optical experiment with the Moonstone by placing it in the sun and then shutting the light out of the drawing room to watch the diamond phosphoresce. The Moonstone is a miniature light show you can play with.

The Moonstone's phosphorescence not only fulfills what Victorians understood as the medium specificity of diamonds but also turns it into a metonym for colonial India. In British hands, the Moonstone is not so much a third eye as a devourer of vision. Although the women at the party are described as "devouring the jewel with their eyes," its racializing "yellow" glow and hypnotic depths suggest that the opposite effect is at work. The diamond is an optical toy with agency, one that subverts the instrumental logic of the optical technology by turning the human body into an instrument for its own ends. We can read this dynamic in the descriptor "yellow deep," with its racial and optical connotations. The phrase pairs yellow, the "color" of Asians according to eighteenth- and nineteenth-century race science, with what Edward Said terms "the distant Oriental deep," mystifying and enchanting India through the metonym of the diamond.[77] At the same time, "yellow deep" expresses the diamond's phosphorescent power to seemingly pull the sunlight into it, charging like a battery. These two meanings come together when the diamond is described as feeding on the gazes around it. The yellow deep swallows the subject's vision, "drawing your eyes so that you saw nothing else." This effect recalls the hypnotic medium, a concept developed by the surgeon James Braid to describe how an ordinary sensory stimulus like a candle flame or pendulum can induce a trance state. The Moonstone seems to draw the eye the way it draws light, however, feeding on those around it for its power. Later, Betteredge remarks that "there was a miserable lack of life and sparkle" at the dinner party and exclaims that the party is "possessed" by "the Diamond" (75). The Moonstone has drawn its light not only from the sun but from the English, siphoning their "sparkle" for itself.

In other words, the Moonstone's optical qualities of sparkling and phosphorescing are racialized as violent and sinister forces that act upon unsuspecting English admirers. While "The Diamond Lens" presented the diamond as an instrument for bearing witness to the colonial scene, *The Moonstone* reverses the logic of optical spectatorship by presenting the diamond as an optical medium that mediates its spectators. Just as its phosphorescence turns sunlight into a "moony glow," the diamond grows in power by turning its spectators into objects for its own use. In this sense, the Moonstone behaves like a colonized subject that exercises sovereignty over its colonizers. Looking at the Moonstone is not a sovereign act but an abdication of self-sovereignty. To look is to be possessed by India.

I will not deny that this construction sets up the diamond as a figure for the Indian Uprising, as Duncan argues. But if the Moonstone represents a counterimperial "invasion" of England by India, it does not figure physical violence so much as the ability of Indians, and India, to "[lay] . . . hold" of English consciousness for a time, an experience that is characterized as both thrilling and temporary. The diamond's phosphorescent glow will fade; the English spectators' ordinary perceptual state will be restored. In the meantime, this laying hold of consciousness is rendered as exciting, frightening, and not wholly unpleasurable. Rachel holds the diamond in her hand "like a person fascinated," a condition that implies she is not only enthralled but rooted in place. In the nineteenth century, the term "fascination" described the way a snake entrances its prey by means of its gaze, and "fascinated" was used as a synonym for being mesmerized or hypnotized.[78] The Moonstone looks back at Rachel, fixing its spectator as the object of its gaze. Following the logic of predator and prey, it could be argued that the diamond fascinates the English spectator so that they will be unaware of attack by the Indian guards who will come to reclaim it. Yet it seems significant that the person the Indians do kill, Ablewhite, is "the only one of us who kept his senses" before the Moonstone—the only one, that is, not to be fascinated. The diamond's ability to fascinate is ultimately not predictive of its capacity for violence but its capacity to entertain.

Rather than an instrument of Indian counterinsurgency, I think of the Moonstone as an Indian optical-perceptual entertainment that lays hold of the conscious mind temporarily through its intoxicating visual effects. This becomes clearer when we consider how the Moonstone is doubled by two other Indian recreations: the mirror of ink and opium. The Moonstone's Indian guards are first seen in England performing the mirror of ink on an English boy. The subject of chapter 2, the mirror of ink was a clairvoyant magic trick performed by a Cairo magician named Sheik Abd al-Qadir al-Maghrabi and made famous in Britain by the Egyptologist Edward William Lane. Although Collins transposes the trick from Egyptian Muslims to Hindu priests, it would have been instantly recognizable to readers from Lane's original description. As I discussed in chapter 2, eminent proponents of mesmerism like Harriet Martineau argued that the trick's centerpiece—a boy was made to see persons and places unknown to him by looking into a circle of ink poured in his hand—was achieved through clairvoyance, with the magician making "mesmeric passes" over the boy's body to mesmerize him. Collins describes the mirror of ink in this way. "Black stuff, like ink" is first poured "into the palm of the boy's hand." The performance proceeds:

> The Indian—first touching the boy's head, and making signs over it in the air—then said, "Look." The boy became quite stiff, and stood like a statue, looking into the ink in the hollow of his hand.
>
> . . . The chief of the Indians said these words to the boy: "See the foreign gentleman from foreign parts."
>
> The boy said, "I see him." (22)

Collins makes clear that the trick is an example of mesmeric clairvoyance by emphasizing the relationship between the anonymous Indian's hands, which both touch the boy's head and make "passes" over it, and the boy's ability to "see." In her account of witnessing the mirror of ink in *Eastern Life, Past and Present*, Martineau argued that Abd al-Qadir was an "unconscious mesmerizer" who did not know that he was performing a fashionable and sophisticated Western medical practice.[79] Collins mimics this colonial dynamic between the unconscious and inept Oriental magician and the enlightened British observer: While "the Indians looks upon their boy as a Seer of things invisible to their eyes," the English characters explain that the "boy is unquestionably a sensitive subject to mesmeric influence" who "no doubt reflected what was already in the mind of the person mesmerizing him."

The racialized epistemic divide between white observers and Brown mesmerist also reflects the British fashion for the mirror of ink and mesmeric demonstrations as forms of entertainment. Martineau visited Abd al-Qadir because his performances of the mirror of ink had become a required stop on any British traveler's Egyptian itinerary, while mesmerism was not only a therapeutic cure but a popular parlor entertainment that invited attendees to speculate on whether they were witnessing authentic clairvoyance or a sophisticated hoax. The mirror of ink thus prefigures the unveiling of the Moonstone in the drawing room several chapters later. Both are forms of visual and perceptual entertainment that turn on a medium—the ink, the diamond—that "draw[s] your eyes" and makes you see things either that are not actually there (visions in the ink) or as they are not (the diamond's virtual depths). Both link visual illusion to Orientalized and racialized practices of perceptual control, as the "yellow" diamond and "black" ink exert epistemic and bodily power over British people. The English boy's "stiff[ness]" as he "[looks] into the ink in the hollow of his hand" and "sees" will recur both when Rachel stands "like a person fascinated" gazing at the diamond in her hand and when Betteredge perceives "the heavens themselves" in a jewel held "between . . . finger and thumb." The racializing yellow of the diamond has its double in the racializing blackness of the ink, both colonial figures for a kind of Indian savagery that infects British consciousness and invades the white body.

Finally, the Moonstone diamond's visual and perceptual powers are represented through opium, the Indian commodity par excellence that eventually offers the solution to the mystery. Although the diamond reaches the villain Ablewhite, who pockets it to pay his debts, it is the hero Franklin Blake who takes the diamond from Rachel's bedroom while sleepwalking under the influence of opium. Like mesmerism, opium shows up in the novel to express the way that the Moonstone diamond takes control of consciousness. Ezra Jennings, an opium addict who solves the mystery with Franklin's help, explains that opium has "intensified" the Moonstone's perceptual power over Franklin: "The latest and most vivid impressions left on your mind—namely, the impressions relating to the Diamond—would be likely . . . to become intensified in your brain, and would subordinate to themselves your judgment and will" (400). In other words, Franklin is anxious that Rachel's life is threatened by the Indians who wish to recover the diamond—an anxiety sparked by seeing them mesmerize the English boy—and under the influence of opium, this overtakes his conscious mind and leads him to steal the Moonstone himself to protect her from harm. Opium most clearly resembles the "black stuff, like ink" that the Indians pour into the boy's hand; it has a similar capacity to "subordinate" a person's "judgment and will" and allow them to "see persons and things beyond the range of human vision" (54). To take Jennings's scientific explanation at face value, however, opium also functions as an "intensif[ication]" of the diamond's "vivid impression" on the mind, releasing the diamond's power over the subject—a power prefigured in its optical effects. At the same time, opium's "intensifi[cation]" of Franklin's impressions turns Franklin into a kind of phosphorescent diamond. He has looked at the diamond, taken in an impression of it, and stored those impressions within him even after the original stimulus is gone.

Are we to understand this perceptual invasion of English minds by Indians and their media—diamonds, magic, opium—as an expression of imperialist panic in the post–Indian Uprising age? Rather than foreclosing this interpretation, I want to propose that we take seriously the representation of Indian "invasion" of British domestic life as Victorian popular entertainment. India enters the English home in the form of theatrical magic, mesmerism, optical spectatorship, and recreational drugs—the arena, put simply, of fun. These media experiences constitute what Susan Zieger has called "the novel's implicit advocacy for irrational states of mind."[80] It is frightening to surrender your body and mind to the mystic emanations of the diamond, but it is also thrillingly desirable—a "sublime intoxication," as Ezra Jennings writes of Franklin's opium high. In this sense, the Moonstone's ability to act on English perception with its "yellow" glow returns us to the Great Exhibition. There, the Koh-i-noor's rude materiality demystified what the British East India Company and the British Crown hoped to present as the wonder of British India. *The Moonstone*'s representation of the Indian diamond as a spectacular medium for virtual encounter with India not only reenchants empire but fulfills the desire for a technological medium that acts on British spectators, providing them with "Indian" experiences of savagery, wonder, and romance. Doubled in opium and the mirror of ink, part Indian commodity and part Indian magic, the Moonstone acts on perception by allowing the English people who possess it to phosphoresce—to take on, temporarily and recreationally, what the novel portrays as Indian self-states. Duncan argues that the Moonstone's invasion of England with Indianness signals a "loss of [English] character," and it is true that the language of loss and enervation recurs throughout the novel as characters are drained of energy after looking at the diamond, lose sight of their own surroundings to see in a drop of ink, and forget their own actions while sleepwalking. But Rachel, Betteredge, the English boy, and Franklin are not emptied out so much as they are filled for a time with new and exotic perceptions, just as the Moonstone is filled for a time with the light of the sun. If the diamond, like opium and Indian magic, "subordinate[s]" to itself the "judgment and will" of the English characters, it is as a form of intoxication that temporarily weakens the body even as it brings the novelty and pleasure of a colonial encounter. This state of possession is a "fever," to borrow Betteredge's word for his irrepressible enthusiasm for detective mysteries, one that will in time burn itself out.

Viewed this way, *The Moonstone* offers a retelling of the Koh-i-noor's possession by the British that sublimates the racialized dangers of India and Indian people as optical and perceptual aesthetic experience mediated by a diamond. The Moonstone's "invasion" of English minds through its phosphorescent optical powers, a reimagining of what King called its "malignant lustre," is less a manifestation of violence than it is a playful harnessing of the trope of Indian savagery for the purposes of wonder and thrill. To be "invaded" or "possessed" temporarily by the Indian diamond—to surrender oneself temporarily to Indianness—is not a sign of waning English sovereignty but rather one of the privileges of English sovereignty in the age of empire, a mode of cultural imperialism comparable to the purchase of tea, shawls, opium, stereographic tours, or admission to a magic show. The Indianization of the optical spectator is an encounter at once as "intensely physical" and embodied as E. M. Collingham describes the English experience of India and as fantastically dematerialized as Bengal tigers and the Taj Mahal seen through a magic lantern.[81]

This chapter has endeavored to show how the aesthetics of virtuality—of seeing what is not there, of experiencing the remote as proximate—informed the way British citizens felt themselves to be part of empire and experienced supremacy over other peoples and places without ever visiting them. The story of the Koh-i-noor's failure to impress spectators at the Great Exhibition and its reenchantment in literary works like "The Diamond Lens" and *The Moonstone* is the story of the emergence of virtual aesthetics as a meaningful framework for making sense of empire's absent presence in everyday life in the metropole. Like the cultural history of the mirror of ink that I offered in chapter 2, the Koh-i-noor diamond functioned as an imaginary medium for "vision at a distance."

In the remainder of this book, I will turn my attention from empire to home by asking how virtual aesthetics shaped representations of the nation. Chapter 4 asks how the phantasmagoria, among the most famous optical shows of the nineteenth century, offered a framework for representing nationalist revolution in French and British culture. Rather than vision at a distance, the phantasmagoria seemed to promise vision through time as the ghosts of history were conjured by a magic lantern in a dark room. In the literary imaginary of the phantasmagoria, the virtual aesthetics of historical copresence is what creates the nation. If participation in the British Empire required the capacity to see and experience other places without ever leaving home, participation in the British nation meant being haunted by ghosts.

CHAPTER 4

Recalled to Life

Phantasmagoria as the History of the French Revolution

For Karl Marx, revolutionary history was a ghostly business. *The Eighteenth Brumaire of Louis Bonaparte*, his political analysis of the coup that led to the formation of France's Second Empire, famously opens with the credo that history "appear[s] twice . . . the first time as tragedy, the second time as farce."[1] This metaphor invokes the tragedy and comedy masks of Ancient Greek theater to satirize Louis Napoleon Bonaparte's (Napoleon III) seizure of power as a "caricature" of that of his uncle Napoleon I half a century earlier. Within the next few lines, however, the genres of tragedy and farce give way to a metaphorics of spectrality and haunting.[2] The reason historical events seem to repeat themselves is not, as one might reasonably expect from Marx, because of unchanging economic conditions or relations of production.[3] Instead, it is because revolutionary change requires an ongoing encounter with historical ghosts. "The tradition from all dead generations weighs like a nightmare on the brains of the living," Marx writes, as revolutionaries "anxiously conjure up the spirits of the past in order to present this new scene in world history in time-honored disguise and borrowed language."[4] History is still a piece of theater—each episode a "new scene"—but now its genre is neither tragedy nor farce. Instead, Marx describes a ghost theater of historical copresence in which the living "conjur[e] up . . . the dead of world history" in an effort to break with the past.[5]

This ghost theater was, like tragedy and farce, a real genre in nineteenth-century culture. It was called the phantasmagoria. Between 1792 and roughly 1830, when it was displaced by newer forms of visual projection and technological magic, the phantasmagoria was an international sensation that popularized the theatrical use of optical technology to create virtual images through the use of a hidden magic lantern that projected ghostly specters in a dark room. Just as Marx described, the phantasmagoria staged a theatrical encounter between the living and the dead, one that often took the form of a "conjuring up of the dead of world history," as ghosts of French national history like Honoré Mirabeau, Voltaire, and Maximillien Robespierre were made to appear. They were also made to disappear, an effect that Marx references when he writes that the political gains of the French Revolution "all vanished like a phantasmagoria [*verschwunden wie eine Phantasmagorie*]" with Napoleon III's coup.[6] More than any other technology I discuss in this book, the phantasmagoria lingered in the popular imagination long after its obsolescence, haunting virtual culture in an appropriately ghostly afterlife. It persisted in new virtual technologies that re-created its chief effects through new technological means and was reconfigured as a complex and multivalent metaphoric figure in nineteenth-century literary discourse.

Much ink has already been spilled on the phantasmagoria as Victorian metaphor, but the relationship of the phantasmagoria to the French Revolution and theories of nationalism in Victorian culture has never been fully explored.[7] For instance, what Marx describes as the ghostly recapitulation of Napoleon I's rise to power in Napoleon III's coup d'état registers a more fundamental spectrality endemic to the modern nation-state in nineteenth-century Europe. His description of revolutionaries who commune with the ghosts of the past in their effort to "creat[e] something that has never yet existed" invokes the revolutionary mass violence that led to the birth of France as a modern republic and the rise of nationalism across the Western world. In chapters 1–3, we have seen how Victorian scientific popularizers, showmen, and writers presented virtual aesthetics as the crowning expression of a rational, liberal, and enlightened nation and its civilizing empire precisely because it makes visual pleasure dependent on practices of reflexivity and scientific disenchantment. Marx offers a window into a different relationship between nineteenth-century nationalism and virtual media, one in which the stewards of the rational, liberal state are necessarily enthralled by the "tradition of dead generations" that they seek to break with—not exemplary disenchanted spectators at an optical show but superstitious fools haunted by ghosts. It is this ineluctable condition of haunting, this need to raise the ghosts of history precisely in order to break with the past, that dooms the nation to repeat its own mistakes.

This chapter traces this discourse of national history as a phantasmagorical ghost theater as it emerged in French and British writing about the phantasmagoria and the French Revolution between 1796 and 1859. For Marx, one "dead generation" in particular haunts the revolution of 1848 like a nightmare: the French Revolution. This is clearly a metaphor, yet it touches on a broader cultural imaginary that originates with the phantasmagoria itself. I argue that the phantasmagoria was conceived as a virtual technology for representing the French Revolution. As early as 1792, when Paul Philidor premiered the first phantasmagoria in Paris with a virtual projection of Mirabeau rising from the floor and advancing toward the audience, the phantasmagoria's optical ghost theater offered a way to represent the birth of the republic through violent revolution as an experience of being haunted by the dead. Philidor's successor Étienne-Gaspard Robertson made the phantasmagoria's ghostly links to history even more explicit when he staged his show in a Capuchin convent that had historical ties to both the ancien régime and the republic. In his popular two-volume autobiography, *Mémoires récreatifs, scientifiques, et anecdotiques* (1831), Robertson described the reception of his phantasmagoria as an exhumation and resurrection of the revolutionary dead that paralleled the way that memory can conjure absent persons.[8] Drawing on Robertson's memoir and contemporary accounts of attending his show, I argue that phantasmagoria spectatorship was constructed as a nationalist pastime that invited French audiences to bear witness to the "dead generations" out of which the modern French nation was born. In other words, the metaphor of French national consciousness as phantasmagoria is not an invention of later writers like Marx: it is a feature of the phantasmagoria's media history.

The second half of the chapter turns to two Victorian narratives of the French Revolution, Thomas Carlyle's *The French Revolution: A History* (1837) and Charles Dickens's *A Tale of Two Cities* (1859), that take up the cultural imaginary of phantasmagoria as a ghostly theater of French history. For Carlyle, the French Revolution is a phantasmagoria that plays out both for the figures who act within its history and for readers. In *A Tale of Two Cities*, Dickens stole liberally from both Carlyle and

Robertson to tell a story about the French Revolution as a phantasmagorical haunting that is structured by metaphors of resurrection and exhumation—most famously by the expression "recalled to life," which he applies to both historical events and people caught in and rescued from history's crosshairs. Like Marx, Carlyle and Dickens are drawn to the phantasmagoria as a means of conceptualizing a national experience of historical copresence, or the haunting of the present by a phantasmal past. Informed by *Mémoires récreatifs, scientifiques, et anecdotiques*, they draw on the nationalist and colonial frameworks of the pedagogy of disenchantment to compare the lived experience of the French Revolution to phantasmagoria spectatorship.

Before I proceed, I want to offer a disclaimer about the capriciousness of the phantasmagoria archive and, in particular, of the chief figures in my chapter, Robertson and Dickens. One of the many connections between them is that they were both successful plagiarists. While Robertson stole most of his innovations from his predecessor Philidor, shamelessly passing them off as his own, Dickens took much of his account of history of the French Revolution as a phantasmagoria from Robertson and Carlyle, only occasionally acknowledging his debts. I have been writing about Robertson and Dickens for the better part of a decade, and I am still discovering new ways that their narratives of their own genius have succeeded in deceiving me into misattributing to them innovations in the exhibition and representation of the phantasmagoria.[9] In this chapter, I try to source forms, ideas, and expressions to their original creators as best as I can, in the process correcting errors of attribution and interpretation—some significant, some minor but revealing—that I and other media and cultural historians have introduced into the scholarly record. At the same time, the chapter considers these instances of theft and copying as an integral feature of the archive: first as tragedy, then as farce; first by Philidor, then by Robertson; first in Carlyle, then in Dickens. The history of the-phantasmagoria-as-history is structured by repetitions, duplications, and recapitulations that reveal its persistence and reinvention across media formats. This persistence is what interests me—this way that the cultural discourse of phantasmagoria as historical haunting seems to haunt Victorian literary culture, appearing everywhere and yet strangely difficult to pin down. Like its virtual images, the phantasmagoria's archival traces in Victorian discourses of the French Revolution, national history, and history writing can seem spectral, hazy, ubiquitous—at once a theme and the very grounds of the discourse itself.

Phantasmagoria as History Show

One Paris evening in December 1792, almost exactly a month before crowds would gather to witness the execution of King Louis XVI in the Place de la Révolution, a mysterious exhibition made its first appearance. At the Hôtel de Chartres, a scenic fifteen-minute stroll from the Place de la Révolution along the northern edge of the Tuileries Garden, audience members could pay three livres to enter a room draped with black curtains and lit by a single funereal lamp. At five o'clock and again at nine o'clock, the lamp was extinguished and ghosts appeared. They moved through the shadowy darkness toward the audience and then, just as spectators thought they might reach out and touch them, they disappeared into thin air. Whether any Parisians doubled up on January 21 to see Louis XVI executed in the morning and ghosts rise at night is unknown to us now. What is clear, however, is that the French writers and showmen responsible for popularizing the phantasmagoria over the course of the decade imagined its astonishingly vivid ghosts as a kind of historical return of the repressed issuing from the authoritarian violence and repression of the French Revolution's Reign of Terror. As Sébastian Mercier would later write, "The ghosts and specters that were conjured in the theaters and that we took pleasure in contemplating were the reflection of revolutionary days."[10]

The phantasmagoria was a nationalist history show from its very beginnings. Paul Philidor launched the exhibition in Paris in the winter of 1792, just three months after the overthrow of the monarchy, as "PHANTASMAGORIE, apparition of Ghosts and invocation of the Shades of famous Persons."[11] *Phantasmagorie*, or phantasmagoria, was Philidor's neologism from the Greek roots *phantasma* ("image," "phantom," "apparition") and *agora* ("assembly"), a term that seems to offer a spectral equivalent to the newly formed National Constituent Assembly by defining the show as "an assembly of ghosts." Among the "famous persons" that Philidor presented to his audiences was Mirabeau, the father of the French Revolution, who rose from the floor as a glowing white wraith and slowly grew in size as he advanced toward the audience. The phantasmagoria thus presented itself as a sort of ghostly national parade, one that reflected the unfolding events of the revolution by representing its martyrs. Philidor's show lasted a scant few months and then was shuttered, probably because his historical specters fell afoul of the newly founded Revolutionary Tribunal at the height of the Reign of Terror. One possible explanation for Philidor's disappearance, offered by the wax sculpture artist Madame Tussaud, says that he was imprisoned for projecting an image of Louis XVI shortly after the king's death.[12] The story points to the discursive relationship between the phantasmagoria's virtual images, the optical resurrection of the dead, and historical recurrence.

Five years after Philidor's phantasmagoria closed, a showman by the name of Étienne-Gaspard Robertson announced his own version of the show. Born Robert—his Anglicized last name was a bid for cosmopolitan prestige typical of nineteenth-century showmen and magicians—Robertson had come to Paris from his native Belgium in 1791, abandoning the ecclesiastical career set out for him by his father to study physics and painting. He worked as a tutor in an aristocratic family during the Reign of Terror, a period during which he later claimed to have invented the phantasmagoria, identifying himself as a new species of "physicist-philosopher" whose exhibitions aimed "to destroy the enchanted world that owes its existence solely to the magic wand of fanaticism."[13] In truth, he was an immensely successful plagiarist. He copied every distinguishing element of Philidor's show, from its name to its technological design, while crediting himself with inventing a legitimate scientific art of apparitions. In the winter of 1798, the Parisian press announced "*Fantasmagoria* at the Pavilion of the rue de l'Échiquier, by cit. E.-G. Robertson: apparitions of Specters, Phantoms, and Revenants, as they must and could have appeared throughout history, in every place and in every nation."[14] It opened at the Pavilion de l'Échiquier, a small theater that held sixty people, to wild success.[15] In an uncanny doubling of the story told about Philidor, Robertson's show was also shut down by the police after a report surfaced that he was asked by an audience member to show the ghost of Louis XVI. Once again, the playful and metaphorical association between the phantasmagoria's virtual images and ghosts, between projection and resurrection, made the show the target of state censorship.

To understand how this nexus of virtual images, ghosts, French nationalism, and historical resurrection emerged, we must look closely at the apparatus of the phantasmagoria itself. The historian Mervyn Heard calls the phantasmagoria "the secret life of the magic lantern," a playful phrase that captures the show's use of a comparatively commonplace optical technology for the startling and mysterious illusion that ghosts were being conjured right before the audience's eyes.[16] The phantasmagoria involved the projection of glass slides in a dark room,

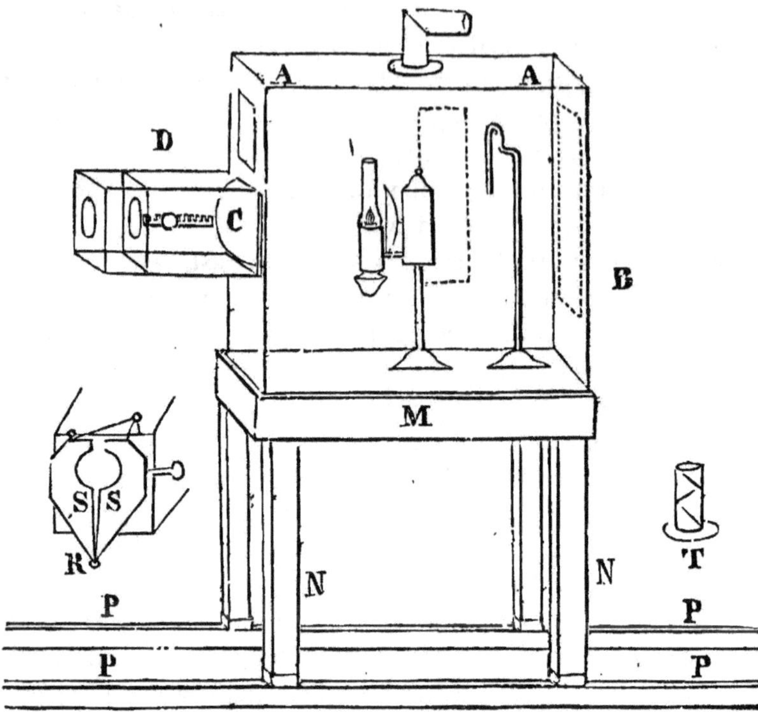

FIGURE 4.1. Robertson's rolling magic lantern. E. G. Robertson, *Mémoires récreatifs, scientifiques, et anecdotiques*, Librairie encyclopédique de Roret, 1840.

but unlike other lantern shows, it made a "secret" of its technology. The slides were rear-projected from a mobile magic lantern hidden behind a curtain, and the complete darkness of the theater disarticulated the luminous images in space, creating the illusion that these ghostly virtual images were moving about the room. The secrecy of the phantasmagoria was more an aesthetic than an epistemic quality of the show; its use of a hidden magic lantern was well known. Rather than mere trickery or deception, the phantasmagoria embodied what Theodor Adorno would later call nineteenth-century art's triumph of illusion through the obscuring of the traces of production.[17] It worked by creating an immersive virtual environment sculpted out of light and shadow, one in which ghosts seemed to soar through the room without the barrier of a stage or screen to separate them from the audience.

At the heart of the show was the use of a hidden magic lantern mounted on wheels (figure 4.1). In the eighteenth and nineteenth centuries, most magic lantern shows used front projection, with both the magic lantern and projectionist visible to the audience. The phantasmagoria used rear projection, with the magic lantern projecting onto the screen from behind it. The magic lantern could be rolled toward and away from the screen with an adjustable focus so that the projected images would remain in focus at any distance, creating the illusion that the images were moving. When the lantern was moved away from the screen, the images seemed to grow; when it was moved toward the screen, they seemed to shrink. The screen was also concealed in the complete darkness of the theater; Robertson even designed a perfectly transparent screen that he hid behind a black curtain until the lights were extinguished. The backgrounds of the slides were treated with lampblack, which removed the usual halo of light surrounding the projected images of the magic lantern and dissolved them into the unvariegated blackness of the theater. The combination of an imperceptible screen and the imperceptible boundaries of the image "had the effect of giving the ghosts a kind of independence," as if they were autonomous beings.[18] It was impossible for audiences to locate where the images really were in space: they seemed to hover and loom, approaching the audience and then retreating, appearing out of nowhere and disappearing into nothing.

The aesthetic experience of the phantasmagoria was therefore one of radical proximity and intimacy between images and spectators, ghosts and living beings—what Thomas Elsaesser calls "an ambient form of spectacle and event."[19] Unlike the cinema, the phantasmagoria does not confine images to a frame. It not only creates virtual images but also virtual space, effecting a perceptual displacement of its images from the screen that supports them to the air itself. Robertson's practice of projecting on smoke made this displacement even more explicit, creating the illusion that the images were hazy floating ghosts, spectrally embodied, at once immaterial and solid. Noam Elcott calls this aesthetic "the assembly of humans and images," a phrase that neatly revises the meaning of phantasmagoria —"an assembly of ghosts"—to reflect the way the illusion configures this spatial intimacy between spectators and projections.[20] Yet by creating the effect of virtual images surging toward the audience or suspended in space, the phantasmagoria did more than simply assemble humans and images in the same room. For comparison, Pepper's Ghost projected virtual images of the human body in a room with audience members, but it relied on a firm spatial separation between ghosts and spectators. The pane of glass that projected images of hidden actors onto the stage was also a barrier, imperceptibly but nevertheless physically separating stage and audience, spatially demarcating the world of spirits as part of the theatrical illusion and therefore distinct from the real world. The phantasmagoria allowed ghosts and spectators to gather even more closely together; the illusion that the images are surging into the audience violated the physical separation we associate with screen aesthetics.[21] It challenged the boundary between ghost and human, image and referent.

The shared space in which humans and images assemble—at once the real space of the theater and the virtual space constructed by the apparently mobile and unbounded spectral images—also compelled an uncanny sense of time. After all, the phantasmagoria does not just project images but a specific kind of image that represents and simulates a ghost. This was evident in two ways. First, while the lantern slides depicted varied types of material, including comic and pastoral scenes, the dominant subjects were dead historical figures, ghosts rising from graves, and women turning into skeletons (figures 4.2 and 4.3). Robertson specialized in adapting gothic painting and literature for the phantasmagoria, such as his representation of the Bloody Nun from Matthew Lewis's novel *The Monk*, and in trick slides that allowed him to project movement and visual transformation, like a dead man emerging from a tomb full of flames.[22] Second, both Philidor and

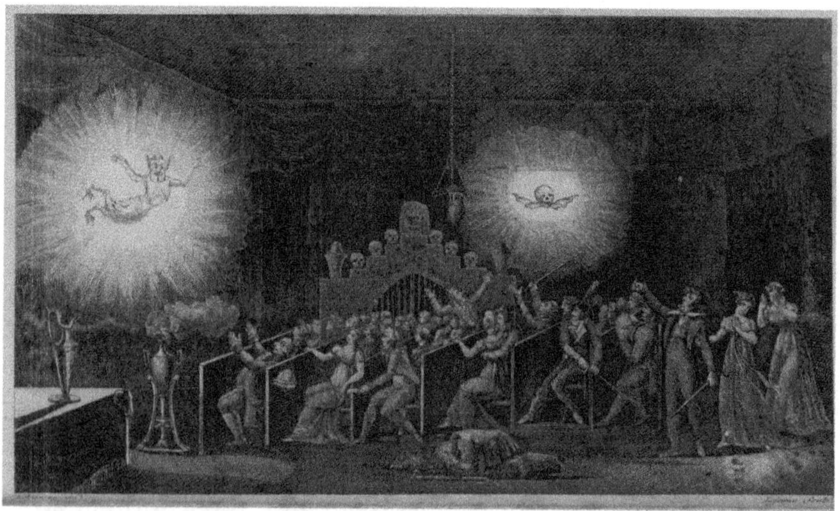

FIGURE 4.2. Engraving of Robertson's phantasmagoria. E. G. Robertson, *Mémoires récreatifs, scientifiques, et anecdotiques*, Librairie encyclopédique de Roret, 1840.

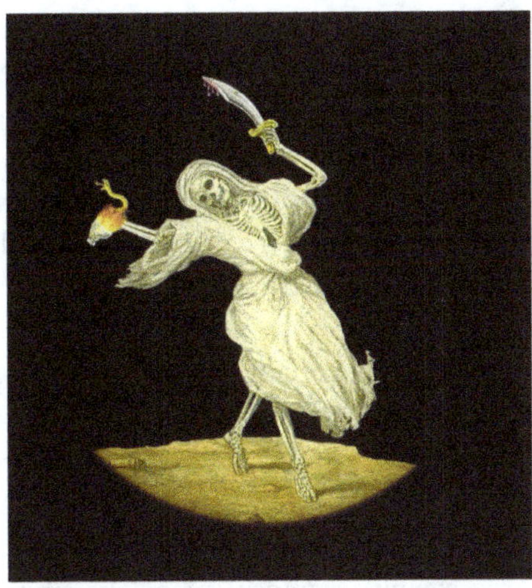

FIGURE 4.3. Phantasmagoria lantern slide. Courtesy of the National Science and Media Museum/Science and Society Picture Library.

Robertson presented the phantasmagoria as a demystified séance, which positioned it within a genealogy of necromantic ghost raisings. To be clear, the phantasmagoria never claimed to be a ghost raising but rather an entertaining representation of a ghost raising. Nevertheless, by assembling the living with apparently free-floating and metamorphosing virtual images of the dead, the phantasmagoria anchored the spectator perceptually and sensorially in the present while seeming to bring them into contact with the past.[23] In the phantasmagoria, time collapses—it becomes as malleable, as strangely sculpted, as space.

The Parisian phantasmagoria's assembly of ghosts and spectators, images and audiences, made it an apt technological medium for producing national consciousness and articulating a shared national identity. The show reflected the violence of the revolution. Its mobile, metamorphosing specters seemed to reverse-engineer temporarily the mass death of the Terror and the revolutionary wars, replaying the birth of the republic as a history of collective loss. At the same time, the show's creation of a space and time in which the living and the dead can assemble turned it into a spectral counterpart to the nationalist populism of the revolution. I want to be clear that when I describe the phantasmagoria's nationalist aesthetics, I am not suggesting that the phantasmagoria was an authorized expression of republican nationalism or that it was endorsed by the government. The phantasmagoria offered a new medium for imagining and visualizing the effects of the Terror on individuals and the nation at large precisely at the moment when explicit representations of the Terror were censored by the authorities.[24] As Ronen Steinberg argues, the trope of ghosts returning from the dead was pervasive in the aftermath of the Terror precisely because of the political project of historical erasure that sought to remove evidence of mass killings from public view.[25]

My argument that the phantasmagoria acted as a virtual theater for nationalist history and identity is prefigured in an oft-quoted 1798 editorial written for the republican journal *L'Ami des lois* by François Martin Poultier d'Elmotte, a member of the National Constituent Assembly, about a night at Robertson's show. Often mistaken by scholars as a reliable eyewitness account of the phantasmagoria, it is actually a political satire that uses the show's apparent resurrections of revolutionary historical figures to portray the phantasmagoria as a riposte to the repressive logic of the Terror.[26] Take the opening line of the essay: "A decimvir has said that only the dead do not return, but go to Robertson's and you will see that the dead return like anyone else" ("*Un decimvir a dit qu'il n'y avait que les morts qui ne revenaient pas; allez chez Robertson, vous verrez que les morts reviennent comme les autres*").[27] This line has been mistranslated in English for over 150 years and, as a result, its political context has been lost.[28] The term "decimvir," or member of the commission established by the Roman Republic for the codifying of laws, refers to Bertrand Barère, a powerful Jacobin member of the National Convention and champion of the Reign of Terror known for his memorable aphorisms. "Only the dead do not return" (*il n'y a que les morts qui ne reviennent pas*) is one such phrase. Originally from a speech to the National Convention of 1794, it formed part of Barère's call for a stronger national defense: he argued that France should have annihilated British troops so they would not "return" in future conflicts. As Barère would later complain in his memoirs, however, the phrase was also taken out of context during that same period as a justification for the massacres of the Terror.[29] This new application was not exactly a stretch: Barère was a founding member of the Committee on Public Safety and responsible for the propaganda that condemned many aristocrats to the guillotine.

Poultier d'Elmotte's use of the phrase "only the dead do not return" plays on these layered meanings. It depicts Robertson's phantasmagoria not just as a return of the dead but as a refutation of the Jacobin justification for the mass violence of the Terror—that the only way to ensure the past does not return is to murder it. Robertson answers Barère's *ne reviennent pas* with his *revenants*, as if to say that murder cannot kill history—it always returns. This idea comes back later in the essay, when the author claims that Barère and his fellow Jacobin Pierre-Joseph Cambon are in the audience. This is impossible—both men were in exile when the essay was written. They were thrown out of the National Assembly after the Thermidorean Reaction, the parliamentary revolt against Jacobin rule that saw the overthrow of Robespierre. Readers would thus have understood the editorial not as an eyewitness report but as a witty parable of internecine republican battles during the Reign of Terror. For instance, Poultier d'Elmotte describes Robertson throwing the proceedings of the National Convention of May 31, 1793, onto the fire—the date when Jacobins purged the more moderate Girondists from the revolutionary leadership—to conjure ghosts "in bloody veils" that encircle Barère and Cambon until they run screaming out of the theater.[30] There is no evidence that Robertson ever performed such theatrics. Instead, the author creates a fictional scene that replays the events of the Thermidorean Reaction by imagining the phantasmagoria as a counterforce to the violent authoritarian radicalism of the Jacobins. He shows Barère surrounded by the ghosts of those he has murdered—ghosts that, counter to his own claim, return like anyone else. Those purged by Barère now purge him.

In spite of its fictional elements, the editorial's political commentary relies on a sophisticated understanding of the phantasmagoria's medium-specific visual and technological effects. More than just identifying the show's virtual images with the revolutionary dead, Poultier d'Elmotte uses the phantasmagoria's capacity to create a space and time in which people and ghosts assemble as a metaphor for an imaginary form of national assembly that would challenge the state policy of censorship to engage in a collective process of political repair. The victims of the Terror are revealed to Barère and Cambon by the "almost universal acclaim" (*une acclamation presque génerale*) of the "assembly," diction that turns the audience into a political body whose cheers constitute a democratic action.[31] The victims themselves are a "mob of shadows" (*la foule des ombres*), or shadow assembly, who join the assembly of the living to run the Jacobins out of the theater.[32] In this imaginary, the phantasmagoria is a political assembly in which the dead and living work together to form a collective that can overcome historical repression.

Robertson preserved Poultier d'Elmotte's editorial on the phantasmagoria by reprinting it in its entirety more than thirty years later in *Mémoires récreatifs, scientifiques, et anecdotiques* (1831), his two-volume memoir of his scientific exploits. He considered it an important part of the history of the phantasmagoria because he believed that it was responsible for the police shutting down his show. Toward the end of the article, Poultier d'Elmotte wrote that an audience member asked Robertson to conjure the ghost of Louis XVI. It was in response to this claim, Robertson believed, that his show was closed and his equipment confiscated later that year. Beyond its value as a historical artifact, it is clear that Robertson favored the article. While he recognized it as "almost entirely a work of the imagination," it neatly complemented the account of the phantasmagoria that Robertson developed in his memoir.[33] His story about the invention and popularization of the phantasmagoria emphasized its use of gothic aesthetics and optical magic to bring the repressed histories of the monarchy and the early years of the French republic to life through the conjuring of ghosts.

Volume I of *Mémoires récreatifs, scientifiques, et anecdotiques* is an anecdotal history of the French Revolution—a narrative of an Enlightenment hero's scientific and artistic triumphs during and after the dark days of violence and unrest. The phantasmagoria is his apotheosis, an invention that he credits as a source of enlightenment for a superstitious and uneducated public even as he clearly revels in its aura of the supernatural. For instance, Robertson echoes Poultier d'Elmotte's language when he celebrates his phantasmagoria as a "kingdom of the dead" that turns the theater into a portal between the ordinary world and an otherworld of ghosts and skeletons.[34] This gothic aesthetic can be understood within the framework of rational magic that I have called the "pedagogy of disenchantment," exemplified in the scientific treatises and showmen's exposés I discussed in chapter 1, such as David Brewster's *Letters on Natural Magic* (1832) and Jean-Eugène Robert-Houdin's *Confidences d'un prestidigateur* (1858). *Mémoires récreatifs, scientifiques, et anecdotiques* shares with both Brewster's treatise and Robert-Houdin's memoir a conviction that even the most supernatural-seeming visual illusions and technological magic possess a rationalizing pedagogy that will liberate audiences from base superstition. Much of the volume is taken up with narrating the history and technology of the phantasmagoria, with Robertson scrubbing Philidor's existence from the historical record and claiming for himself—at times defensively—full credit as the illusion's singular inventor. At the same time, Robertson develops an account of the historical and affective relationship between the French Revolution and the phantasmagoria by constructing the phantasmagoria's technologically mediated encounter with the dead as a virtual haunting that serves the purpose of historical representation. By appearing to bring the dead back to life, the phantasmagoria enables audiences to experience the suppressed historical past of the ancien régime and the Terror as present.

Playful allusions to historical resurrection coursed through Robertson's phantasmagoria. The show was divided into two parts, the first representing "imaginary specters" and the second "known shadows."[35] The latter included a combination of historical figures like Mirabeau, Henry IV, and Voltaire and audience requests, with Robertson adapting a technique first used by the German necromancer Johann Schiller of inviting audience members to submit in advance detailed requests for "ghosts" that they wished to see and then rapidly commissioning portraits on glass slides. The show ordinarily culminated with a climactic apparition that reflected "some event of the day"; examples included Robespierre hit by lightning as he climbs out of his tomb and the crowning of Napoleon beneath a star bearing the words "18 Brumaire."[36] The spatial illusion of the bright moving images soaring through the dark room styled these "known ghosts" as temporary resurrections of the dead, the lantern's mobility turning the projections into, in Robertson's words, "the veritable proceedings of ghosts."[37] This imaginary of historical resurrection was enhanced by Robertson's incorporation of galvanic demonstrations into his show. Galvanism, which Robertson called "a new fluid . . . which temporarily restores movement to bodies which have ceased to live," was part of his earliest concept for the phantasmagoria and served a dual function.[38] It established the phantasmagoria within the genre of the scientific lecture-demonstration rather than that of the necromantic séance, all the while "planting subliminal messages" about the reanimation of the dead "in the minds of his audience."[39] Spectators watched the showman first apply an electrical current to the legs of dead frogs to make them twitch as if alive, and then unfurl phantoms and revenants. The galvanic demonstration and the projection of "known shadows" mirrored each other, both "temporarily restor[ing] movement to bodies which have ceased to live." Audiences might rightly ask, as David J. Jones puts it, "If dead frogs could move again, could Robespierre rise?"[40]

As we know, this question really was asked—not about Robespierre but instead about Louis XVI. After a temporary exile in Bordeaux while his show was closed down by police, Robertson launched a new and improved Parisian phantasmagoria that seemed calculated to defy state censorship by making the metaphoric association between his optical ghosts and historical resurrection even more explicit. Instead of appearing at the Pavilion de l'Échiquier, Robertson moved his exhibition to a larger and more dramatic location: the Couvent des Capucines, or Capuchin convent. Occupied by the Order of the Capuchin Poor Clares, the Couvent des Capucines was built in 1602 by Henry IV to house the remains of Queen Louise de Lorraine. In 1698, it became the site of Place Vendôme, constructed by Louis XIV, who rebuilt the convent as part of his renovations. The convent was abandoned in 1790 after the National Constituent Assembly seized the properties and lands held by the Catholic Church, and later it was used to interrogate perceived royalists, including Robertson.[41] In 1793, the National Assembly renamed the square Place des Piques, after the pikes used to impale the heads of victims of the guillotine during the Reign of Terror.

By staging the phantasmagoria anew at the Couvent des Capucines, Robertson turned it into what Jones calls "the first totally self-contained entertainment."[42] Although the architectural style was Baroque, the crumbling ruins and garden studded with the tombstones of dead nuns fit in with the gothic aesthetics of the show. In the dark of night, audience members had to cross the garden and walk among the graves to reach the two-story cloisters that Robertson had rented. They entered a long corridor painted with fantastical images; passed into the *salon de physique*, where Robertson now housed his demonstrations of galvanism; and then opened a door decorated with Egyptian symbols to reach the theater. Not only was the phantasmagoria now an immersive and site-specific experience, but the site itself also associated the spectacle of optical projection and its imaginary of ghostly resurrection with Catholic religious belief. At the same time, the convent embodied the revolutionary history that Robertson's slides portrayed. The convent was not only built during the ancien régime, a monument to its splendor, but it was also associated with the violent excesses of the revolutionary republic. In this space, the phantasmagoria became a site-specific performance of historical resurrection that was meant to exploit the audience's lived historical experience of the Terror as part of its affective charge.

In *Mémoires récreatifs, scientifiques, et anecdotiques*, Robertson portrayed the phantasmagoria's optical ghosts as emanating from the convent's material traces of the ancien régime and making visible the convent's historical connection to the mass violence of the Terror. He begins by attempting to justify his choice of site as part of the rationalizing project of the phantasmagoria. To replace blunt credulity and fear of ghosts with philosophical skepticism and disenchantment, Robertson claims that he must first inspire in his audience "a kind of religious terror," for which "a vast chapel in the middle of a cloister" is the ideal location.[43] However, he goes on to specify that the cloister not only inspires religious contemplation but also evokes the historical memory of the revolutionary exhumations. In 1793, the National Convention ordered the exhumation and destruction of ancient royal tombs, the majority of which were in the basilica of St. Denis, a shocking ritual meant to consolidate the new republic symbolically.[44] The cadavers were deposited in a trench and covered with quicklime; those that were not already pure ash, as the most ancient were, were dismembered and corroded. Robertson claims that the Capuchin convent, which held the remains of Louise de Lorraine, inspired memories of these exhumations, waxing poetic about "the tombs expelled from this sanctuary, as they had been from all the temples, from all the convents, and which we had seen piled up by the hundreds on the steps of the church squares." These memories conspired with "the ancient belief in shadows" to make it seem as if the optical ghosts he projected issued "from real sepulchers" and fluttered around the "mortal remains which they had animated."[45] In other words, Robertson imagines his Capuchin phantasmagoria as an exhumation and resurrection of the dead. Rather than trying to convince his audiences that they are witnessing a supernatural event, he describes how the show played on the audience's conceptual associations to manufacture a site-specific and medium-specific experience of national history. By evoking both the audience's primal ghost belief—"the ancient belief in shadows"—and their historical memory of the Reign of Terror's exhumations, the phantasmagoria would create the illusion that the revolutionary dead were emanating from the Capuchin crypt. The phantasmagoria is thus not only a visual illusion but also an imaginative fiction that works by activating a chain of associations between churches and the afterlife, relics and souls, the Capuchin Church and the National Assembly, tombs and the Reign of Terror.

This passage exemplifies Robertson's tendency to exaggerate his accomplishments. The tombs of the Capuchin Church were not actually exhumed by the revolutionary authorities—the remains of Louise de Lorraine lay peacefully in their crypt until they were rediscovered and relocated to the Basilica of Saint-Denis in the early nineteenth century. But whether the phantasmagoria succeeded in exploiting historical trauma for aesthetic effect is immaterial to my argument. What interests me is how Robertson imagines himself as manipulating an audience's collective perceptual experience to portray the phantasmagoria as itself a kind of exhumation and resurrection—an unearthing and making visible of a history that has been buried and killed by the revolution through the optical aesthetics of moving virtual images. Because the exhumation of tombs occurred in 1793, in one instance as a prelude to the public execution of Marie Antoinette, Robertson clearly ties this aesthetic to the public acts of violence and historical erasure that marked the Terror and its aftermath.[46] He imagines the phantasmagoria as a show that can cultivate national consciousness through an optical return of the repressed.

Robertson's imaginary of the phantasmagoria as a historical ghost show that rebuilds the nation in the wake of mass violence aligns with that of Poultier d'Elmotte in his editorial of more than thirty years earlier. Poultier d'Elmotte fictionalized the phantasmagoria as a political assembly in which the raising of ghosts challenged the state policy of historical repression. Robertson portrays the phantasmagoria as a form of perceptual and technological magic that represents the process of historical memory itself and, by extension, parallels the construction of the nation from collective acts of historical memory. In this sense, Robertson returns us to Marx's *The Eighteenth Brumaire of Louis Bonaparte* and the "dead generations" that haunt the French Revolution of 1848. He imagines the phantasmagoria as a history show not only because of its "known shadows" but, more importantly, because its medium-specific effects of creating a virtual space and time of encounter with the dead expressed a postrevolutionary national condition of living with ghosts.

History as Phantasmagoria Show

I have offered a detailed media history of the phantasmagoria to demonstrate that its practices of optical magic and cultivation of a new form of virtual mass spectatorship were discursively and imaginatively connected to the rise of nationalism and representation of national history. In the second half of this chapter, I will consider the work of two British writers whose narratives of the French Revolution reveal the persistence of this structure in Victorian culture. Thomas Carlyle's *The French Revolution: A History* and Charles Dickens's *A Tale of Two Cities* draw on existing French discourses of the phantasmagoria to develop a phantasmagorical metaphorics that describes and evokes the lived experience of the Reign of Terror. As it did for Marx in *The Eighteenth Brumaire of Louis Bonaparte*, phantasmagoria offers these writers a framework for representing historical copresence—the way the past haunts the present like a ghost. For Carlyle and Dickens, the phantasmagoria of the French Revolution serves as a dramatic scene of exigency and crisis out of which English national identity can be forged and renewed.

Before I turn to an analysis of the texts in question, I would like to address three methodological problems that scholars confront when tracing the influence of the phantasmagoria on Victorian literary culture. References to the phantasmagoria abound in Victorian literature. The first problem scholars encounter is that the phantasmagoria was not a Victorian media spectacle; in fact, its legacy in nineteenth-century Britain was early and brief. It arrived in England in 1801 with Paul de Philipstahl's phantasmagoria show at the Lyceum Theater in London, but its popularity peaked just a few years later, and it died out as a headline entertainment by the 1830s.[47] Its technology and visual effects were adapted or absorbed into new media spectacles that outstripped the phantasmagoria in popular appeal, such as dissolving views, Pepper's Ghost, spirit photography, and theatrical special effects. For instance, in the 1820s, Philipstahl's one-time assistant Henry Langdon Childe used a magic lantern dissolve to create theatrical special effects of the ghost ship the *Flying Dutchman* and the eruption of Mount Vesuvius on the London stage.[48] Known as a dissolving view, this effect is created when light is slowly stopped down on one lantern lens and raised on the other to create the illusion that one image dissolves into another on the screen. At the Royal Polytechnic Institution, which housed London's premier optical theater, Henry Dircks named his original patent for what would become Pepper's Ghost the "Dircksian Phantasmagoria," positioning his free-floating, realistic, spectral simulacra as a technological update of Robertson's magic lantern show.[49] When a writer like Thomas Hardy describes Eustacia Vye in *The Return of the Native* (1878) as "a figure in a phantasmagoria—a creature of light surrounded by an area of darkness," he is not drawing on his direct experience with a show like Robertson's; Hardy was born long after the phantasmagoria's heyday.[50] Hardy is more likely ascribing to the phantasmagoria the media effect of a luminous, spectral moving body engulfed in darkness that he knew from cultural discourse and from the later media forms that the phantasmagoria inspired. A luminous image "surrounded by an area of darkness" describes many Victorian magic lantern slides, which were often composed of circular paintings against black backgrounds, while the emphasis on Eustacia as a "creature of light" recalls Pepper's Ghost's creation of spectral bodies made of light. As a result of this chronology, literary allusions to the phantasmagoria can reflect a cultural imaginary of the show that does not align with its actual media effects or that reinterprets its media effects through a contemporary framework. To say that Hardy is influenced by the phantasmagoria is to miss the critical mediating role of Victorian projection formats in his visual imagination.

A second related problem is that, as cultural memory of the phantasmagoria show waned, the term "phantasmagoria" assumed new meanings, referring to an evolving set of visual effects and perceptual experiences with which the show was broadly associated in the cultural imagination.[51] Take *Reuben Sachs* (1889), in which Amy Levy's Judith Quixano reflects that emotions are treated as "mere phantasmagoria conjured up by silly people, by sentimental people, by women." The term "phantasmagoria" has not entirely lost its association with the ghost show, but it is being used to refer more broadly to a regime of visual deception. Levy deploys "phantasmagoria" to evoke marginalized and feminized superstitious belief in immaterial or spectral illusion, not unlike the "magic panic" in Elizabeth Gaskell's 1853 novel *Cranford*, contrasting it with the sober, serious, and masculine realm of "material relationships."[52] *Reuben Sachs* shows us that phantasmagoria does not always refer reliably to the media format it was invented to describe, one characterized not by the shallow trickery of women but by the masculine and disenchanted realm of rational recreation.

The third problem is that reliable media histories of the phantasmagoria are hard to come by and are skewed by the prominence of Robertson's *Mémoires récreatifs, scientifiques, et anecdotiques* in archival records of the show. Nineteenth-century literary scholars and historians continue to attribute the invention of the phantasmagoria incorrectly to Robertson, circulate mistranslated passages from his memoir, and misinterpret key primary sources like Poultier d'Elmotte's editorial.

I have come to understand these features of the archive not as obstacles but as opportunities. The phantasmagoria operated as an imaginary virtual medium for Victorians. They related to the phantasmagoria through cultural discourse about the show, sometimes more boastful and bombastic than strictly correct; its reconstruction in newer media formats; and the transforming meanings of the term "phantasmagoria" as it came to be attached to new media technologies, forms of spectacle and illusion, and psychological states. It is in this spirit that I consider the work of Thomas Carlyle and Charles Dickens. These writers are not necessarily responding to the phantasmagoria's "actual" media history but to its mythologization by French writers like Poultier d'Elmotte and Robertson and the reimagination of some of its key effects in contemporary projection formats like the dissolving view. Rather than viewing the phantasmagoria as a media spectacle that had a true history and a metaphoric afterlife, I propose that the phantasmagoria was always an imaginary medium for thinking about the haunted and ghostly condition of national history, memory, and identity. Its metaphoric uses are inextricable from and constitutive of its media history.

The imaginary of the phantasmagoria as national haunting formalized in *Mémoires récreatifs, scientifiques, et anecdotiques* was not lost on the Victorians. If Robertson and Poultier d'Elmotte proposed the phantasmagoria as a revolutionary history show, nineteenth-century theorists of history reflected this back by describing the history of the French Revolution as a phantasmagoria. I began this chapter with a brief discussion of Marx's theory of historical-psychological copresence in *The Eighteenth Brumaire of Louis Bonaparte*, arguing that his account of national history as a phantasmal haunting was structured by a metaphorics of the phantasmagoria. Marx's interest in tropes of spectrality, haunting, and optical technology can be found across his oeuvre, from the "specter haunting Europe" in *The Communist Manifesto* (1847) to the description of ideology as a camera obscura in *The German Ideology* (1845), to the account of the commodity as a "phantasmagorical form" in *Capital, Volume 1* (1867). The specific connections that *The Eighteenth Brumaire of Louis Bonaparte* makes between history and haunting, phantasmagoria and the French Revolution, are prefigured in the historical writings of Thomas Carlyle.[53] Six years after Robertson's *Mémoires récreatifs, scientifiques, et anecdotiques* was released, Thomas Carlyle published his monumental *The French Revolution: A History* (1837), which traced the revolution from 1789 to the height of the Reign of Terror. While I cannot prove that Carlyle read *Mémoires récreatifs, scientifiques, et anecdotiques*, I believe it is likely. *The French Revolution* seems to respond directly to Robertson in its articulation of revolutionary history in a way that Terry Castle calls "a kind of spectral drama—a nightmarish magic-lantern show playing on without respite in the feverish, ghostly confines of the 'Historical Imagination.'"[54] The language of phantasms and phantasmagories, specters and spectrality, and magic lantern slides pervade Carlyle's grandiloquent, dramatized, and intensely visual descriptions of historical actors, sites, and events.

Like Robertson in *Mémoires récreatifs, scientifiques, et anecdotiques*, Carlyle draws a metaphoric equivalence between the lived experience of the French Revolution and phantasmagoria spectatorship. To bear witness to the unfolding of revolutionary history, whether as an actor or a reader, is to be a spectator at a "Scenic Phantasmagory." Before the storming of the Bastille, when the Jacobin leader Thuriot enters the prison to negotiate with its governor, Carlyle portrays him looking down into the street at the thronging masses ready to lay siege: "Such vision (spectral yet real) thou, O Thuriot, as from thy Mount of Vision, beholdest in this moment: prophetic of what other Phantasmagories, and loud-gibbering Spectral Realities, which thou yet beholdest not, but shalt!"[55] Of the September Massacres at the Prison de l'Abbaye, Carlyle speaks directly to "the Reader, who looks earnestly through this dim Phantasmagory of the Pit" but "will discern few fixed certain objects."[56] Thuriot looks down from one prison, the reader looks into another, but both are confronted with "spectral realities"—with a reality defined by its spectrality and radical state of transmogrification. Nothing is "fixed" or "certain" in the phantasmagoria, or in revolutionary history: all is in a state of change so rapid and unceasing that reality seems incorporeal, pure shadow and light.

The French Revolution's account of history as phantasmagoria evolved out of two essays from the 1830s: "On History" (1831) and "The Diamond Necklace" (1837). In "On History," Carlyle contrasted the historian as "Seer" from the historian as mere "onlooke[r]."[57] The onlooker is incapable of recognizing the sublime nature of history as "an ever-living, ever-working Chaos of Being, wherein shape after shape bodies itself forth from innumerable elements" that can never be fully tamed by the linearity and successive format of historical narrative. The "Seer" is an "Artist in History" characterized by his penetrating insights into this "Chaos of Being," his ability to perceive and arrange it into historical narrative.[58] "Chaos of Being" evokes a primordial and metaphysical state, like the "formless void" out of which God creates the world in the Book of Genesis. Its infinite bodying forth of shapes from infinite sources constructs historical process as, in Hayden White's terms, "a panorama of happening in which the stress is on the novel and emergent," turning history into "an arena in which new things can be seen to appear."[59] White's metaphoric use of the panorama, a nineteenth-century immersive visual media format, is telling: while the "Chaos of Being" itself is not described in explicitly visual terms, the role of the "Artist in History" as a "Seer" implies that it can and must be visually apprehended.

In "The Diamond Necklace," published the same year as *The French Revolution*, Carlyle developed this trope of history writing as seeing by rewriting the "Chaos of Being" as a phantasmagoria. The essay opens by characterizing the history of "our own poor Nineteenth Century" as "the lordliest Real-Phantasmagory, which men name *Being*." This phantasmagoria "rose and vanished, in perpetual change":

> Oak-trees fell, young acorns sprang: Men too, new-sent from the Unknown, he met, of tiniest size, who waxed into stature, into strength of sinew, passionate fire and light: in other men the light was growing dim, the sinews all feeble; they sank, motionless, into ashes, into invisibility; returned *back* to the Unknown, beckoning him their mute farewell.[60]

In this passage, we can see how Carlyle revises his "Chaos of Being" as a phantasmagoria "which men name *Being*," one that characterizes the metaphysical process of history through the phantasmagoric visual effects of images that rise, vanish, and metamorphose. The "Real-Phantasmagory" fulfills what White describes as history's arena of novel appearances, as images rise and transform and dissolve into new images before the historian's eyes. At the same time, what I have described as the phantasmagoria's construction as a virtual space and time sculpted out of darkness and light makes it a fitting expression of the primordial "Chaos of Being." This God's-eye view of history—Carlyle goes on to specify that it is "a sight for angels, and archangels"—is what the historian should aim to represent.

The examples of the oak tree and the "new-sent" men evoke medium-specific features of the phantasmagoria and dissolving view to metonymize history through instances of death and rebirth. Jonathan Potter has argued that the dissolving view functioned as a metaphor for history in the work of Carlyle and Dickens, noting how its principal effect of one image melting into another provided them with a framework for conceptualizing the transitory moments of history.[61] Carlyle's direct reference to the phantasmagoria should be heeded, however: the dissolving view was a successor to the phantasmagoria that used or re-created many of the phantasmagoria's techniques of visual transition and superimposition. "Oak-trees fell, young acorns sprang" references the way both the phantasmagoria and dissolving view show one object transforming into another.[62] The metaphysical scenes Carlyle describes here, of organisms growing and dying and seeding new organisms, builds on the macabre slipping slide sequences that the phantasmagoria was best known for, like a woman turning into a skeleton or Robespierre evaporating into dust. The men growing from tiny babies, "wax[ing] into stature," and then "[sinking], motionless, into ashes, into invisibility," also recalls the phantasmagoria's effect of enlargement created by rolling the magic lantern away from the screen, as in Philidor's Mirabeau growing in size, as well as its virtual images disappearing into thin air. Carlyle maps the birth, maturation, and death of a human being and, by extension, the mysterious and sublime nature of historical being, onto the magic lantern's metamorphic specters. If history is a process in which "shape after shape bodies itself forth," as he wrote in "On History," the shapes are images bodied forth from a magic lantern.

In *The French Revolution*, Carlyle extends this metaphor by portraying the events of the French Revolution as scenes from a phantasmagoria. At the same time, he develops an account of history writing as a kind of "See[ing]" that recognizes the fundamentally spectral and metamorphic nature of historical reality. Note the echoes of Carlyle's "Real-Phantasmagory" of history in *The French Revolution*'s description of the Pont Louis XVI. Several chapters after his account of the storming of the Bastille, in which Thuriot looks down from the prison on the "Phantastmagor[y]" in the streets below, Carlyle describes how the Bastille's stones have been recycled in a bridge built over the Seine:

> Vanished is the Bastille, what we call vanished: the *body*, or sandstones, of it hanging, in benign metamorphosis, for centuries to come, over the Seine waters, as *Pont Louis Seize*; the soul of it living, perhaps still longer, in the memories of men.[63]

Like the phantasmagorical specters of history in "The Diamond Necklace" that "rose and vanished, in perpetual change," in *The French Revolution*, the Bastille has "metamorphos[ed]" into the Pont Louis XVI, a physical reconstruction that mirrors France's metamorphosis from monarchy to republic built from the rubble of the past. Here, Carlyle applies the penetrating form of historical perception that he outlines in "On History" and "The Diamond Necklace." The figures of the "Seer" and the "onlooker" haunt his description of the Bastille as "what we call vanished"—seemingly absent but actually transfigured into a new form. An onlooker, with his superficial and ordinary ocular perception, might say that the Bastille had vanished because he trusts only in bodies as they immediately appear. The Seer, an Artist in History, recognizes the spectral and metamorphic nature of the apparently physical world. He sees the prison in the bridge, the oak in the acorn, the adult in the infant. By perceiving the world as it is endlessly transfigured and transformed, the Seer recognizes history for the "Real-Phantasmagory" it is.

Unlike in *The Eighteenth Brumaire of Louis Bonaparte*, where history is an inescapable realm of haunting, *The French Revolution* portrays the phantasmagoria of history as a primal, ontological condition of transformation and change that can be disciplined into narrative as long as a Seer—a heroic individual characterized by his optical-epistemic virtuosity—applies his talents to the cause. In this sense, Carlyle returns us to the Victorian discourse of disenchanted spectatorship that I discussed in chapter 1. In Carlyle's metaphor, the present is a virtual image—it is what appears to vision, what is immediately perceptible, yet it is also an illusion. History is the technological apparatus that produces the endless stream of present-as-virtual-image—the always unfolding phantasmagoria that transforms infants into adults and prisons into bridges. The Seer or Artist in History is thus a variant of the disenchanted spectator who can simultaneously appreciate virtual images and identify their technological basis—the sovereign spectator who sees the illusion without being tricked. While the Artist in History is not an explicitly British figure, Carlyle's rationalizing perspective and God's-eye view in *The French Revolution* is imbued with a nationalist partisanship. Disenchanted spectatorship is here an attribute of the British historian, master of the chaos of the French revolutionary scene.

Carlyle's Artist in History is also a magician in his own right: a master showman who makes history's phantasmagorical structure perceptible to his readers, at once enthralling them with images of the past and enlightening them in how those images came to be. In other words, the Artist in History is a British phantasmagoria showman—an Enlightenment hero like the one Robertson makes himself out to be in his memoir. Carlyle therefore works within the tradition of British writers like George Eliot who turned to the framework of virtual images to portray the literary text as an optical technological prosthesis that extends vision into new times and places. Like Eliot, Carlyle appeals directly to "the Reader" as a witness to the scenes he creates, presenting the historical narrative as a virtual scene constituted by virtual images.[64] Nina Foster argues that Carlyle's historical reconstruction of the events of the French Revolution "involves a dynamic three-way interaction among the author, the reader, and the dead but once living actors of history . . . a 'willed fellowship of the dead.'"[65] Another way of describing this fellowship of the dead would be "an assembly of ghosts"—a phantasmagoria. Like Robertson's show, which allows spectators to share space with ghosts, Carlyle's text mediates an encounter between the reader and this fellowship of the dead, rendered as ghostly figures bearing witness to ghostly scenes.[66]

Recalled to Life

To say that Charles Dickens based *A Tale of Two Cities* on Carlyle's *The French Revolution* is not, on the face of it, to say anything especially new. Generations of scholars have noted that Dickens used Carlyle's chronology of the revolution, rewrote several of his most memorable historical set pieces, and adopted his key images and metaphors. Carlyle's influence is felt so comprehensively in *A Tale of Two Cities* that the critic G. K. Chesterton asserted that "it is not entirely by Dickens."[67] What concerns me in this final section of the chapter is how *A Tale of Two Cities* continues in the lineage of Robertson and Carlyle by writing the history of the French Revolution as a phantasmagoria. What Carlyle names the "Spectral Phantasmagory" of French revolutionary history, Dickens prefers to call a "bright continuous flow."[68] This is his description of a procession of the carriages of the nobility "whirling by in quick succession" early in the novel, and it represents the carriages as a single spectral optical illusion, one that blends the luminous, quick-changing images of the phantasmagoria with the illusion of motion in persistence of vision toys (117). In an oft-cited passage from the final chapter, Dickens offers his own version of Carlyle's Pont Louis XVI in his description of another procession, this time of tumbrils on the way to the guillotine:

> Change these back again to what they were, thou powerful enchanter, Time, and they shall be seen to be the carriages of absolute monarchs, the equipages of feudal nobles, the toilettes of flaring Jezebels, the churches that are not my father's house but dens of thieves, the huts of millions of starving peasants! (385)

The Soviet filmmaker Sergei Eisenstein famously described this moment as a cinematic "dissolve."[69] Rather than anticipating the formal techniques of cinema, the passage offers something more backward-looking: a descriptive equivalent of a magic lantern dissolving view modeled on Carlyle's Romantic history of phantasmagorical metamorphosis. Just as the Pont Louis XVI hangs as a "benign metamorphosis" of the Bastille, reconstructed from its stones, the tumbrils are built out of the hacked-up accoutrements of the ancien régime, the carriages, churches, and huts that represented and upheld the political system that the French Revolution had overturned. Dickens's ancien régime is, like Carlyle's Bastille, only "what we call vanished." Rolling toward the scaffold, the tumbrils represent the ineluctable forward momentum of history; but imaginatively metamorphosing into their old forms, like Cinderella's enchanted carriage turning back into a pumpkin, they stand in for a nonlinear historical process structured by spectral returns.

When Dickens analogizes history as a dematerialized visual sequence characterized by visual transformations—when he writes the French Revolution as phantasmagoria—Carlyle's influence is all too clear.[70] Yet Dickens was not only a devoted reader of Carlyle; he also read Robertson. Fluent in French, Dickens read *Mémoires récreatifs, scientifiques, et anecdotiques* closely four years before the publication of *A Tale of Two Cities* and wrote a two-part essay on Robertson's life for *Household Words*, loosely summarizing the volumes of Robertson's memoir. The phantasmagorical motif in *A Tale of Two Cities* shows his indebtedness to both Robertson and Carlyle. But unlike the intertextuality of *A Tale of Two Cities* and *The French Revolution*, the influence of *Mémoires récreatifs, scientifiques, et anecdotiques* on Dickens's spectral and metamorphic approach to representing the history of the French Revolution remains unexamined in Dickens scholarship. Robertson's depiction of the phantasmagoria as a historical return of the repressed in which the ghosts of the revolutionary dead converge on the living is embedded in the narrative structure of *A Tale of Two Cities*. The novel turns history into a series of spectral recursions in which people and events are "recalled to life."

To make this case, let us look first at narrative structure. The central characters in *A Tale of Two Cities* are French émigrés living in London: Lucie Manette, a young woman believing herself to be an orphan; Alexandre Manette, her long-lost father, discovered by the revolutionaries M. and Mme. Defarge after his release from the Bastille; and Charles Darnay, pseudonym of Charles Evrémonde, a French aristocrat who abandons his title in sympathy with the revolution and becomes Lucie's husband. Their relations with one another are fraught with secrecy. While Darnay hides his true identity, Manette keeps secret the true cause of his imprisonment: he was privy to the rape and murder of a young woman by Darnay's uncle, a powerful marquis, who threw Manette in prison to protect himself from exposure. A famous early passage of the novel reflects that "every human creature is constituted to be that profound secret and mystery to every other," a condition that is not unlike death. Death, the narrator reasons, is "the inexorable consolidation and perpetuation of the secret that was always in that individuality" (14–15). This description of the mysteries locked away inside each person is immediately ironic because it opens a scene that sees the banker Jarvis Lorry journeying to Paris to "dig someone out of a grave." That someone, Manette, is described as "buried alive" and "recalled to life," at once exhumed and resurrected, a set of metaphors that are literalized in a subplot in which Lorry's porter moonlights as a "Resurrection-Man" (17). Not only does no secret stay secret in *A Tale of Two Cities*, but the dead do not even stay buried—or dead.

Although "Recalled to Life" is the title of the brief first volume of the novel, which concerns Manette's discovery by Lorry and Lucie, the phrase and concept is woven through the rest of the book. At the beginning of the second volume, Darnay, like Manette, is introduced into the novel as "recalled to life" after being acquitted of the charge of treason in London and saved from the death penalty. In the final volume, he is recalled to life once again. Darnay returns secretly to Paris at the height of the Terror to try to make amends for his uncle's and father's wrongdoing and is immediately imprisoned in La Force by the revolutionaries. Lucie and Manette follow him to Paris, attempting to rescue him, but a manuscript that Manette left in his prison cell detailing the crimes of the Evrémonde family has been discovered during the storming of the Bastille and is used by the revolutionary tribunal to condemn Darnay to death. Darnay is finally rescued from prison by Sidney Carton, the dissolute lawyer who redeems himself through self-sacrifice when he takes Darnay's place at the guillotine. Both Manette's letter and Darnay are, like Manette, "buried" (263), exhumed, and brought back to life. Carton, meanwhile, envisions at his death the new life he will live in Lucie and Darnay's future son, who will "[win] his way up in that path of life which once was mine" (390). Even this final death—the death that recalls Darnay to life—is not a true death, as Carton anticipates becoming a ghost that will haunt the future. "Recalled to Life" is thus more than a motif in *A Tale of Two Cities*—it is a narrative structure of recursion in which secrets and persons are buried and exhumed, killed and resurrected. The novel's true thesis is not that secrets are like the dead because they are unknowable but rather that secrets are like the dead because they never truly die. "The dead return like anyone else," Poultier d'Elmotte wrote in the editorial reprinted in *Mémoires récreatifs, scientifiques, et anecdotiques*, and secrets return like the dead. The more they are suppressed, buried, or kept from sight, the more reliably they will, like the specters of Robertson's phantasmagoria, be "recalled to life."

The language Dickens uses to describe this process of recalling to life is also drawn from the visual effects of the phantasmagoria. Lorry first imagines Manette as recalled to life on the long coach ride to Dover, in a sequence that plays out like a phantasmagoria show of the mind. The coach is drenched in "night shadows," which have their double in Lorry's dreamlike musings, the "night shadows within" (18). These shadows present to him "a multitude of faces," all of which resolve into "the ghostly face" and "specter" of Manette (17–18). Lorry then imagines himself digging Manette out of his grave, only for him to "suddenly fall away to dust" (18). The diction here mirrors Robertson's, who refers to the virtual images of the phantasmagoria as "shadows" and "ghosts." Manette's status as both specter and corpse—at once metamorphosing like a shadow and grossly material as he collapses into dust—recalls Robertson's description of his phantasmagoria as an exhumation that produces ghosts. At the same time, the graveyard imagery recalls specific phantasmagoria slide sequences that Robertson lists in *Mémoires récreatifs, scientifiques, et anecdotiques*, such as human figures metamorphosing into skeletons, spirits rising out of tombs, and gravediggers searching for treasure.[71] The image of Manette "fall[ing] away into dust" seems to re-create a slide sequence from Robertson's phantasmagoria in which Robespierre rises from his tomb and then is hit by lightning, causing him to evaporate into dust.[72] The fact that this scene replays in Lorry's mind over the course of the journey, "the ghostly face ris[ing]" again each time after Manette's corpse crumbles and decays, associates it all the more with the infinitely repeatable narrative slide sequences projected in the phantasmagoria.

Although this scene takes the form of a dreamlike vision, the same phantasmagorical imagery is applied to Manette and Darnay throughout the novel to describe the way their near-death experiences turn them into ontologically liminal beings, at once alive and dead. Lucie's first meeting with Manette is described as a kind of ghost show in which Lorry and Defarge—the wine merchant and revolutionary who houses Manette after his release from prison—are variously identified as "spectators" and "beholders" as they bear witness to the encounter between Manette and Lucie (46, 48). While Manette is "spectral" and "transparent," Lucie stands near him "like a spirit," turning them both into ghosts who communicate through glances that pass between them "like moving light" (43–46). What Lorry and Defarge "behold," in other words, is not only two ghosts but the source of the phantasmagoria's ghosts in "moving light."

A second ghost show plays out at Darnay's trial at the Old Bailey. The Old Bailey is "a deadly inn-yard" from which those accused of crimes "set out . . . on a violent passage to the other world" (63)—like the rooms in which Robertson exhibited the phantasmagoria, it is a liminal space between life and death. Darnay is introduced into the novel standing beneath a mirror positioned "above the prisoner's head . . . to throw the light down upon him" (66). Thus illuminated, Darnay becomes one of the "crowds of the wicked and the wretched [that] had been reflected in it," crowds that would have "haunted" the Old Bailey "in a ghastly manner . . . if the glass could ever have rendered back its reflexions, as the ocean is one day to give up its dead" (66). This narrative interjection compares a mirror that could unleash all that has ever been reflected in it to the resurrection of the dead on the Day of Judgment. Read in the context of Robertson's *Mémoires récreatifs, scientifiques, et anecdotiques*, a mirror that resurrects the dead references the phantasmagoria's media effect of projecting a "mob of shadows" that sweep through the theater. As Dickens would have known, Robertson called the transparent screen onto which he rear-projected his lantern slides—the very surface upon which he made the dead return to life—his "mirror."[73] Mediated by this mirror-screen, turned into "a sight" for all to behold, Darnay temporarily joins the crowds of the dead before he is "recalled to life" (61).

In *The Historical Novel*, Georg Lukàcs offers what is now a well-known critique of *A Tale of Two Cities*: that its portrayal of the French Revolution is merely "romantic background . . . a pretext for revealing [the] human-moral qualities" of the central characters.[74] *A Tale of Two Cities* does not meet Lukàcs's criteria for a historical novel, which should integrate characters with their historical circumstances by representing "the social and human motives which led men to think, feel and act just as they did in historical reality."[75] My reading of phantasmagoria in *A Tale of Two Cities* challenges this view. The liminality and spectrality of Dickens's characters, the way their lives are structured by a logic of resurrection, is an index of their complete integration with their historical circumstances. When Lucie, Manette, and Darnay appear as ghosts, oscillating between death and life, they are touched by the same "bright continuous flow" of revolutionary history that turns the carriages of the nobility and the peasants' huts of the ancien régime into the tumbrils of the Reign of Terror. It is not that the novel segregates the human from the historical but that motives and decision making are not the critical point at which they intersect. Indeed, *A Tale of Two Cities* is largely uninterested in "social and human motives"—characters are driven instead by a broad, single-minded purpose to commit or reduce harm, from the primal vengefulness of the Jacobins and Lucie's salvific purity.

Why characters do what they do is simply not the right question to ask about the novel's approach to historical representation. We might ask instead how characters are reduced to ghostly specters, dematerialized into an optical "flow" by the violent and sudden political transformations of the revolutionary period, regardless of what they do and why they do it. Fredric Jameson, in his response to Lukàcs in "The Historical Novel Today, or, Is It Still Possible?," identifies a mode of historical representation that captures Dickens's approach—one that foregrounds the collective over the individual character and is characterized by "phantasmagoric state[s] . . . a dissolution of individuality and a loss of self in the crowd."[76] In *A Tale of Two Cities*, the Jacobins literally lose their individuality to the crowd by taking on nicknames of Jacques 1, Jacques 2, and Jacques 3, absorbing themselves into the collective will of the popular uprising. But so are British characters like Lucie, Manette, and Darnay stripped of their individuality—not as an ideological choice, but as a necessary result of living through revolutionary history.

I have proposed that Dickens's representation of revolutionary history as a "phantasmagoric state" is informed not only by Carlyle's phantasmagoric diction and imagery in *The French Revolution* but also—and equally—by Robertson's imaginary of the phantasmagoria as resurrection medium in *Mémoires récreatifs, scientifiques, et anecdotiques*. The seeds of Dickens's portrayal of the French Revolution as phantasmagoria can be found in an essay Dickens wrote on Robertson for *Household Words* four years before the publication of *A Tale of Two Cities*. "Robertson, Artist in Ghosts," tells the story of Robertson's supposed invention of the phantasmagoria against the backdrop of the Reign of Terror. "Robertson, Artist in Ghosts" could be described as something between a translation, a précis, and an editorial. It summarizes many of the important anecdotes and events covered in Volume I of *Mémoires récreatifs, scientifiques, et anecdotiques*, but it does so in Robertson's own words, which Dickens translates and freely adapts into his own narrative.[77] The profound line-by-line similarities between "Robertson, Artist in Ghosts" and passages from *Mémoires récreatifs, scientifiques, et anecdotiques*, including occasional lines and phrases taken from E. Roche's introduction to the 1840 edition, tells us how closely and faithfully Dickens read this book. At the same time, the very coinage "Artist in Ghosts" seems to deliberately echo Carlyle's "Artist in History," turning Robertson and Carlyle—the phantasmagoria showman and the historian, respectively—into doubles of each other. In *A Tale of Two Cities*, Dickens seems to develop and deepen Carlyle's optical model of history by turning "ghosts" and "history" into synonyms. For Dickens, writing history and staging a phantasmagoria are ultimately two different ways to do the same thing: resurrect the dead. "Robertson, Artist in Ghosts" shows the development of this structure in Dickens's thinking.

Dickens's interest in Robertson's phantasmagoria comes as no surprise. He is among the most flamboyantly optical of Victorian writers, and scholars, including Helen Groth, Joss Marsh, Christopher Pittard, and Grahame Smith, have documented his enthusiastic engagement with stage magic and optical technology.[78] "Robertson, Artist in Ghosts" betrays his knowledge of and participation in the discourse of natural magic when he lauds the phantasmagoria as a technology designed to demystify the supernatural and promote rational thought. The passages that Dickens chooses to translate or paraphrase from *Mémoires récreatifs, scientifiques, et anecdotiques* reveal his sympathy for Robertson's self-presentation as an Enlightenment hero, destroying mass superstition through optical entertainment. In "Robertson, Artist in Ghosts," Robertson is a man living "in an age of superstition" who refuses to "trad[e] on the public ignorance by any false pretense," making "a great point . . . that his entertainments were to show how easily superstition could be worked upon—what dire visions could from very simple causes spring—how groundless, in fine, was the common dread of apparitions."[79] Revolutionary France, meanwhile, is characterized by its angry, anti-intellectual peasant mobs "determined upon cheap bread and no optics," who turn their magic panic into political action when they send the aristocrats and nobility, a "white-headed race of people" at once decadent and guileless, to the guillotine.[80] The French Revolution appears as a regrettable mass delusion that finds its expression in the fear of ghosts.

Even though Dickens uses many of Robertson's own words while paraphrasing his ideas, his own perspective emerges in the anti-French bent of these descriptions. France and French people are characterized by their inherent superstition, and Robertson is a hero who transcends his proximity to Frenchness through his superior rationality. Dickens applies what I described in chapter 1 as the gendered and colonial framework of disenchanted spectatorship to the Anglo-French context. The "public ignorance" and "common dread" of French people translates the feminized hysteria and restless natives we saw in chapter 1 into a nationalist paradigm. Just as French colonial officials in Algeria understood Algerian magic belief to fuel anticolonial violence, so does

Dickens portray French superstition and the policy of "no optics" as the grounds for violent revolution. Like Jean-Eugène Robert-Houdin, sent to dismantle the anticolonial movement by first tricking and then disillusioning his Algerian audiences with his magic show, Robertson is presented here as an advocate of law and order. "His entertainments were to show how easily superstition could be worked upon": to guard, in other words, against revolutionary mass hysteria.[81]

Dickens's initial portrayal of ghost seeing as the product of a French disposition toward the supernatural is in tension with a second explanatory framework. Throughout the essay, his chauvinistic British nationalism gives way to a complex view of superstition as a historical-psychological condition resulting from the lived experience of the French Revolution. In this framework, superstition is not in the essential nature of French people but rather a contingent historical phenomenon affecting visual and mental perception. This second framework comes into view when we look at how Dickens translates and editorializes on a seemingly incidental passage from *Mémoires récréatifs, scientifiques, et anecdotiques* about modern ghost belief. In its original context, the purpose of the story is to defend Robertson's false claim that he was the sole originator of the phantasmagoria against the thesis that modern optical spectacles like the phantasmagoria had their origin in the supposed miracles of Egyptian, Greek, and Roman antiquity. Robertson is keen to discredit this argument because it challenges the narrative of his supposed originality and genius. He does so by inviting his readers to reflect on the persistence of superstition in modern culture: "Have we not seen the shadow of a chimney outline the figure of Louis XVI so strikingly as to attract a large crowd of people daily to the garden of the Palais-Royal?" Among the crowd, he explains, the rumor had spread that the ghost of the king "came every day to show himself to the Parisians. A commissioner of police, followed by some masons, had to put an end to this appearance, and made it vanish in the presence of the astonished spectators."[82] Robertson's point is that the history of ghost seeing does not necessarily imply the presence of optical technology. Even in the modern age, in a city like Paris, a visual illusion as tenuous as a shadow on a chimney can strike fear in the hearts of a crowd.

The story about the Parisians and the shadow of Louis XVI has had a textual afterlife as a parable of modernity. In *Pensieri* (1837), the Italian poet and philosopher Giacamo Leopardi rewrote it to take place in Florence, where "on a corner by the Piazza del Duomo" he claims to have seen "a crowd of people gathered beneath the ground-floor window of what is now the Palazzo Riccardi." The crowd is "terrified" of the "Phantom"—a "motionless shadow flailing its arms"—seen through a window illuminated only by a streetlamp. A police officer is called to look inside the room, where he discovers that the "Phantom" is in fact the combined shadows of a distaff and a smock flailing in the wind. "In the nineteenth century," Leopardi editorializes, "in the very heart of Florence, which is the most learned city in Italy and whose inhabitants are particularly discerning and sophisticated, people still see ghosts that they believe to be spirits—ghosts that are distaffs."[83] Tom Gunning has argued that Leopardi's story represents the phantasmagoria's legacy as "an art of total illusion that also contained its own critique," one in which modernity inheres in "the explanation of the ghosts as a visual phenomenon."[84] His analysis is more apt than he perhaps appreciated because Leopardi's story is effectively plagiarized from Robertson's account of the phantasmagoria.[85] Florence replaces Paris and the Piazza del Duomo replaces the Palais Royal, while the shadow of Louis XVI becomes that of an ordinary woman, but the message is the same: superstition persists in modernity, lurking within the urban crowd, but it can be destroyed through acts of technological and visual demystification.

In "Robertson, Artist in Ghosts," Dickens reproduces Robertson's anecdote about the Parisians who mistake the shadow of a chimney for that of Louis XVI. But by taking it out of its original context, he changes its meaning even more than Leopardi does in his much bolder rewriting. Instead of supporting the claim that people throughout history have always been credulous and easily deceived, Dickens uses the story to establish Paris during and after the Reign of Terror as uniquely prone to magic panic:

> [Robertson] was bent upon reproducing some of the miracles worked by the priests of old. It was very easy to excite the wonder of the town, even without any great dexterity or conjurer's tools of a refined description. Crowds were flocking daily to the gardens of the Palais Royal to gape at the shadow of a chimney, which, at a certain hour of the day, resembled the figure of Louis the Sixteenth. Thousands believed that the shadow of the king upon whom they had trampled haunted the Parisians by appearing daily in his garden. A commissary of police, by the help of a few masons, at last caused the demolition of the august shade in the presence of a concourse of astonished people. It does not take much to produce a ghost.[86]

This is, in one sense, a quite faithful translation of the original passage in *Mémoires récreatifs, scientifiques, et anecdotiques*. However, Dickens reverses Robertson's original meaning by portraying the phantasmagoria not as a wholly original invention but as a reproduction of the miracles of antiquity: Robertson is "bent upon *reproducing* some of the miracles worked by the priests of old" (emphasis added). In Dickens's rewriting, the shadow of Louis XVI does not reveal the persistence of credulity throughout history but rather presents revolutionary Paris as a time and place unusually ripe for an optical deception like the phantasmagoria—a place in which "wonder" is "easy to excite." This diction is Dickens's own addition, as is his remark, "It does not take much to produce a ghost." It is not so remarkable that Parisians are drawn to the phantasmagoria, Dickens intimates, because they are already seeing ghosts everywhere.

For Robertson, the story of the shadow of Louis XVI is proof of the persistence of ghost belief in the modern age, and for Leopardi it is a parable of modernity's dialectic of skepticism and credulity. For Dickens, the story offers something else entirely: an analogy between phantasmagoria spectatorship and the lived experience of revolutionary history. French people do not see ghosts because they are French; they see ghosts because they lived through the Reign of Terror. For instance, in another addition to Robertson's story, Dickens specifies that the crowds are drawn to "the shadow of the king *upon whom they had trampled*" (emphasis added), turning what in Robertson's account is simply an especially convincing visual illusion into the projection of a collective guilty conscience. The people who killed Louis XVI now see him wherever they go. Read this way, the line "it does not take much to produce a ghost" is not an indictment of how the French superstition makes audiences easy marks for the phantasmagoria. Instead, it is ironic: if producing a ghost requires an organized popular uprising that executes a king, it is in fact tremendously difficult. Rather than a symptom of the French national character, seeing ghosts is the product of a contingent historical circumstance: revolution.

Although it changes the original meaning of the passage, Dickens's rewriting is true to the general spirit of *Mémoires récreatifs, scientifiques, et anecdotiques*. It captures Robertson's mythographic account of the phantasmagoria as a simultaneous exhumation and resurrection of historical figures killed during the Reign of Terror, seen both in his description of audiences perceiving his virtual moving images as manifestations of the spirits of the dead buried in the Capuchin graveyard and in his reprinting of Poultier d'Elmotte's editorial on the phantasmagoria as an assembly place for revolutionary ghosts. Where Dickens differs from Robertson is in his emphasis on the psychological dimensions of historical experience. He represents the scene at the Palais Royal as a collective folly resulting from collective historical action. The "crowds" that executed Louis XVI are now "haunted" by his shadow, their guilt expressing itself in ghost seeing. Dickens's presentation of the execution of Louis XVI as crowd action—not attributable to any specific historical actors or even specific groups of actors, but dispersed broadly across "crowds"—defines the collective experience of history as a shared state of haunting.[87] Georg Lukàcs wrote that the French Revolution "made history a *mass experience* . . . on a European scale," one that made apparent "that there is such a thing as history, that it is an uninterrupted process of changes and finally that it has a direct effect upon the life of every individual."[88] For Dickens, history as mass experience is history as mass delusion. Like Marx's historical ghosts that weigh on the brains of the living, Dickens's Reign of Terror leaves behind a phantasmal residue in the minds of those who experienced it, whether as witnesses or actors. The scene at the Palais Royal is analogous to the phantasmagoria show—it is another kind of assembly of ghosts and spectators, one that reveals Robertson's projection of virtual moving images to be an expression of an already existing historical condition that sees the past returning to life in spectral form.

"Robertson, Artist in Ghosts" can be read as developmental writing toward *A Tale of Two Cities*—an essay on phantasmagoria and the French Revolution that served as a blueprint for Dickens's phantasmagorical French Revolution novel. Like *The Eighteenth Brumaire of Louis Bonaparte*, "Robertson, Artist in Ghosts" proposes that ghost seeing is endemic to the context of nationalist revolution. *A Tale of Two Cities* builds on this theory further when it suggests that revolutions not only make people see ghosts but also make people undergo an uncanny condition of spectralization. Characters not only witness ghosts—as Lorry does when he digs Manette out of a grave—but they become ghosts, as Manette, Lucie, Darnay, and Carton all do at various moments. Becoming a ghost is no longer reserved for major historical actors like Louis XVI. In *A Tale of Two Cities*, both seeing and becoming ghosts is a condition of living within the historical scene of revolutionary transformation. We do not need the evidence of this essay to place Dickens within a genealogy of writers like Robertson, Carlyle, and Marx who portrayed the French Revolution as a phantasmagoria. What it offers us instead is a map for how *A Tale of Two Cities* is grounded in Robertson's account of the phantasmagoria as a historical ghost show structured by optical resurrection and spectral returns of the dead. "Robertson, Artist in Ghosts" helps us see that the mode of historical representation that Fredric Jameson calls the "phantasmagoric" is related to the virtual aesthetics of the phantasmagoria show in more than name. *A Tale of Two Cities* not only draws on the Carlylean phantasmagoric motif but also on the media history of the phantasmagoria and its imaginative associations with the French Revolution.

"Robertson, Artist in Ghosts" returns us to the question with which we began: How is the phantasmagoria bound up in the nationalist imaginary? *A Tale of Two Cities* is often read as a novel of national difference, written in an era when British national identity was defined—as Linda Colley has shown—against real and perceived military threats from France.[89] In this argument, France and England are juxtaposed like the "streaky bacon" of tragedy and comedy in *Oliver Twist* (1838), alternating combustive scenes of revolutionary Paris with the unshakeable orthodoxies of British life. Priti Joshi has challenged the view that the novel is structured by "the old Anglo-French antipathy" that defines English against French.[90] *A Tale of Two Cities* is about the making of Britons, she writes, but in this novel "one is not born a Briton but *becomes* one" through noble acts of adventure and self-sacrifice.[91] French-born characters like Lucie, Manette, and Darnay all become Britons through such acts. Yet if *A Tale of Two Cities* is not nationalist in the old ways—if it does not define national belonging in terms of geographic boundaries or racial essence—it is imperialist in some new ways. Joshi argues that the novel displaces onto the Reign of Terror the scene of the Indian Uprising of 1857–1858. After the Indian Uprising, France was no longer the primary foil against which British identity was articulated. Now, to be British was to be the erstwhile victims and ultimate conquerors of Indian savagery. Joshi's framework offers one explanation for why *A Tale of Two Cities* fails to meet Lukàcs's criteria for historical fiction, in spite of how closely Dickens studied Walter Scott: the novel is not a work of historical realism so much as an imperial fairy tale about British heroes triumphing over a savage colonial mutiny.

Although "Robertson, Artist in Ghosts" was written two years before the Indian Uprising, its complex and nuanced representation of that "old Anglo-French antipathy" prefigures the colonial logic of heroes and villains, Britons and natives, that structures *A Tale of Two Cities*. Dickens defines France as Robert-Houdin defined Algeria and

Harriet Martineau and Wilkie Collins defined India—as superstitious and ungovernable. Ungovernable *because* superstitious, the French are preternaturally prone to magic panic, mistakenly believing they can exchange optics for bread and then becoming what David Brewster called "the dupes of supernatural imposture" precisely because they refused to learn optics.[92] In other words, we can see how Dickens reanimates the colonial tropes of the pedagogy of disenchantment when he displaces the figure of the savage Indian onto the superstitious French citizen. At the same time, and on closer examination, the bounds of nation dissolve in "Robertson, Artist in Ghosts" just as they do in *A Tale of Two Cities*. Ghost seeing is not the province of the French but the province of those who have lived through and participated in a revolution, a condition that produces credulity through trauma and guilt. Dickens thus comes remarkably close to Elizabeth Gaskell's position in *Cranford* when she observes how female magic panic is produced by patriarchal social norms: he implies that seeing ghosts is a structural condition created by contingent historical circumstances, not an essential marker of nationality or race. For Robertson, Carlyle, Marx, and Dickens, phantasmagoria provides an optical framework for historical representation on a grand European scale: "the dead of world history" on ghostly parade, the "Real-Phantasmagory" of the nineteenth century in unceasing spectral metamorphosis.

In chapter 5, I will turn to a quite different optical model for history—the moving-image toy, which I argue serves as a cultural trope for the repetitive and circular rhythms of daily life under industrial capitalism. This is virtual aesthetics in its least exotic and most provincial form—not the imperial gaze of the mirror of ink, the mystical portal of the Indian diamond, or the bright continuous flow of Anglo-French history, but the spinning toy made of paper and its evocations of the urban factory, the agricultural village, and the neurotic compulsions of the working body. Yet in all its humility and stripped-down technological form, the moving-image toy gives rise to a virtual aesthetics of industrial modernity that helped to create the aesthetic and technological conditions for the emergence of cinema at the end of the century.

CHAPTER 5

Spinning in Place

Trapped in the Moving-Picture Machine

Among the most iconic scenes in the history of cinema is Charlie Chaplin's Tramp caught in the rotating gears of a steel factory machine (figure 5.1). The film is *Modern Times* (1936), and the gag occurs during the Tramp's stint at a futuristic factory where the boss and his workers communicate through a video screen. While screwing nuts onto steel plates on the assembly line, the Tramp's own lithe, fidgety body is fed into the machine. He is carried down by the conveyor belt where cogs and wheels spin him slowly but surely around, in a visual echo of the repeated twists of the wrench and circular tightening of the nuts that characterized his work on the assembly line. Film scholars have noted the resemblance between this fantastical industrial machine and the film projector, the Tramp moving through the gears like the film strip through the sprockets.[1] Seen in this light, the scene can be read as meta-cinematic: Chaplin-the-director operates the camera-machine that records and distributes Chaplin-the-star's image.[2]

This chapter proposes a different but related visual and technological reference point for this film image. The flat, pictorial quality of the sequence in the film; the rotation of industrial wheels; and the scene's governing motif of cyclicality, seriality, and repetition recall the first moving-image device ever created: a paper-and-print-based technology called the phenakistoscope (figure 5.2). Unlike cinema, which is

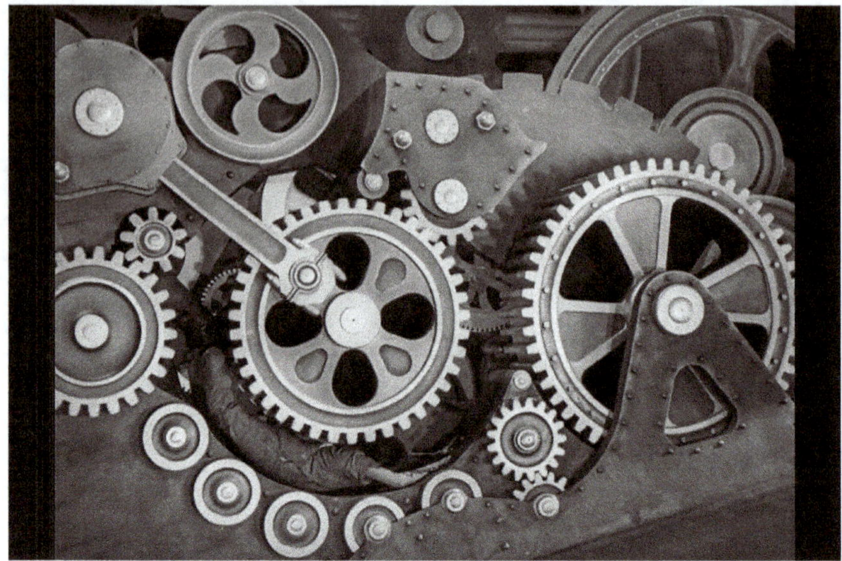

FIGURE 5.1. Film still from *Modern Times*. Charlie Chaplin, 1936.

structured by the linear temporality of the film strip, the phenakistoscope is spun to create what Nicolas Dulac and André Gaudreault call a circular and repeating image with neither beginning nor end.[3] The Tramp is similarly constrained. His dizzying journey through the machine seems to automate his body, as if it has internalized the rhythm of the machine.[4] The circular repetition of the wheels in which he spins cause him to compulsively tweak every nut-shaped object he sees, from the foreman's nipples to the buttons on a lady's dress. If his actions mark his body as a film image, an automaton created by the circular cranking of the projector, they equally evoke the men and

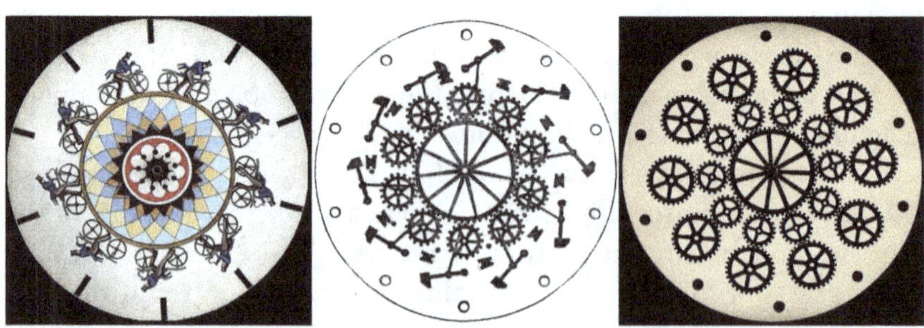

FIGURE 5.2. Assorted phenakistoscope disks.

women fated to spin on nineteenth-century phenakistoscope disks. Like those figures, the Tramp is not only doomed to move in circles but also becomes the embodiment of both the technological moving image and industrial automation, and more properly of the moving image *as* automation, of cinema as perpetual motion machine.

Why does a 1936 film about the American factory look so much like an optical toy made in 1833? And what can this comparison tell us about the visual, technological, and discursive continuities between early moving-image toys and the first decades of cinema—between Victorian virtual aesthetics and the film narratives of the twentieth century? This chapter makes the case that we can answer these questions only when we attend closely to an easily overlooked *discontinuity* between moving-image toys and cinema. Film history usually positions nineteenth-century moving-image toys like the phenakistoscope as precinematic devices that precede and lead to the development of the cinema through their transformation of static pictures into an unbroken series of virtual moving images. These histories often gloss over the fact that the history of moving pictures does not begin with the unfolding linear action that we associate with cinema but with the representation of repetitive and cyclical action. Beginning with the phenakistoscope in 1833 and continuing through the zoetrope and praxinoscope, almost all nineteenth-century moving-image devices were circular and worked only when spun. Their effect of virtual movement was inextricable from their physical movement, which forced all represented actions to repeat themselves until the device wound slowly to a stop. Narrative is impossible in the first moving pictures because the form of the apparatus refuses linear unfolding.[5]

Rather than treating the circular repetitions of the phenakistoscope and its kin as a primitive stage in cinema's evolution as a narrative medium, I consider these devices on their own terms, as moving-picture instantiations of non-narrative, ahistorical time—time without progress or development. In this sense, my reading of the phenakistoscope builds on my discussion of the phantasmagoria's nonlinear temporality in chapter 4. As we saw in the work of writers like Étienne-Gaspard Robertson, Karl Marx, and Charles Dickens, the phantasmagoria's projected virtual images became a cultural touchstone for a theory of history as structured by haunting and recursion, "conjure[d] up" as a spirit or "recalled to life" as a ghost. However, this chapter turns from history in its epic and spectacular scale—what Thomas Carlyle called the "Real-Phantasmagory" of the nineteenth century—to the banal, mundane, and everyday temporality of the English working body. I argue that nineteenth-century virtual moving images and their representation in literary culture expressed the technological and industrial scene of capitalist labor from the viewpoint of the worker—the Chaplinesque figures automated by the machines they are meant to operate, turned into human cogs or wheels. Against the dominant view of modernity as an era of civilizational progress and technological development, the phenakistoscope and the spinning optical toys that followed it depicted the labor on which such visions of progress depend as cyclical, repeating, and infinite, without beginning or end.

I trace this optical motif of circularity and repetition from the phenakistoscope to the work of Thomas Hardy, whose late fiction of the 1880s and 1890s offers a historical midpoint between the invention of the phenakistoscope and *Modern Times*. Hardy's investment in visual culture and optics is the subject of numerous studies,[6] but he is more often viewed as a nostalgic chronicler of rural and village folkways as they are displaced by the arrival of industrial modernity than a writer who engages deeply with modern technology itself.[7] I contend that Hardy wrote *with* technology, not just against it. His technological motifs underscore a nuanced critique of industrial modernity, one that is grounded not in rural nostalgia but an analysis of the politics of capitalism. The cyclicality of moving-image toys offered a model for his representation of embodied labor as perpetual motion. Like Chaplin, Hardy's work is full of people caught in a state of circularity and repetition from which they cannot free themselves. Read through the lens of *Modern Times*, we can see how his stories and novels bring the capitalist logic of the late nineteenth-century factory to his representation of the early nineteenth-century country town.

I begin the chapter with a discussion of phenakistoscope disks from the 1830s and 1840s, taking seriously these examples of print ephemera as meaning-bearing texts that reflect on the device's formal principles and the relation between spectator and spectacle through visual themes of bodies being acted on by outside forces. Analyzing the visual rhetoric of the disks allows me to read the phenakistoscope as a device that commented on industrial capitalism's mechanization and automation of the body and emerging psychoanalytic concepts of the body as propelled by unconscious drives. Next, I demonstrate how these same themes are transposed into the late fiction of Thomas Hardy, where they function as representations of the life and labors of the English working classes. I trace the motif of circularity and repetition in "On the Western Circuit" and "The Fiddler of the Reels," two short stories that were published in 1894 in the collection *Life's Little Ironies* and that depict the fast-paced spectacles of modern urban life, and *The Mayor of Casterbridge* (1886), a novel about a small English town built on top of Roman ruins. These case studies all feature characters who repeatedly move or are moved in circles, either by machinery, the mechanistic remote control of bodies by another person's will, or a mechanical unconscious, a structure that Hardy renders through reference to the circular and repeating format of the phenakistoscope. The idea that Hardy, with his fine-tuned English tragedies, should have anything to do with Chaplin, the quintessential Hollywood slapstick comedian, might sound bizarre. But by the end of the chapter, it will become clear that *The Mayor of Casterbridge* and *Modern Times* are closely linked works that reflect and participate in an alternative history of the moving image as industrial and technological animation of the body. What Hardy and Chaplin see through the phenakistoscope is that modern life is characterized by spinning in place.

Spinning in Place

Modern Times tells the story of the Little Tramp, Charlie Chaplin's indefatigable silent screen persona, "spectacularly failing" to fit into the dehumanizing automated world of the 1930s industrial city, with its skyscrapers, factory plants, and assembly lines.[8] A Great Depression comedy about the capitalist machine and one worker who perpetually gums up the works, *Modern Times* is also haunted by Chaplin's childhood. Although he became a Hollywood icon, Chaplin was a Victorian, born in London's poverty-ridden neighborhood of Walworth in 1889, and he fashioned the Tramp after the real-life tramps he saw growing up on East Street.[9] The opening factory sequence of *Modern Times* reflected the brutal conditions on American assembly lines, including reports Chaplin heard of men having nervous breakdowns after years of performing the same repetitive work, but it was also inspired by an earlier era of industrialization. The scene of the Tramp pulled into the machine was based on Chaplin's memory of the twenty-foot-long Wharfedale printing machine that he feared would devour him when he worked in a London printshop as a boy.[10] The Wharfedale was an iron giant of a printing press invented in 1856 in response to the growing demand for newspapers and magazines in Britain (figure 5.3). It revolutionized printing through the use of a rotary process known as the

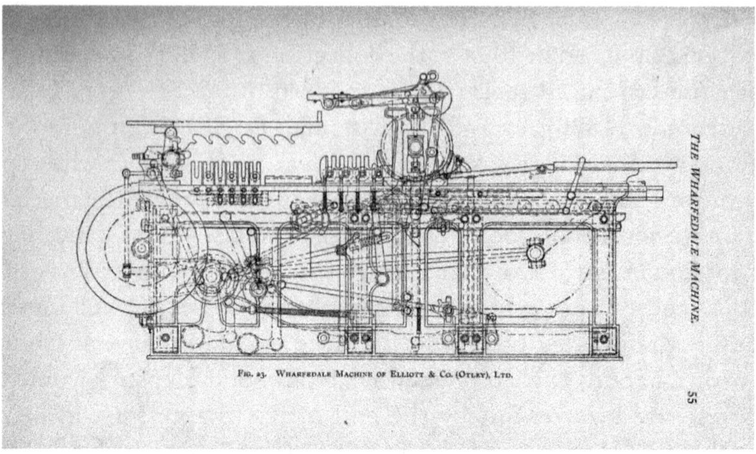

FIGURE 5.3. Wharfedale printing press. John Southward, *Modern Printing: A Handbook of the Principles and Practice of Typography and the Auxiliary Arts*, 3rd ed. (Raithby, Lawrence, 1912–1913).

stop-cylinder, in which paper is fed into a rotating cylinder on a plate bed that rocks backward and forward. It is not difficult to picture a young Chaplin dwarfed by the Wharfedale and frightened that he could be sucked beneath the rotor and flattened into newsprint.

In *Modern Times*, Chaplin layers the depression-era US factory on top of the late Victorian industrialized workplace. The rotating wheels that power the conveyor belt are a slick technological reconfiguration of the stop-cylinder rolling over the long, flat plate bed. Comparing *Modern Times* to Charles Dickens's *Hard Times*, Garrett Stewart points out that the film is part of the genre of industrial fiction that anxiously and satirically explores the industrial regulation and automatization of labor and the mechanization of human behavior under capitalism.[11] My argument is that *Modern Times* also participates in a nineteenth-century visual history of representing the body-in-machine and body-as-machine through structures of circularity and repetition, and the body as spinning, twisting, and whirling to the rhythms of steam-powered wheels. This history begins, like Chaplin's career, in the printshop, with an unassuming toy called the phenakistoscope.

Invented in 1832 by Belgian physicist Joseph Plateau, the phenakistoscope is an optical toy composed of a large spinning disk mounted on a handle (figure 5.4).[12] A sequence of figures is arranged around the circumference of the disk and interspersed by small apertures. The spectator plays with the toy by holding it up to their eye in front of

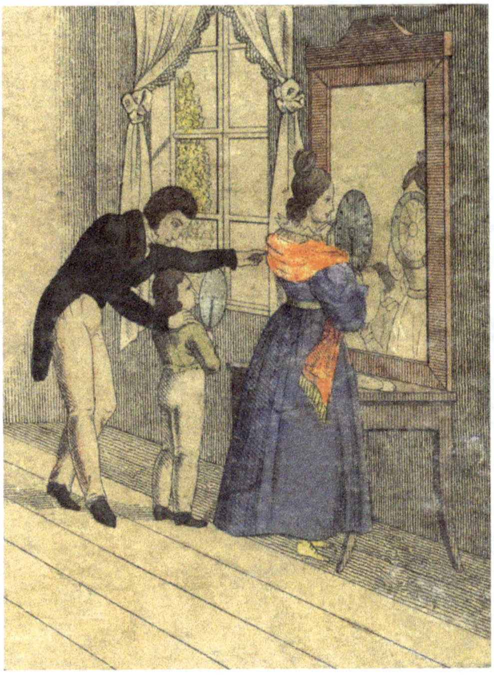

FIGURE 5.4. A family plays together with phenakistoscopes. Detail of an illustration by E. Schule on the box label for Magic Disk, Disques Magiques, ca. 1833.

a mirror, looking through an aperture, and spinning the disk. When these three actions are performed at the same time, the spectator will perceive the sequence of figures on the disk reflected in the mirror as an unbroken animated flow. The phenakistoscope thus demonstrated the perceptual illusion that nineteenth-century scientists called persistence of vision.[13] The term was coined by eighteenth-century physicists and taken up by Plateau in his study of retinal afterimages. Like Aristotle and Isaac Newton before him, Plateau was interested in the way the retina retains light impressions after the visual stimulus disappears and the way these impressions can seem to fuse or blend with one another when perceived in quick succession.[14] In Plateau's words, this effect of light impressions "blend[ing] together without confusion" creates an illusion that "a single object is gradually changing form and position."[15] His 1829 doctoral dissertation at the University of Liège, "Dissertation on Some Properties of the Impressions Produced by Light on the Eye," fixed the length of a light impression on the eye at roughly one-third of a second, with slightly different durations for impressions of different colors. This meant that if objects or

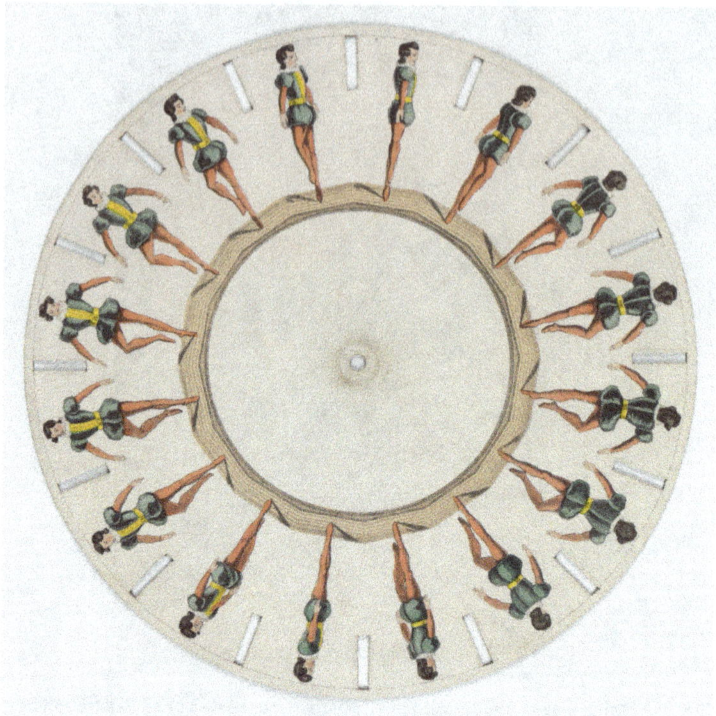

FIGURE 5.5. Phenakistoscope disk designed by Joseph Plateau. Courtesy of the National Science and Media Museum/Science and Society Picture Library.

images were presented to the eye every one-third of a second, the illusion called persistence of vision would occur.

The phenakistoscope, a neologism composed of Greek roots that means "deceptive view," was Plateau's proof of concept for this theory. His original disk, printed the following year by the London print seller Ackermann & Co., depicted a ballet dancer drawn in sixteen different poses (figure 5.5).[16] When you spin the disk, you see the dancer turn en pointe with lifted arm and leg. Your eye is not limited to seeing a single twirling dancer; instead, you see at least three twirling dancers in a row. Rather than a singular virtual moving image, the phenakistoscope created a series of virtual moving images simultaneously. As Plateau described it in his first public announcement of the invention in January 1833, "When one subjects this disk to the experiment in question, one sees with surprise, and the illusion is complete, all these little dancers turning round, with the direction of their pirouette depending on the speed and direction of the rotation of the disk."[17] The result is what film critic David Robinson has called "the earliest form of moving picture."[18] It is important to distinguish the moving images of the phenakistoscope from those of the phantasmagoria. As I discussed in chapter 4, the phantasmagoria simulated motion in two ways: by progressively enlarging or shrinking the virtual image, creating the effect that it was approaching or retreating, or through trick slides that substituted one image for another, creating the effect of a single image metamorphosing. The phenakistoscope, by contrast, broke down movement into distinct pictorial phases and reconstructed it as an optical illusion of motion. Film historians generally agree that the phenakistoscope is the first moving-picture machine. David Bordwell, Kristin Thompson, and Jeff Smith's *Film History: An Introduction*, the definitive film history textbook, begins the story of cinema with the phenakistoscope, while Deac Rossell considers the phenakistoscope, along with later moving-image toys like the zoetrope and praxinoscope, among a handful of devices that represent "the origin of the movies."[19]

While these film scholars are not wrong to see the phenakistoscope as a technological precursor to the cinematographic apparatuses of the late nineteenth century, the emphasis on the phenakistoscope's "cinematicity" risks overlooking its quite distinct virtual effects and modes of spectatorship. For instance, film historians and theorists have wrongly associated the phenakistoscope's moving images with a mode of spectatorship in which visual experience is produced *for* a passive spectator.[20] In fact, the phenakistoscope was designed and marketed as a reflexive pedagogical toy that made the creation of virtual images an actively engaged and embodied process on the part of a user who, unlike a spectator at the cinema, was always in control of their visual experience. A product of the tradition of rational recreations and natural magic, the phenakistoscope was meant to demonstrate an optical illusion that occurs at the intersection of technological and physiological optics, of apparatus and eye. Like the stereoscope, it is a pedagogical device that operates through playful interaction—a precursor to what we might today call active learning. This is reflected in Plateau's description of the phenakistoscope's virtual images as the result of an "experiment." Spinning a phenakistoscope is a science experiment that simultaneously creates an entertaining series of moving images and yields insights into the nature of vision.

The phenakistoscope gave birth to the paradigmatic form of the spectator as showman. Unlike the magic show's strict separation between showman and audience, and cinema's separation between apparatus and image, the phenakistoscope is meant to be both operated and appreciated by one person who has complete control over the speed, direction, and duration of the virtual moving images that they see. Even representations of cospectatorship, such as the many drawings and prints from the period that show lovers or families looking through the apertures of the phenakistoscope together, emphasize the agency of users to create and manage their own visual experience. The spectator's visual and manual participation is as necessary to the creation of virtual moving images as the apparatus itself. This format would continue throughout the nineteenth century in a succession of hand-operated optical toys that refined the phenakistoscope's basic technique through new and innovative technological designs, from the zoetrope and praxinoscope, which retained the circularity and repetition of the phenakistoscope by replacing the spinning disk with a spinning drum, to the flip-book, which introduced a linear and developmental logic to moving pictures.

Throughout the 1830s, printshops in London, Paris, and other European cultural capitals responded to the craze for moving pictures by manufacturing and selling phenakistoscopes as well as artist-designed folios of disks. Their advertisements and packaging often capitalized on the reality effect of the phenakistoscope's animations by declaring them "Living Pictures." The term acknowledges the discursive association between spinning a phenakistoscope and animating its pictures, coding the process of making still pictures move as infusing representations with life. We also see this connection between the moving picture and the living picture in William George Horner's blueprint for a device based on the phenakistoscope, one that would later be called the zoetrope. Horner called his invention the Daedaleum, after Daedalus, the craftsman of Greek myth whose statues were so lifelike they moved by themselves. Writing in *The London Edinburgh Philosophical Magazine and Journal of Science* in 1834, two years after Plateau's invention, he explained that the Daedaleum would imitate "the practice which the celebrated artist of antiquity was fabled to have invented, of creating figures of men and animals endued with motion."[21] The slippage here between the two senses of animation—giving static pictures motion and giving inanimate objects life—can help us speculate about the imaginative dimensions of early moving-image spectatorship. Phenakistoscope spectatorship is active, embodied, physical; it relies, as Tom Gunning puts it, on the spectator's coordination of hand and eye.[22] By making pictures move, the person who spins the phenakistoscope disk or the drum of the zoetrope becomes an animator, an endower of life.

Yet as we have seen, the phenakistoscope does not simply make images move—it makes them move in a circle that repeats as the disk spins. To account for the imaginative dimensions of phenakistoscope play, as well as the role of this device in film history, it is critical that we appreciate the formal and phenomenological affordances of this confined and confining serial format. Dulac and Gaudreault write of the phenakistoscope:

> The subjects are like Sisyphus, condemned *ad infinitum* to turn about, jump, and dance. In another sense, the figures are machine-like: untiring and unalterable. They are "acted-upon subjects" rather than "acting-out subjects."[23]

Dulac and Gaudreault base their account on a formal and technical analysis of the apparatus, the way its circularity strips the figures it portrays of agency and condemns them to perpetual motion. I take this argument even further. From the moment of its invention, the phenakistoscope did not simply produce but explored the idea of a mechanical or automated human body as a figure for technological modernity through motifs of manual labor, machines and tools, and behavioral and psychic compulsion. In a literal sense, it is the spectator who *acts upon* the subjects of the phenakistoscope by spinning the disk, and the act of spinning that "condemn[s]" the subjects to this "acted-upon" position. The spectator is at once animator of the moving image and operator of the figures represented on the disk. By visualizing working bodies and industrial machines whose constrained and repetitious movements are controlled by the leisurely spectator, phenakistoscopes enacted a cyclical temporality expressive of the technological and industrial scene of capitalist labor.

To understand this more fully, we must consider the visual rhetoric of the disks themselves. The imagery of early phenakistoscopes was varied, not only across publishers and the artists they commissioned to design folios of disks but also within folios themselves.[24] For example, the first of three folios published by Rudolph Ackermann consisted of six disks designed by Plateau with artist Jean-Baptiste Madou. These included not only Plateau's ballet dancer but also showy and formally

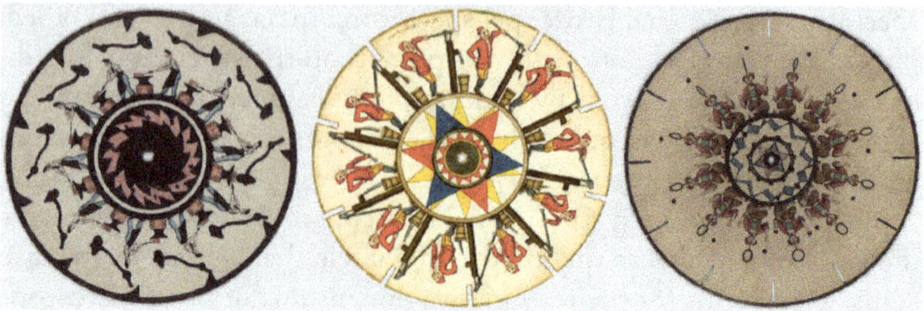

FIGURE 5.6. Assorted phenakistoscope disks.

innovative designs like "Serpent Disappearing over the Edge," in which the snakes seem to emerge from the center of the disk and slither out beyond the frame. While much of the scholarship on the phenakistoscope focuses on this type of phantasmagorical disk, with its "unnerving effect of the world of the illusion overlapping on one's own," the preponderance of disks did not feature gothic imagery or the illusion of the moving image breaching the boundary between disk and world.[25] As Meredith Bak puts it, phenakistoscope disks instead "are densely populated by gears propelled by people and animals or running autonomously, modeling relationships between men and machines and lauding the tireless efforts of industrial technologies."[26] Subjects include men and women smelting iron, chopping wood, juggling balls, and performing acrobatic and contortionist feats, and machines made of cogs, wheels, and pulleys (figure 5.6).

This is particularly true of two folios produced by Simon Stampfer, the Austrian mathematician who invented an almost identical device to Plateau's in February 1833 and called it the stroboscope. In contrast to Plateau's focus on the human body and phantasmagorical transformation, Stampfer's disks foregrounded machinery and laboring bodies and included subjects like mechanical hammers, toothed wheels, women pumping water, and men sawing.[27] Designers working after Plateau and Stampfer, including Thomas Talbot Bury, Thomas Mann Baynes, Alphonse Giroux, and the anonymous designers of London folios published by W. Soffe and E. Wallis, often used a layered composition to make the most use of the space of the disk, with a main subject, usually involving human activity, forming the topmost circle, and smaller inner circles featuring animals, dancing devils, spirals, or wheels.

The phenakistoscope transforms all bodies into working bodies, regardless of subject matter. While many of the disks represent recreational human behavior like horseback riding and men playing leapfrog, I agree with Bak that the disks "synchronize" work and play "to the same tempo."[28] Bodies on the phenakistoscope appear mechanized, automated, moving "with the same precision and fluidity as the workings of machinery."[29] The man who pumps water from a well and the man who tosses his ball to a frog are both condemned to repeat this action again and again; each time the water will flow from the pump into a wooden bucket, the frog will catch the ball in his mouth and swallow it, and each sequence will repeat. The bucket never overflows, and the frog is never full; the working man never tires or takes a break, and the playing man never runs out of balls; the sense of perpetual motion is the same. Just over a century before *Modern Times*, in which the Tramp's body becomes regulated by the circular and repeating rhythms of the mass production line and is swallowed up by the strange clockwork of the industrial machine, the circular and repeating phenakistoscope "formally replicated the tireless logic of mass production" and depicted the factory worker as "another cog in the larger industrial apparatus."[30] Chaplin picks up on the phenakistoscope's collapsing of the distinction between work and play when he has the Tramp spin through the cogs of the machine to the sound of merry-go-round music, scoring a workplace accident to the cadences of holiday fun.[31]

A close examination of phenakistoscope disks reveals shades of Chaplin's Tramp: men and women fated to move in circles by the requirements and psychic compulsions of factory labor and the industrial machine. More than a dancing man, Plateau's original phenakistoscope disk seems to show a windup toy or ballerina in a mechanical music box. He is stiff and expressionless, and when the disk is spun, he turns on pointed toes with inhuman precision, as if moved by clockwork. His movement is perfectly circular, echoing the shape of the disk as well as its circular motion as it is spun by the spectator. Plateau's dancer reflects the device of which he is an icon: a machine that moves in circles (the mechanical dancer) as the visual representation of a machine that moves in circles (the phenakistoscope). The integration of and symmetry between human and machine is similarly represented in a much-copied disk by the London publisher E. Wallis that imagines a mechanical sawmill, turning the human labor of chopping or sawing wood into a feat of industrial machinery, and in a disk published by W. Soffe in which a large, heavy black hammer hovers above a piece of hot metal on an anvil and rhythmically hits it, dwarfing the blacksmith and seemingly rendering him obsolete (figure 5.6). Such disks reflect the effects of the industrial revolution, which moved artisan labor performed in homes and workshops into the factory and streamlined manual labor with the use of machines. Just as Plateau's dancer appears automated, a mechanical toy within a mechanical toy, the E. Wallis and W. Soffe disks explore the mechanization of human labor—the requirement that workers become machines or be displaced by them.

Plateau's first disk not only alludes to the phenakistoscope's mechanization of the human body, what Bak refers to as the synchronizing of human movement to the rhythm of the factory, but equally to the phenakistoscope's circular and repeating format. The dancer does not leap in the air or move from first to second position; he spins in place, embodying Dulac and Gaudreault's insight that the moving figures of the phenakistoscope are "hostage[s]" to circularity and repetition. The phenakistoscope presents spinning in place as the temporality of workers under capitalism and as a fundamental condition of industrial modernity. We see this thematized in the repeated motif of rodents running in wheels, a visual idiom—"like a hamster in a wheel"—that reflects the temporal conditions of the phenakistoscope itself. For example, Alphonse Giroux's "*Le bûcheron et le souris*" ("The Woodcutter and the Mouse") layers a mouse running in circles inside a small compartment beneath its main subject of a woodcutter repeatedly chopping a piece of wood on a stump. Giroux thus connects the man's labor to the scurrying of the mouse and implies that both activities are equally fruitless to the one performing them.

The hamster-in the-wheel trope can help us identify a second theme of bodies moving in circles in phenakistoscope disks, one in which the body can be held hostage to spinning in place not by the logic of mass production but by universalizable behavioral or psychological traits. In a disk designed by Thomas Talbot Bury for Ackermann's second folio, a woman grabs a man by his coattails and beats him over the head with a paddle; beneath this plane of action is an interior wheel populated by smaller wheels; inside each of these smaller wheels, a squirrel runs in circles. Unlike the mouse in the wheel in Giroux's disk, Bury's squirrel is the peanut gallery commenting on the man and woman's unresolvable conflict and turning it into a comic parable of shrewish wives and foolish husbands: "it was ever thus, and ever will be thus." A *Punch* cartoon from 1848 builds on this trope when it satirizes parliamentary conflict through a phenakistoscope disk depicting two members of Parliament meeting, poised in fisticuffs, and shaking hands: "The following are the points of the circle around which Members revolve," the accompanying text states, "chasing one another, with as much result as a dog running after his tail; that is to say, only exciting the merriment of those who look on."[32] Like the squirrel in the wheel or the dog that chases its tail, the married couples and politicians that revolve in the phenakistoscope disk are driven by their own folly to repeat themselves again and again without learning from their mistakes.

At the broadest level, the bodies of phenakistoscope disks are in thrall to invisible forces beyond their control, forces that act through them and determine their fate. In this regard, phenakistoscope disks mediate between traditional conceptions of the Wheel of Fortune drawn from medieval philosophy—the wheel spun by Fortuna to determine the fates of men—and its nineteenth-century interiorization in the theory of the unconscious. The spinning men and women on phenakistoscope disks simultaneously evoke medieval paintings of men and women sitting on or clinging to a rotating wooden wheel and what Sigmund Freud would later call the "*passive* experience" of the psychoanalytic patient, "over which he has no influence, but in which he meets with a repetition of the same fatality."[33] The "compulsion to repeat," which Freud described in *Beyond the Pleasure Principle* (1920) as a state in which the patient unconsciously engineers the same fate for himself again and again, draws on the very notion of an "acted-upon" subject while proposing that the forces that act upon us and that we externalize in the form of enemies, antagonists, or even social and economic conditions, are ultimately psychic and interior. Phenakistoscope disks present us with a vision of acted-upon bodies, bodies compelled to repeat, that is unrulier and more ambiguous than Freud's. The figures on the disks are at once mechanized, automated, animated, and compulsive; compelled by economic relations, machine capitalism, social convention, and human nature; driven by cultural imperatives and unconscious needs.

These visual references to compulsion, mechanization, animation, and remote control come together in a phenakistoscope disk of unknown origin made around 1840 (figure 5.7). As became common after Bury's folio for Ackermann in 1833, the disk is divided into three pictorial planes that all reference the phenakistoscope's logic of circularity and repetition. In the outer ring, a small, elfin fellow in a ruffled collar and red cap spins a top by means of a string coiled around its axis. When pulled quickly, the string sets the top spinning. This kind of top is featured in Pieter Bruegel the Elder's painting *Children Games* (1560), where the players include a boy in a red cap similar to that worn by the child

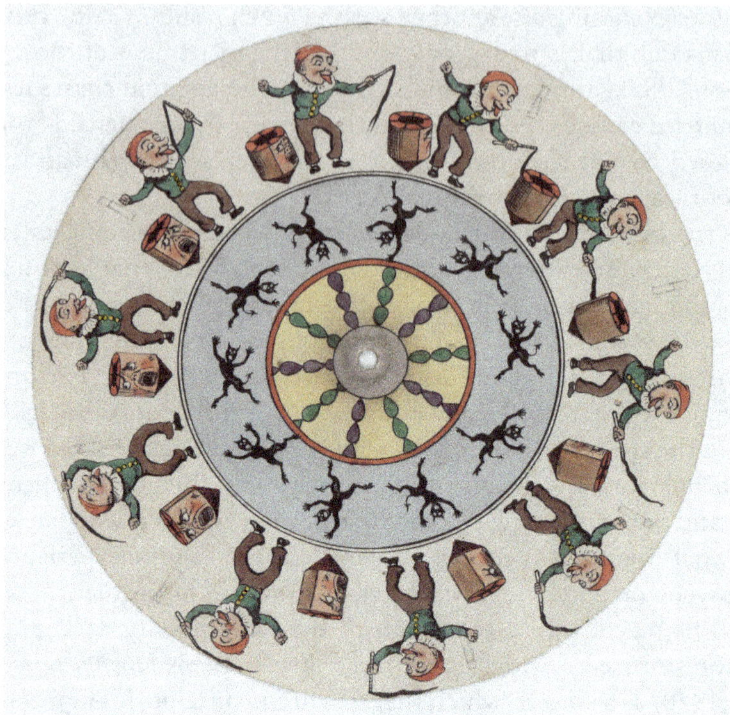

Figure 5.7. Phenakistoscope disk depicting a boy and a spinning top. Courtesy of the National Science and Media Museum/Science and Society Picture Library.

on the disk, suggesting that we might read him as a boy at play. The top, meanwhile, is personified with a human face, and as it spins, it quakes in horror, open-mouthed as if screaming, eyes tilted upward to the face of his tormenter. The string, which the boy raises in the air before bringing it back down around the top, reads distinctly as a whip, turning the act of spinning into an assault. The middle ring features black devils, as if in silhouette, cartwheeling against a pale blue background. They turn cartwheels over a center ring made to look like a wooden wheel with alternating green and purple spokes.

This is the most explicitly reflexive phenakistoscope disk that I have come across in my research because it not only references the device's status as a spinning toy but also explores the role of the active spectator in creating "living pictures" through the act of spinning. The boy stands in for those who play with the phenakistoscope, while the uncannily personified spinning top, with its pug nose and full set of teeth, can be read as a commentary on the marketing of the phenakistoscope by Soffe and others as a "Living Picture." Like the boy who spins the top, the spectator who spins the phenakistoscope brings pictures to life. Here we have a representation not only of the manual and perceptual process of animation—persistence of vision achieved through the coordination of hand and eye—but equally of Dulac and Gaudreault's characterization of the figures on the phenakistoscope as "acted upon." While the boy plays gleefully and absorbedly, his tongue stuck out irreverently, the top's obvious terror implies a relation of dominance and submission, even of master and slave. The top spins because it is captive to the player, under his control. In this tongue-and-cheek disk, to play with a phenakistoscope is to possess and exercise control over the life and movements of another by making it work—making it spin—for your pleasure. The devilish imps are a common trope in moving-image toys as well as in nineteenth-century stage magic and early cinema, likely drawing on the many variants of the Faust story that depicted Mephistopheles as a visual conjurer and master of illusions.[34] Here, the devils subject the image to overdetermination. The top is controlled by the child who spins it, but the devil may have possessed the child to perform this action in the first place—indeed, the devil serves as a figure for the compulsion to sadism that animates the boy to animate the top. The disk imagines the moving images of the phenakistoscope as subject to and possessed by mysterious forces—not coming to life but brought to life, not acting but acted upon.

I have offered a reading of the phenakistoscope as a toy that comments on labor and power under industrial capitalist modernity through its serial format, circular and repeating structure, and representational content. The phenakistoscope and the spinning moving-image toys that followed it prefigure and contextualize the factory scene in *Modern Times* not only by depicting "acted upon" bodies subjected to forces outside their control, bodies like machines activated through buttons and levers, but more specifically bodies technologically conditioned to move tirelessly in circles. The motif of the wheel, at once evoked through the phenakistoscope's circular design and reflexively represented on the disks themselves, is an overdetermined figure for the industrial machine, civilizational and technological progress, compulsive hamster-in-the-wheel behavior, the Wheel of Fortune, and unconscious drives. In the following section, we will see how these ideas come together in new configurations in the late fiction of Thomas Hardy.

Hardy develops an account of what I call the mechanical unconscious as a driving force in the operations of industrial capitalism. He draws his account from the visual rhetoric and procedural logic of phenakistoscopes and other spinning moving-image toys.

Circuits and Reels

The factory is not a scene in the fiction of Thomas Hardy, but it is a presence. Hardy's novels and short stories take place in Wessex, his fictional Dorset, among woodsmen and dairy maids, pig farmers and corn threshers—the preindustrial agricultural laborers whose lives were being uprooted by the industrial revolution. Because of his nostalgia for and identification with the culture and the lifeways of a rapidly disappearing rural England, Hardy is sometimes misread as a Luddite disengaged from the forces of urbanization and mechanization that his novels critique.[35] The second half of this chapter challenges this characterization by tracing the phenakistoscope's logic of spinning in place through the final decade of Hardy's career as a fiction writer, from the mid-1880s to mid-1890s. As Margaret Kolb has noted, Hardy's Wessex novels have circular structures driven by the circular movements of their characters.[36] Her chief example is Michael Henchard, the protagonist of *The Mayor of Casterbridge*, whose journey through the novel takes him back to where he started, "the precise standing which he had occupied a quarter of a century before," after having lost his position as mayor and his distinguished station in the town following a scandal.[37] Rather than what Kolb calls "plot circles," circularity as a narrative form for the novel, I am interested in circularity and repetition as a representation of technological or automated human behavior across Hardy's fiction. Following Caroline Lesjak's description of Hardy as a chronicler of "the local, lived experience of emergent capitalist relations," I argue that Hardy turns to the motif of circling bodies to show how human lives and labors are automated by the machinery of modernity.[38] By placing *The Mayor of Casterbridge* (1886) alongside the short stories "On the Western Circuit" (1891) and "The Fiddler of the Reels" (1893), I reveal how Hardy builds human narratives structured by the phenakistoscope's formal logic of circularity and repetition—narratives that are suggested by the phenakistoscope but that this device, with its inherently non-narrative structure, is unable to develop itself. These narratives generate an account of the mechanical unconscious, or unconscious drives expressed through mechanical motion, that are incipient in the phenakistoscope disks that I discussed in the previous section.

Through Henchard and his circular journey, *The Mayor of Casterbridge* develops the relation between circular repetitions and unconscious drives. This latter term is obviously anachronistic, and I realize that it risks incorrectly conflating Hardy's strange and complicated account of human behavior with Freud's later definition, so let me be more specific. In speaking of unconscious drives in Hardy, I am referring to a structure of nonconscious motivation that he described in his notebook variously as "human automatism" and "people moving under enchantment." This force "works to make a person, a people, &c., do one set of things while believing another"[39] and leads to "human action in spite of human knowledge."[40] These notes, all from the mid to late 1880s, describe Hardy's interest in a split consciousness that drives people to act in opposition to what they know or believe. "Automatism," a term drawn from the world of technology (automata) to describe actions undertaken mechanically rather than from consciousness or will, leads to what Dulac and Gaudreault call in the phenakistoscope "acted-upon subjects." In this case, however, a person can be acted upon by themselves. One can act in spite of one's "knowledge"; that is, action can be driven by something other than conscious knowledge.

Henchard's circular trajectory exemplifies this "automatic" state of being. When he finds himself on "the road by which his wife and himself had entered . . . five-and-twenty years ago," a reference to the opening scene of the novel, he means merely to "visit."[41] But Henchard's intention to "go on from this place" is overpowered by "thoughts of Elizabeth," his stepdaughter:

> Out of this it happened that the centrifugal tendency imparted by his weariness of the world was counteracted by the centripetal influence of his love for his stepdaughter. As a consequence, instead of following a straight course yet further away from Casterbridge, Henchard gradually, almost unconsciously, deflected from that right line of his first intention; till, by degrees, his wandering, like that of the Canadian woodsman, became part of a circle of which Casterbridge formed the center.[42]

The circle that Henchard "almost unconsciously" walks around Casterbridge is not only in opposition to the "straight course" but also to "that right line of his first intention." In other words, his circling is a symptom of that "automatism," or unconscious drive, that makes people act in spite of their intentions, decisions, or plans. This description of automatism draws, like the term itself, from the mechanical world. Henchard's "unconscious" movement is governed by "centripetal" and "centrifugal" forces, the opposing forces that cause an object to rotate. The "tendency imparted by his weariness of the world"—the desire to move farther from Casterbridge but also the desire to die—is "centrifugal," while the "influence of his love for his stepdaughter"—the desire to return to Casterbridge but also the desire to live—is "centripetal." Henchard's circling is a paradoxical form of stasis—immobilized movement that comes from ambivalence and contradictory desires. Henchard not only traces a circle from the beginning of the novel to the end, as Kolb has argued; he spins in place.[43]

The Mayor of Casterbridge takes place in the historical past, beginning "before the nineteenth century had reached one-third of its span" and continuing eighteen years later, probably around mid-century. If the action occurs at a distance from the factories, production lines, and industrial machines referenced in phenakistoscope disks, it is also set during the period of the phenakistoscope's popularity. The novel's depiction of human agency evokes the phenakistoscope's connection between spinning and acted-upon bodies, the compulsion to repeat and the mechanization of human activity. Henchard is governed by the physics of spinning bodies, an invisible pair of forces that metaphorically represent the equally mechanistic, invisible, and totalizing effects of unconscious motivation. In this regard, we should read this scene of walking as an example of what Elaine Scarry, in the well-known essay "Work and the Body in Hardy and Other Nineteenth-Century Novelists," describes as Hardy's technique of representing work through displacement so that even when "labor is suspended . . .the motion of the body at work seems to surround [Hardy's characters] like a ghost of perpetual action."[44] For Scarry, what interests Hardy about work is precisely this sense of perpetual motion. "Work is action rather than discrete action," she writes, and "has no identifiable beginning or end . . . It is the essential nature of work to be perpetual, repetitive, habitual."[45] When we look closely at Henchard's circular walk, it becomes clear that Hardy draws on the logic of the spinning moving-image toy as a "solution" to what Scarry calls "the deep problems" in the representation of work as an ongoing activity.[46] The phenakistoscope not only offers a model for action without beginning or end but, as I have argued, it is deeply engaged in the representation of labor as a "perpetual, repetitive" activity.

Even as it seems to map so neatly onto Scarry's essay, my reading of Henchard's walk also poses an important challenge to hers. Scarry views both the activity of work and Hardy's perspective on it in romantic terms. To work, by threshing corn or trussing hay or cutting down trees, is to experience a sublime integration of self and world that analogizes the act of writing a novel, to be an "embodied human consciousness" and "embodied maker" who is "immersed in his interaction in the world, far too immersed to extricate himself from it."[47] Yet the centrifugal and centripetal forces that act on Henchard more powerfully than his own will do not point to an experience of work as embodied, conscious making but rather of work as the body being divided from the mind so that it can be made use *of*. In the scene of Henchard walking, as in the other examples I will discuss in the remainder of this chapter, Hardy draws on the language of physics and automation and the visual and technological procedures of the moving-image toy to represent embodied labor as alienated labor. These scenes have very little to do with the experience of plenitude that Scarry finds elsewhere in Hardy's representation of work and the body. Instead, they show bodies governed by forces that are at once externally and internally generated, beyond conscious control.

Hardy's representation of the alienated working body that spins in place finds its most articulate form in two of Hardy's short stories. Originally written for magazines, "On the Western Circuit" and "The Fiddler of the Reels" were republished in *Life's Little Ironies* (1894), a collection that Martin Ray calls "an alternative fictional world" to Wessex novels like *The Mayor of Casterbridge.* Instead of "the world of rural occupations and traditional craft" that takes center stage in his novels, the stories in *Life's Little Ironies* are populated by urban professionals—"outsiders" to the country villages where they predominantly take place.[48] "On the Western Circuit" and "The Fiddler of the Reels" are set in the present day (when Hardy wrote the stories) and feature tropes of urban and industrial modernity like steam-powered machines, technologized popular culture, and world's fairs. Through optical and mechanical motifs drawn from the modern world and registered by the "circuits" and "reels" of their titles, these stories represent working people in thrall to the compulsion—at once technological, economic, and psychic—that drives them to move in circles.

"On the Western Circuit" opens with Charles Braford Raye "endeavoring to gain amid the darkness [of night] a glimpse" of the ruins of a cathedral.[49] Raye, whom the narrator immediately warns us will "[play] the disturbing part" in the story, is a judge on the West Country judicial circuit who has stopped over in Melchester on business and is doing a bit of sightseeing. Despite his name, Raye is unable to see much of the cathedral, but the walls "reflected sharply a roar of sound" from the city square and draw him into the tumult of a fair replete with the noises of "steam barrel-organs, the clanging of gongs, the ringing of hand-bells" and the kinetic technological activity of rides like "swings, see-saws, flying-leaps" (244–45). The centerpiece of the fair is "three steam roundabouts," or steam circuses, better known today as merry-go-rounds (245). Raye stops in front of the largest roundabout to watch its brilliant musical revolutions; among the many "gyrating personages" on the ride he spots the "prettiest girl," Anna (245–46). They spend the evening together, later have sex, and after Raye has moved onward on the Western Circuit, she finds herself pregnant. She is illiterate, so she asks her employer Edith Harnham to write Raye love letters on her behalf. Raye falls in love by correspondence with the writer of the letters; he marries Anna, only to realize his mistake.

"On the Western Circuit" points through its title to the story's central metaphors: circuits and circling. While the narrative mostly deals with letter writing, and indeed was nearly called "The Writer of the Letters," Hardy's ultimate choice of title places the thematic emphasis on the opening scene of the fair and its powerfully realized central figure of the roundabout: another sort of "Western circuit" powered, like industrial capitalism itself, by steam.[50] The roundabout registers industrial modernity's disruptions and transformations of traditional English life and particularly its effects on the body. Like the merry-go-round music that scores the Tramp's twirl through the machine, Hardy's roundabout collapses technologies of work and play. The pleasure-seekers Raye sees on the rides, like the conveyor-belt workers in *Modern Times*, are "so rhythmical that they seemed to be moved by machinery" (245). Of course, as Raye notices a moment later when the riders themselves come into view, the riders *are* moved by machinery. Yet the momentary ambiguity about the motion of these bodies registers the story's broader concern with how industrial modernity "seems" to mechanize the body. As Michael Niblett argues, the scene at the fair conveys "the dislocating, estranging effect of the contemporary modernization of the English countryside" on those who traditionally worked the land—laborers now "reduced . . . to lifeless bodies animated only by the movement of the machinery."[51] The condition of being "moved by machinery" applies as well to Raye, the professional man: a circuit judge travels in circles powered by another kind of steam engine, the train.

The circular nature of the roundabout is critical to Hardy's representation of the industrial animation and automation of the body. Unlike the train, the paradigmatic symbol of technological and industrial modernity, the roundabout is a steam *circus*, meaning that it is incapable of moving forward. Its inexorable circling not only literalizes the "circuitry" of the West England circuit court that Raye traverses by train but also provides a metaphorical framework for Hardy's diagnosis of the acted-upon body, compelled to circle and repeat, as a product of capitalist industrialization. This laboring body is made to work in service of the capitalist ideal of technological and civilizational progress, but progress is precisely what it is incapable of. There is no progression, no forward movement, in Hardy's vision of capitalism. His Western civilization is a Western circuit.

Hardy develops these themes by styling the roundabout as a kind of large-scale, interactive moving-image toy. John Plotz has compared the scopic dimensions of Hardy's roundabout, which spins in circles repeatedly for the pleasure of the "idle spectator," to the experience of playing with a phenakistoscope.[52] There are some obvious drawbacks to this comparison, which runs the risk of collapsing the discrete contexts of the parlor room and the fairground and flattening the differences in technology, scale, and qualities of movement between the two devices. Not all circular, spinning devices are phenakistoscopes after all. Yet Plotz's observation is an important one and even richer than his analysis bears out because Hardy's description of the roundabout actually sees him drawing on two dimensions of Victorian moving-image culture. First, the roundabout reflects the cultural imaginary of the phenakistoscope as a medium through which the spectator mechanizes and remotely controls the laboring body by making the apparatus spin. When Raye pays for Anna to take another ride, "producing his money" so that "she was enabled to whirl on again," the situation recalls both the capitalistic and industrial imaginary of phenakistoscope spectatorship and the portrayal of the phenakistoscope's moving bodies as working bodies (248). It reimagines what phenakistoscope disks portrayed as the fraught and controlling relationship between the spinner and the spun, the spectator and the body in motion, as a narrative situation structured by dynamics of gender and class. Second, Hardy draws on the language of optical technology to portray the roundabout as a technology that produces virtual images.

Rather than viewing the roundabout as a kind of phenakistoscope, I want to propose that Hardy's roundabout is constructed out of the moving, mechanical, and virtual effects of a variety of optical toys.

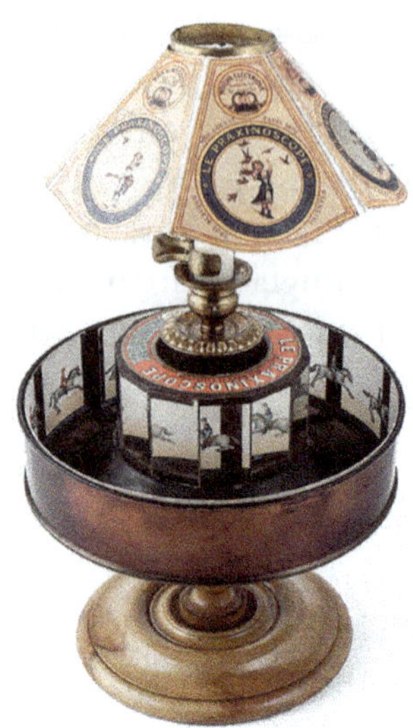

FIGURE 5.8. The praxinoscope. Courtesy of the Bill Douglas Cinema Museum.

For instance, the story clearly invokes the optical and technological regime of persistence of vision in its description of the roundabout's mechanical horses. They move with "a galloping rise and fall, so timed that, of each pair of steed, one was on the spring while the other was on the pitch," like Eadweard Muybridge's instantaneous serial photographs of a galloping horse in *Animal Locomotion* (1887) and their reconstruction as moving images through the zoopraxiscope, his combination phenakistoscope/magic lantern (245–46). With its "long plate-glass mirrors set at angles" that "revolved with the machine" and "flashed the gyrating personages and hobby-horses kaleidoscopically into [Raye's] eyes" (245) the roundabout also resembles the praxinoscope, a toy that creates circular and repeating moving images when a paper strip with pictures of successive motion is placed inside a spinning drum with long flat mirrors forming a circle at the center (figure 5.8). Just as Raye sees the horses and people moving in the mirrors at the center of the roundabout, so do the static pictures on the paper strip transform into moving images when seen reflected in the central mirrors. The term "kaleidoscopic" derives from the kaleidoscope, an optical toy that reflects small pieces of glass in an infinite array of luminous patterns. Its use here makes it explicit that Raye does not see Anna herself, "the prettiest girl out of the several pretty ones revolving," but a virtual image mediated by mirrors and light.

The construction of the object of desire as a virtual image is a motif across Hardy's work, as is the encounter between lovers mediated by mirrors.[53] "On the Western Circuit" modulates this theme of erotic desire as visual and perceptual illusion through the roundabout's spectral mechanics.[54] Anna is not just a mirror image—she is a persistence of vision illusion created at the intersection of the roundabout's circuitry, the mirror, and Raye's observing gaze. Like Muybridge's horse or the merrymakers and horseback riders on a phenakistoscope disk, Anna is part of a series composited into an animated moving image when the roundabout spins. The narrator claims that "the observer's eye centered on the prettiest girl out of the several pretty ones revolving," positioning her as one in a series of girls on the ride, only to interject in Raye's free indirect discourse that "it was not that one with the light frock and light hat whom he had been first attracted by; no, it was the one with the black cape, grey skirt, light gloves and—no, not even she, but the one behind her." Hardy implies that Anna is not "selected" as the "prettiest"; rather, she is a product of all the women fusing together in the "kaleidoscopic" whirl of images (246). Anna is, as her name evokes in this context, an *animation*, a lifelike illusion produced at the interface of the spinning, mirrored roundabout and Raye's "observer's eye." This basic idea undergirds the story as it progresses: Raye will fall in love not with Anna herself, but with the composite figure of Anna and Edith produced by Edith's ghost-written letters.

In *The Mayor of Casterbridge*, Henchard's "centrifugal" and "centripetal" condition of spinning in place represents his psychological state. With "On the Western Circuit," Hardy is less concerned with individual psychology than with modern experience broadly conceived. He turns to the visual and technological imaginary of moving-image toys and to the tropes of circularity, repetition, and optical illusion to express a vision of industrial modernity as a condition of spinning and being spun. Raye, Anna, and Edith all emerge from and are characterized by Hardy's infernal fairground, an "eighth chasm of the Inferno" in which "human figures" swing up, down, and around "like gnats against a sunset" (244–45). This is a world in which men and women do not move and act deliberately but rather are moved and acted upon—a world in which you are either riding the roundabout, subject to its illusions, or compelled, like the wealthy Edith, to fuel the engine to keep the machine running. The "Inferno" referenced here is, of course, Dante's; the "eighth chasm" is the eighth circle of hell that Dante reserved for fraudsters. The hell of modernity is its technological circularity, its steam circuitry, that dooms those who dwell in it to endless repetition and to the illusions (visual frauds) that circularity and repetition produce. Put another way, in "On the Western Circuit," the hell of modernity is a virtual moving-image toy.

A year after Hardy published "On the Western Circuit" in *Harper's Weekly* and *The English Illustrated Magazine*, he started work on a second story that centers even more explicitly on acted-upon bodies that move in circles. "The Fiddler of the Reels" was commissioned by *Scribner's* for a special number of the magazine devoted to the 1893 Chicago World's Fair. The story begins with a group of men who recall London's Great Exhibition of 1851 while "talking of Exhibitions, World's Fairs, and what not" in the present day.[55] This leads them to remember the story of three South Wessex people "whose queer little history was oddly touched at points by the Exhibition" (286). Car'line is a young Mellstock woman engaged to marry the mechanic Ned Hipcroft, but she is seduced by the itinerant fiddler Mop Allamoor after hearing him play his violin. Car'line's response to Mop is physiological and involuntary. When he plays the fiddle, "the aching of the heart seized her simultaneously with a wild desire to glide airily in the mazes of an infinite dance." Mop, in effect, possesses her to dance to his music: "her tread convulsed itself more and more accordantly with the time of the melody" and "her gait could not divest itself of its 'compelled capers'" (289). Thrown over by Car'line, Ned moves to London where he helps to build the Crystal Palace, the structure that housed the Great Exhibition. Shortly after the opening day of the Great Exhibition, he receives a letter from Car'line begging him to take her back, and she surprises him by arriving in London to marry him with a small child in tow: Little Carry, her daughter by Mop, who has abandoned her. Charmed by the child, Ned marries her anyway, and three years later they decide to leave London and return to Mellstock as a family. On the way, Car'line and her daughter stop at a pub, where she discovers Mop playing his fiddle. Her susceptibility to Mop's music undiminished by time, she finds herself dancing at the center of a reel, "weak" and "overpowered with hysteric emotion" but unable to stop (299). She faints; Ned arrives in time to revive her; but Mop disappears with the child. Their whereabouts are never discovered, but the "general opinion" finds that they have emigrated to America, the girl now trained "to keep him by her earnings as a dancer" while he plays his jigs and reels (304).

Like "On the Western Circuit," "The Fiddler of the Reels" signals its interest in circular movement in the title. A reel is a folk dance in which the dancers form traveling figures, circling one another in a figure eight. The climax of the story sees Car'line Aspent "lose her power of independent will" (299) as she dances the center, or "axis," of a five-handed reel to the violin strains of her ex-lover, moving in circles and unable to stop until she collapses in exhaustion. She is "the axis of a dizzily rotating human wheel," Isobel Armstrong writes of Car'line, the dance's pattern "form[ing] a human zoetrope that becomes the center of the narrative."[56] Although it is not clear to me that Hardy's dancers take the specific form of a zoetrope as opposed to another related optical toy, like the phenakistoscope, the reference to moving-image technology is clear. The title puns on the "reels" of many nineteenth-century moving-image devices, with strips of images wound or placed around a spinning drum, wheel, or cylinder—the term would soon be used, of course, to refer to the celluloid strips used to record film images. However, Hardy's description of Car'line is decidedly noncinematic. For instance, the dance is not a tableau or spectacle produced for the patrons of the bar: she moves at Mop's pleasure and for his pleasure alone. If she is like Plateau's mechanized dancer, Mop is the paradigmatic showman-spectator who both watches and sends her reeling:

> She thus continued to dance alone, defiantly as she thought, but in truth slavishly and abjectly, subject to every wave of the melody, and probed by the gimlet-like gaze of her fascinator's open eye; keeping up at the same time a feeble smile in his face, as if a feint to signify it was still her own pleasure which led her on. (301)

Mop's gaze recalls what Armstrong calls the "voluntary" dimensions of optical spectatorship—the act of peering through the aperture—as well as the way playing with an optical toy creates movement out of static images in a manner that phenakistoscopes thematized as "involuntary," or forced.[57] A gimlet "pierces," and Mop's eye simultaneously immobilizes her and forces her to move. Car'line is spinning in place.

The subjugation of Car'line's body in this scene—indeed, the bodily violence of Mop's fiddling—is a critical dimension of the story's use of and reflection on moving-image toys. The "slavish" and "abject" nature of Car'line's dance recalls the phenakistoscope disk of the spinning top, with its visual ambiguity that turns the child's act of spinning the top by uncoiling the rope into a violent whipping (see figure 5.7). Hardy reimagines this relationship between toy and slave, play and torture, in the story's portrayal of dance as what Shannon Draucker terms "musical rape." As Draucker notes, Mop's music has distinct and violent "bodily effects" that are "at once unwanted and uncontrollable," causing Car'line literal pain and leaving her "in convulsions, weeping violently."[58] Like the spinning top in the phenakistoscope disk, personified through its horrified demeanor, Car'line's distress is the human face of the objectification and automation enacted in moving-image toys.

We can better understand these dynamics of violence and subjugation when we attend to the layered meanings of the word "reel." As a noun, "reel" refers both to the song Mop plays and the dance Car'line performs, exposing the way they are deterministically linked by the mysterious power that flows from the strains of Mop's instrument to Car'line's body. Dancing is not a matter of choice or will because Car'line "did not want to dance" (299). She is "seiz[ed]," instead, by a "saltatory tendency"—a tendency, that is, to dance, although the word's secondary meanings (leaping, abrupt movement) convey a physiological reaction to the music like a seizure or spasm. As a verb, "reel" doubles down on the power asymmetry that allows Mop to act on Car'line's body—Mop reels her (as a picture made to move) and reels her in (as a fish on the line), the result of which is that Car'line reels (spins, whirls, sways, staggers, shakes, becomes giddy, collapses).

The story hints that the mysterious power Mop has over Car'line's body is supernatural—he is after all "elfish," "impish," "wizardly," and "fantastical," a purveyor of "devil's tunes" and "witchery," a character Frank Giordano calls "a composite folk and mythical figure" who is at once a "gypsy fiddler" and the devil himself.[59] If Car'line's "slavish" dance recalls the involuntary spinning of the top, Mop's "elfish" appearance and devilish power to bewitch is strikingly similar to the boy with the spinning top on the phenakistoscope disk I discussed in the last section (refer again to figure 5.7). Meanwhile, the narrator of the story disenchants these explanations by marshaling the evidence of modern science, comparing Mop's ability to control Car'line's body remotely to galvanism and mesmerism. Hardy's choice of names reveals a third possible explanation for Mop's capacity for remote control. Mop's given name, Wat, is a homonym for "Watt," the inventor of the steam engine that powered the industrial revolution as well as what was at the time the recently coined name for a unit of electrical power. The apostrophe in "Car'line" turns her into a line of train cars powered by steam or electricity. The story thus coordinates sciences of mind like mesmerism, which allow one person to exercise their will over another, with the force that animates machines to illustrate a condition like Freud's compulsion to repeat, rendering Car'line as the passive subject possessed to act in the same way again and again in spite of the harm it causes her. (It is worth mentioning here that in his notebooks, Hardy uses "mesmerism" interchangeably with "automatism" and "enchantment" to name the force he describes as "human action in spite of human knowledge."[60]) Like the Dantean circling of the roundabout in "On the Western Circuit," this story's vision of human bodies "driven" by an unseen and immaterial mesmeric-mechanical force is mediated by the atavistic motif of the devil. Devilry is not an explanatory mechanism for Hardy. As in the phenakistoscope disk of the spinning top, with its devilish imps turning cartwheels, devilry in Hardy is a signifier for the will to perpetual motion, to circularity and repetition, a drive that is at once technological and industrial (watts, cars) and physiological and psychic (mesmeric, unconscious). In this sense, Mop is less of a character than he is an expression of social, psychic, economic, and technological forces that make people spin.

We have seen that "On the Western Circuit" and "The Fiddler of the Reels" turn to the optical structure of circling and repetition to explore the relationship between determinism and free will and the way people are "whirled" by forces beyond their control. In doing so, Hardy critiques and reimagines the late Victorian civilizational ideology of capitalist, industrial, and technological progress. Rather than the linear, evolutionary, and teleological trajectories implied by the notion of progress, Hardy turns to the circular and repeating format of the phenakistoscope and the Sisyphean perpetual motion of its moving pictures to represent the temporality of bodies laboring under the requirements of industrial capitalism and the internalization of its requirements as drives. In both stories, machines and the unconscious are collapsed into a single force that simultaneously animates people and alienates them from themselves. Through characters compelled to circle and repeat—Anna, who spins on the roundabout for Raye's pleasure and coin; Raye, who spins along the western circuit for a wage; and Car'line, who spins on the dance floor transfixed by Mop's will—the stories play on the phenakistoscope's correlation of the optical animation of static bodies and the mechanization of working bodies by the requirements of industrial capital. Yet like the figures on phenakistoscope disks whose dancing and playing corresponds to the rhythms of the production line, Hardy's characters are pleasure seekers who find that fairgrounds, dances, courtship, and sex are mediated by and hold them hostage to the mechanical logic of the factory. For Hardy, there is no freedom from circling and repetition, compulsions that are at once imposed from without and generated from within.

The Mayor and the Tramp

What has any of this to do with *Modern Times*? I acknowledge the strangeness of claiming a Chaplin comedy as a genealogical descendent of the naturalist tragedies of Hardy. But what Hardy and Chaplin both offer us, I argue, is an industrial vision of the compulsion to repeat, in which the body is at once estranged from itself and animated by industrial modernization. The Tramp is not just compelled to repeat the same action, tightening nuts on a steel plate with a twist of his wrist, by the orders of the overseer; the repetitions begin to infect his body like a twitch, his shoulders and hands seizing up with the urge to keep moving in the same patterns. Once he is rescued from his revolution through the machine, this tendency to repeat the same circular action of twisting and tightening the nuts becomes compulsive. At first, it is as if the machine has automated his body. He cannot resist an opportunity to twist the tiny nutlike circles that now appear to him everywhere: as nipples, buttons, the handles of a fire hydrant. But eventually, this mechanistic behavior resolves into a paradoxical grace: the Tramp begins to dance, twirling about the factory and elegantly kicking his leg in the air as he squirts oil on the assembly line workers, no longer able to tell the difference between man and machine. What both versions of this "mad" routine have in common is the compulsive repetition of circular motion, whether twisting or twirling. Like Hardy's characters, the Tramp moves to the rhythms of the machine—he is the acted-upon subject of the factory's seemingly infinite rotating wheels and endlessly revolving conveyor belts.

Rather than thinking of the Tramp having a "nervous breakdown," as the narrative instructs when the Tramp is loaded into an ambulance and committed to an asylum, we might read the opening factory sequence as a slapstick representation of the compulsion to repeat seen in the phenakistoscope and developed in the novels and short stories of Thomas Hardy. The circularity and repetition of the assembly line and its symptomatic manifestation in his body express the transformation of industrial capitalism's requirements into internal compulsions and drives. By associating the attempt to automate the Tramp's body with madness, Chaplin underscores what Hardy views as the close relationship between repetitious labor, the mechanics of spinning, and unconscious motivation. The Tramp's "breakdown" allows us to read him as a comic variation on Michael Henchard in *The Mayor of Casterbridge*. His spinning in place in the factory literalizes Hardy's proto-psychoanalytic notion of "human automatism," a psychic and embodied condition that he illustrates through Henchard's circular walk around Casterbridge buffeted by competing "centrifugal" and "centripetal" desires.

On closer examination, we can see how *Modern Times* develops its opening motif of the Tramp caught in the moving-picture machine by creating its own versions of some of Hardy's key metaphoric figures. Hardy's "circuit" and "reel"—the roundabout of "On the Western Circuit" and the dance of "The Fiddler of the Reels"—appear in the film's final act. The Tramp's companion, the Gamin, will find both of them jobs when she is spotted dancing outside a café and hired as a showgirl. The segment fades in on children riding a merry-go-round and then pans right, past the entrance of an establishment called the Red Moon Café, to show the Gamin dancing on the street; she twirls and leaps in circles to the sound of the carousel music for the pleasure of a group of bystanders, as if embodying its technological revolutions. Of course, the merry-go-round is also a callback to the Tramp's revolution through the factory machine. The scoring of the Tramp's workplace accident to the sounds of calliope music turns the Gamin's dance and the Tramp's assembly line work into doubles of each other, an association that is reinforced by the Tramp's own dance through the factory after he emerges from between the cogs. It also connects the Gamin's free-spirited movement to the mechanistic workings of the factory and the determinism of capital. Like the children who exchange a coin for a spin on the carousel, the man who runs the café—a white-haired capitalist smoking a cigar who recalls the factory owner at the Tramp's first job—will offer her a wage in exchange for dancing.

Spinning returns in the film's climax. This sequence of the film, in which the Tramp works as a singing waiter at the Red Moon Café, is famous because of the first use of the Tramp's voice, not only in the film but in more than twenty years on the screen. The nonsense language in which the Tramp sings is often read as a tribute to silent cinema as a universal visual language. The sequence also pays tribute to the serial technological formats out of which the cinema was born. The scene begins when the Tramp takes the order of an angry patron—another wealthy, white-haired man—who has been waiting for his roast duck. But just as he emerges from the kitchen with the tray, piled precipitously with dishes and a bottle of wine and held high above his head, all the customers have stood up to dance. As couples crowd the floor of the restaurant, the Tramp is trapped in the middle; jostled from side to side, all he can do is spin in a circle. Like Car'line in "The Fiddler of the Reels," the Tramp is dancing involuntarily, against his own will. In a callback to the opening of the film, the silver tray that spins above his head begins to resemble one of the cogs or wheels from the steel factory. Chaplin's choice to transpose the comedy of automation from the factory into the dance hall shows the invariability of capitalist labor conditions and the requirement that workers perform with the regularity and ease of machines. Whether the Tramp is caught in the gears of the machine while working on an assembly line or caught in a crush of dancers while trying to serve dinner, spinning in place is the ineluctable condition of his life as a working man. Spinning in place at once shows the comic breakdown of human-as-machine, as in his failure to perform the seemingly simple task of walking a straight line from the kitchen to the patron's table, and represents its apotheosis: his infinitely repeating labor has separated the movements of his body from his will, turning him into a cog spun by and for the machine.

Alongside the phenakistoscope and the late fiction of Thomas Hardy, I propose that we read *Modern Times* as part of an alternative genealogy of moving pictures as non-narrative animation. Lev Manovich famously argues in "What Is Digital Cinema?" that we see the return of cinema's disavowed origin in animated loops, visual plasticity, and attractional forms of the optical toy in digital cinema, a claim that has only become more relevant with the rise of TikTok and the resurgence of the moving-picture loop as a popular form.[61] But *Modern Times* reminds us that the virtual aesthetics of the loop and the format of the spinning toy never entirely disappeared from the twentieth century's imagination of the moving picture. By returning moving pictures to their origin in the noncontinuous, fragmented, looping, and iterative motion of the phenakistoscope, Hardy and Chaplin both reproduce and reimagine the phenakistoscope's circular and repeating structure textually and cinematically. They put non-narrative moving images to narrative purposes, building out the phenakistoscope's association between the loop, the industrial machine, factory labor, and the unconscious to tell stories about bodies under capitalism. They help us understand what the spinning and looping virtual moving image means.

Epilogue

Arrival of a Train

I began this book with *Arrival of a Train at La Ciotat* (1896), a film that many historians read as heralding the arrival of cinema. The actuality films of Auguste and Louis Lumière could be read as a fusion of many of the forms of virtual aesthetics that I have explored across chapters 1–5 of this book. While cinema's debt to magic and spectacle is more commonly traced through the work of early film pioneer Georges Méliès, a Lumière actuality like *Arrival of a Train at La Ciotat* is also styled as an illusion: its deep staging reminiscent of stereoscopic photography, its deeply realized ethnographic sense of time and place as transporting as the mirror of ink, even its projection a kind of rational recreation or magic trick because showmen liked to begin with a still image on the screen that suddenly leaps into motion. Early film projection formats also challenge what we tend to think of as the linearity, the finality of the train's arrival. In the variety show programs that were among cinema's first exhibition contexts, films were often repeated and could even be screened both forward and backward. Thomas Elsaesser notes that the Lumière films were designed "to be seen over and over again," formally constructed "to be experienced as both 'closed' and 'open' at the same time, thus improving on, but also commenting on the loops of Thomas Edison's kinetoscope."[1] Or, we might say, Joseph Plateau's phenakistoscope.

For instance, a Lumière film like *Horse Trick Riders* (1896–1897) replicates the serial format of the phenakistoscope by depicting a sequence of men trying to jump on the back of a horse. The attraction of the film lies in its repetitions. We see some version of the trick twenty times: most performers land sitting on the horse, some smash into the horse, others break form by performing cartwheels next to it. Because the men are identically dressed, it is difficult to tell how many of them there are—whether there are twenty men or a smaller number who each repeat the trick several times. Like the women on the roundabout in Thomas Hardy's "On the Western Circuit" (1891) who transform under Raye's gaze into a single, composited, virtual woman, or the moving images of the phenakistoscope represented in sequential pictures, the horse trick riders are at once one man and many men, cycling through the film as the film cycles through the sprockets. *Horse Trick Riders* reimagines the circular and repeating format of the phenakistoscope for a new medium that could combine narrative development with the attractions of the loop. Read in this same way, *Arrival of a Train at La Ciotat* is at once a straight shot across the tracks and a circuit. The train arrives and is always in the process of arriving.

In his famous essay, "The Myth of Total Cinema," the film theorist André Bazin made a similar claim about cinema in the twentieth century. Cinema, he wrote, is not a technological form but a myth, an imagined medium for the "total and complete representation of reality," for "the recreation of the world in its own image," that technology has imperfectly realized.[2] Cinema's technological development does not take the medium farther from its nineteenth-century origins but paradoxically "nearer and nearer" to the totalizing illusion technological pioneers like Plateau and Eadweard Muybridge dreamed of. "In short," Bazin declares, "cinema has not yet been invented!"[3] I do not think of cinema as a proleptic invention, imagined decades before its appearance on the world stage, or of the nineteenth-century showmen and inventors I have covered in this book as its prophets. Instead of the birth of cinema in nineteenth-century media culture, I am arguing for virtual experience—for *seeing things*—as a modern aesthetic and cultural paradigm that emerged in the nineteenth century. In a sense, this book reimagines Bazin's myth of total cinema by displacing cinema from its own history. Virtual aesthetics is a Victorian invention that is still in the process of arriving because it continues to be reconstituted through new technological forms and imaginaries in the present. Like Bazin, I have represented virtual aesthetics as an ideal that transcends its technological instantiations. When I say that virtual aesthetics emerged in the nineteenth century, what I mean is that thinkers, writers, inventors, and scientific practitioners from George Eliot and Elizabeth Gaskell to David Brewster and John Henry Pepper were engaged in a cultural project of imagining it into existence.

To call Victorian virtuality imagined is not to say that it is unreal. Rather, it is to take seriously what the methods of literary study offer to the field of media history: the rigorous analysis of the cultural imaginary that underlies and gives shape to technological forms. From a visual portal to another time and place made out of ink to a mesmeric diamond that penetrates consciousness, from a magic lantern show that raises the dead to a moving-picture toy that remotely controls human bodies, it would be easy for me to announce: virtuality has not yet been invented! But I do not see these Victorian media imaginaries as dreams meant to be realized in technological form. They are simply the ideas, discourses, and practices that make media experiences like attending a phantasmagoria show, looking through a stereoscope, or spinning a phenakistoscope culturally meaningful. They may drive technological innovation, but they are also attempting to make sense of technology—through technology. What I am calling a media imaginary could also be described as a media theory, an explanatory framework for the cultural relevance of media experiences and forms. To approach nineteenth-century virtual aesthetics as imaginary and theoretical; as plural and messy; and as appearing in partial form across a diverse range of texts, objects, and performances, is to refuse the narrative of media history as neutral technological development. It is to recognize instead the ways that the virtual is deeply embedded in and inextricable from the century's dominant cultural and political formations—at once shaped by and giving shape to imperialism, industrial capital, and civilizational ideology.

In the opening to this book, I promised an analysis of what the virtual was—a history of virtual aesthetics before the arrival of the Lumière train. I have avoided transhistorical comparisons between nineteenth-century media forms and discourses and the contemporary models you may have been thinking of as you read these chapters: open world video games, virtual reality headsets, augmented reality, video calls, interactive television shows. But I know that history does not belong in the past. My hope is that this relentlessly nonpresentist approach to the nineteenth century will enable you to consider how we are still imagining the virtual today. I hope that you will take this book as an invitation to ask how we might still be dreaming a Victorian dream: a dream of imaginative transportation and control, of visual derangement and epistemic sovereignty, of immersion and detachment, and of the individual perceptual management of illusion as a civilizational ideal.

Notes

Introduction

1. Not least because *Arrival of a Train* was not actually shown at the first public screening of films by the Lumières at the Salon Indien du Grand Café on December 28, 1895, a date that is often associated with the birth of cinema. For an explanation of why audiences for *Arrival of a Train* were extremely unlikely to have panicked, see Martin Loiperdinger, "Lumiere's Arrival of the Train: Cinema's Founding Myth," trans. Bernd Elzer, *Moving Image* 4, no. 1 (Spring 2004): 89–118; Tom Gunning, "An Aesthetic of Astonishment: Early Film and the (In)Credulous Spectator," in *Film Theory and Criticism: Introductory Reading*, 6th ed., ed. Leo Braudy and Marshall Cohen (Oxford University Press, 2004), 862–76.

2. Laurent Mannoni, *The Great Art of Light and Shadow: Archaeology of the Cinema*, trans. and ed. Richard Crangle (University of Exeter Press, 2000), 267.

3. This effect is most frequently referred to today as flicker fusion. See Barbara Anderson and Joseph Anderson, "The Myth of Persistence of Vision Revisited," *Journal of Film and Video* 45, no. 1 (Spring 1993): 3–12.

4. W. J. T. Mitchell, *Picture Theory: Essays on Verbal and Visual Representation* (University of Chicago Press, 1995), 16.

5. See Rachel Teukolsky, *Picture World: Image, Aesthetics, and Victorian New Media* (Oxford University Press, 2020); Susan Zieger, *The Mediated Mind: Affect, Ephemera, and Consumerism in the Nineteenth Century*, Fordham University Press, 2018); Isobel Armstrong, *Victorian Glassworlds: Glass Culture and the Imagination, 1830–1880* (Oxford University Press, 2008).

6. Teukolsky, *Picture World*, 8.

7. Nicholas Dames, *The Physiology of the Novel: Reading, Neural Science, and the Form of Victorian Fiction* (Oxford University Press, 2007), 30.

8. Richard Menke, *Telegraphic Realism: Victorian Fiction and Other Information Systems* (Stanford University Press, 2008), 139. Other examples of scholarship that place the novel in the context of Victorian "new media" include Nancy Armstrong, *Fiction in the Age of Photography: The Legacy of British Realism* (Harvard University Press, 1999); Kate Flint, *The Victorians and the Visual Imagination* (Cambridge University Press, 2008); Aaron Worth, *Imperial Media: Colonial Networks and Information Technologies in the British Literary Imagination, 1857–1918* (Ohio State University Press, 2014).

9. Work on nineteenth-century literature and optical media includes Helen Groth, *Moving Images: Nineteenth-Century Reading and Screen Practices* (Edinburgh

University Press, 2014); John Plunkett, "Optical Recreations and Victorian Literature," *Literature and the Visual Media* 58 (2005): 1–28; Stefan Andriopoulos, *Ghostly Apparitions: German Idealism, the Gothic Novel, and Optical Media* (Zone, 2013); David J. Jones, *Gothic Machine: Textualities, Pre-Cinematic Media and Film in Popular Visual Culture, 1670–1910* (University of Wales Press, 2011); Meegan Kennedy, "'Throes and Struggles . . . Witnessed with Painful Distinctness': The Oxy-Hydrogen Microscope, Performing Science, and the Projection of the Moving Image," *Victorian Studies* 62, no. 1 (2019): 85–118; Jonathan Potter, *Discourses of Vision in Nineteenth-Century Britain: Seeing, Thinking, Writing* (Palgrave Macmillan, 2018); Grahame Smith, *Dickens and the Dream of Cinema* (Manchester University Press, 2003). Two excellent studies of eighteenth-century literature and optical media also deserve mention here: Julie Park, *My Dark Room: Spaces of the Inner Self in Eighteenth-Century England* (University of Chicago Press, 2023); Peter Otto, *Multiplying Worlds: Romanticism, Modernity, and the Emergence of Virtual Reality* (Oxford University Press, 2011).

10. See Alison Byerly, *Are We There Yet? Virtual Travel and Victorian Realism* (University of Michigan Press, 2012); John Plotz, *Semi-Detached: The Aesthetics of Virtual Experience Since Dickens* (Princeton University Press, 2018); Timothy Gao, *Virtual Play and the Victorian Novel: The Ethics and Aesthetics of Fictional Experience* (Cambridge University Press, 2021); Michael Saler, *As If: Modern Enchantment and the Literary Prehistory of Virtual Reality* (Oxford University Press, 2012); Jules Law, "Virtual Evidence," *Victorian Studies* 56, no. 3 (Spring 2014): 411–24; Jules Law, "Victorian Virtual Reality," in *BRANCH: Britain, Representation and Nineteenth-Century History*, ed. Dino Franco Felluga, https://branchcollective.org/?ps_articles=jules-law-victorian-virtual-reality, accessed December 13, 2023; Jonathan Farina, "Dickens' 'As If': Analogy and Victorian Virtual Reality," *Victorian Studies* 53, no. 3 (Spring 2011): 427–36.

11. For instance, optical media are given strikingly short shrift in *Are We There Yet?*, a study of virtual travel in the Victorian period that has barely a passing mention for the stereoscope, the paradigmatic virtual travel medium of the nineteenth century. Byerly's claim that virtual reality entails "a projection of the self into a fictive environment" grounded in "a sense of locatedness" that provides "a crucial connection between the physical self and the imaginative environment" would be significantly enhanced through a discussion of travel stereographs. See Byerly, *Are We There Yet?*, 15–16. While Plotz's *Semi-Detached* includes a chapter on William Morris's use of the magic lantern, it focuses on the relationship between the lantern and printing press as visual technologies, not the lantern's role in a growing virtual media culture. In his essay "Victorian Virtual Reality," Jules Law gestures promisingly toward the relationship between virtuality in *Middlemarch* and technologies of visual illusion like the stereoscope, with an emphasis on "enhanced visual depth of field" as a reality effect in Victorian fiction. However, the discussion is brief and not fully conceptualized.

12. On the relationship between Western magic and colonialism in the nineteenth century, see Graham M. Jones, *Magic's Reason: An Anthropology of Analogy* (University of Chicago Press, 2017); Simon During, *Modern Enchantments: The Cultural Power of Secular Magic* (Harvard University Press, 2002); Peter Lamont

and Crispin Bates, "Conjuring Images of India in Nineteenth-Century Britain," *Social History* 32, no. 3 (August 2007): 308–24; Peter Lamont, *The Rise of the Indian Rope Trick: How a Spectacular Hoax Became History* (Abacus, 2005).

13. For an overview of media archaeology, see Jussi Parikka and Erkki Huhtamo, eds., *Media Archaeology: Approaches, Applications, and Implications* (University of California Press, 2011); Jussi Parikka, *What Is Media Archaeology?* (Polity, 2012).

14. Parikka and Huhtamo, *Media Archaeology*, 3.

15. Andreas Fickers and Annie van den Oeve, "Doing Experimental Media Archaeology: Epistemological and Methodological Reflections on Experiments with Historical Objects in Media Technologies," in *New Media Archaeologies*, ed. Ben Roberts and Mark Goodall (Amsterdam University Press, 2019), 45–68. See also Andreas Fickers, "How to Grasp Historical Media Dispositifs in Practice," in *Materializing Memories: Dispositifs, Generations, Amateurs*, ed. Susan Aasman, Andreas Fickers, and Joseph Wachelder (Bloomsbury, 2018), 85–102.

16. Meredith Bak, "The Ludic Archive: The Work of Playing with Optical Toys," *Moving Image: The Journal of the Association of Moving Image Archivists* 16, no. 1 (Spring 2016): 1–16.

17. See Eric Kluitenberg, ed., *The Book of Imaginary Media* (Nai, 2006); Eric Kluitenberg, "On the Archaeology of Imaginary Media," in *Media Archaeology: Approaches, Applications, and Implications*, ed. Erkki Huhtamo and Jussi Parikka (University of California Press, 2011), 61–63; Erkki Huhtamo, "Elements of Screenology: Toward an Archaeology of the Screen," *ICONICS: International Studies of the Modern Image* 7 (2004): 31–82.

18. On the afterlife of nineteenth-century optical toys in contemporary children's media, see Meredith Bak, *Playful Visions: Optical Toys and the Emergence of Children's Media Culture* (MIT Press, 2020), 209–26. The artist and educator Robby Gilbert remakes optical media like the zoetrope as art installations; see his reflections on teaching animation with optical toys in Robby Gilbert, "The Concrete Zoetrope: Engaging Students in Pre-Cinema with an Eye to the Future," *Early Popular Visual Culture* 18, no. 1 (2020): 44–57. In our panel "Beyond Pre-Cinema: Archaeology of Eighteenth- and Nineteenth-Century Visual Media" at the 2022 conference of the Society for Cinema and Media Studies, Robby Gilbert, Julie Park, Patrick Ellis, and I proposed the term "paracinematic" as a corrective to "precinematic."

19. "How to See Pictures," *National Magazine*, ed. John Saunders and Westland Marston (London, 1856): 23.

20. "How to See Pictures," 23–24.

21. On the virtual image, see especially Tom Gunning, "The Play Between Still and Moving Images: Nineteenth-Century 'Philosophical Toys' and Their Discourse," in *Between Stillness and Motion: Film, Photography, Algorithms*, ed. Eivind Røsaak (Amsterdam University Press, 2011), 27–44; Tom Gunning " 'We Are Here and Not Here': Late Nineteenth-Century Stage Magic and the Roots of Cinema in the Appearance (and Disappearance) of the Virtual Image," in *A Companion to Early Cinema*, ed. André Gaudreault, Nicolas Dulac, and Santiago Hidalgo (Wiley-Blackwell, 2012), 52–63; Tom Gunning, "Hand and Eye: Excavating a New Technology of the Image in the Victorian Era," *Victorian Studies*

54, no. 3 (April 2012): 495–516; Tom Gunning, "To Scan a Ghost: The Ontology of Mediated Vision," *Grey Room* 26 (2007): 94–127. Gunning's interest in an aesthetics of optical trickery that unites cinema with nineteenth-century stage magic and optical devices is a through line in his work from his earliest publications. See Tom Gunning, "The Cinema of Attractions: Early Film, Its Spectator, and the Avant-Garde," in *Early Cinema: Space, Frame, Narrative*, ed. Thomas Elsaesser (BFI Publishing, 2006), 56–62; Gunning, "An Aesthetic of Astonishment."

22. Gunning, "The Play Between Still and Moving Images," 33.

23. Anne Friedberg, *The Virtual Window: From Alberti to Microsoft* (MIT Press, 2009), 7.

24. Friedberg, *The Virtual Window*, 8. Friedberg claims that Brewster was the first to use the term "virtual" in English, but according to the *Oxford English Dictionary* (*OED*), he was predated by William Molyneux by more than one hundred years.

25. Friedberg, *The Virtual Window*, 9. For an example of this usage, see the discussion of images formed by convex mirrors in David Brewster, *A Treatise on Optics: First American Edition, with an Appendix, Containing an Elementary View of the Application of Analysis to Reflexion and Refraction, by A. D. Bache* (Carey, Lea, & Blanchard, 1833), 24–25.

26. John Henry Pepper, *Light: Embracing Reflection and Refraction of Light, Light and Colour, Spectrum Analysis, the Human Eye, Polarized Light* (Scribner, Welford, and Armstrong, 1876), 68.

27. Teukolsky, *Picture World*, 3.

28. Bill Brown, *The Material Unconscious: American Amusement, Steven Crane, and the Economics of Play* (Harvard University Press, 1997).

29. On this, see Tom Gunning's theory of the optical toy as a device that produces images through the coordination of hand and eye in Gunning, "Hand and Eye."

30. On the relationship between the optical toy and the philosophical toy, see Gunning, "The Play Between Still and Moving Images."

31. For instance, Laura Burd Schiavo argues that the stereoscope lost its connection to experimental science by the mid-nineteenth century, while Meredith Bak demonstrates how stereoscopes were used in American children's education. See Laura Burd Schiavo, "From Phantom Image to Perfect Vision: Physiological Optics, Commercial Photography, and the Popularization of the Stereoscope," in *New Media, 1740–1915*, ed. Lisa Gitelman and Geoffrey B. Pingree (MIT Press, 2003), 113–38; Bak, *Playful Visions*, 181–208.

32. On the use of optical instruments and experiments in eighteenth-century visual education, see Barbara Stafford, *Artful Science: Enlightenment, Entertainment, and the Eclipse of Visual Education* (MIT Press, 1994).

33. Jonathan Crary, *Techniques of the Observer: On Vision and Modernity in the Nineteenth Century* (MIT Press, 1992).

34. For a robust critique of *Techniques of the Observer*'s historical method and use of evidence, see Mitchell, *Picture Theory*, 21–22. Julie Park and Laura Burd Schiavo each make the case that Crary overstates the epistemic paradigm shift between objective and subjective models of vision by pointing to the

technological and aesthetic continuities between "old" media like the camera obscura and "new" media like the stereoscope. See Park, *My Dark Room*, 23–24; Schiavo, "From Phantom Image to Perfect Vision," 119–21.

35. For a complete list, see note 11.

36. Byerly, *Are We There Yet?*, 15.

37. Byerly, *Are We There Yet?*, 5.

38. Gao, *Virtual Play and the Victorian Novel*, 3.

39. Law, "Victorian Virtual Reality."

1. Magic Panic

1. Notable instances of this argument can be found in Tom Gunning, "An Aesthetic of Astonishment: Early Film and the (In)Credulous Spectator," in *Film Theory and Criticism: Introductory Reading*, 6th ed., ed. Leo Braudy and Marshall Cohen (Oxford University Press, 2004), 862–76; Tom Gunning, "The Long and Short of It: Centuries of Projecting Shadows, from Natural Magic to the Avant-Garde," in *The Art of Projection*, ed. Stan Douglas and Christopher Eamon (Hatje Cantz Verlag, 2009), 23–35; Colin Williamson, *Hidden in Plain Sight: An Archaeology of Magic and the Cinema* (Rutgers University Press, 2015); Iwan Rhys Morus, "'More the Aspect of Magic Than Anything Natural': The Philosophy of Demonstration," in *Science and the Marketplace: Nineteenth-Century Sites and Experiences*, ed. Aileen Frye and Bernard Lightman (University of Chicago Press, 2007), 336–70.

2. Gunning, "An Aesthetic of Astonishment," 819.

3. This line of inquiry is influenced by two books that make explicit, in different ways, the civilizational politics of magical and optical spectatorship in the eighteenth and nineteenth centuries. On optical illusions and citizenship in the American context, see Wendy Bellion, *Citizen Spectator: Art, Illusion, and Visual Perception in Early National America* (University of North Carolina Press, 2011). On stage magic and colonialism in the contexts of France and Algeria, see Graham M. Jones, *Magic's Reason: An Anthropology of Analogy* (University of Chicago Press, 2017).

4. For a study that challenges the theory of a disenchanted modernity, see Jason Ananda Joseph Storm, *The Myth of Disenchantment: Magic, Modernity, and the Birth of the Human Sciences* (University of Chicago Press, 2017).

5. As Karl Bell has demonstrated, most nineteenth-century audiences held a range of occult and magical beliefs, a context often overlooked by media historians who take Victorian magic's appeals to skepticism at face value and as a representation of how magic spectatorship worked in practice. See Karl Bell, *The Magical Imagination: Magic and Modernity in Urban England, 1780–1914* (Cambridge University Press, 2012).

6. The narrative arc of Signor Brunoni's magic show and its aftermath was originally printed in *Household Words* as "The Great Cranford Panic. In Two Parts," and appeared in two consecutive weekly issues in January 1853. When *Cranford* was printed as a novel, Gaskell configured the episode as a three-chapter arc: "Signor Brunoni," which represents the magic show; "The Panic," about the fears that it engenders; and "Samuel Brown," in which the magician

is revealed to be an impoverished soldier and his wife. These chapters tell the story of her sojourn from India back to England. Gaskell further signals the importance of stage magic to the novel in the final scene, which takes place at the Cranford Assembly Rooms as a second performance of Signor Brunoni's magic is about to begin.

7. My account of this event is taken from Jones's detailed and conceptually rich analysis in Jones, *Magic's Reason*, 27–43, but it is a well-known story and cited frequently in the literature on nineteenth-century stage magic. Other discussions can be found in Michael Mangan, *Performing Dark Arts: A Cultural History of Conjuring* (Intellect, 2007), 109–12; Murray Leeder, "M. Robert-Houdin Goes to Algeria: Spectatorship and Panic in Illusion and Early Cinema," *Early Popular Visual Culture* 8, no. 2 (May 2010): 209–25.

8. Robert-Houdin in Jones, *Magic's Reason*, 28.

9. Cited in Jones, *Magic's Reason*, 35.

10. Robert-Houdin cited in Jones, *Magic Reason*, 34–35.

11. Bell, *The Magical Imagination*, 92.

12. Jean-Eugène Robert-Houdin, *Les secrets de la prestidigitation et de la magie: comment on deviant sorcier* (Michel Lévy Frères, 1868), 54. My translation. Legerdemain, from Middle French, literally translates as "lightness [or nimbleness] or hand," whereas prestidigitation, of Middle French and Latin roots, breaks down to the "nimbleness [or quickness] of fingers." In early modern discourses of magic, such as Ronald Scot's *The Discoverie of Witchcraft* (1584), he distinguished witchcraft from what he called "juggling," an entertainment that required manual agility. For more on manual dexterity in magic, see Tom Gunning, "'We Are Here and Not Here': Late Nineteenth-Century Stage Magic and the Roots of Cinema in the Appearance (and Disappearance) of the Virtual Image," in *A Companion to Early Cinema*, ed. André Gaudreault, Nicolas Dulac, and Santiago Hidalgo (Wiley-Blackwell, 2012), 54.

13. Gunning, "We Are Here and Not Here," 55.

14. Jim Steinmeyer, *Hiding the Elephant: How Magicians Invented the Impossible and Learned to Disappear* (Da Capo, 2004), 61.

15. Steinmeyer, *Hiding the Elephant*, 34.

16. Steinmeyer, *Hiding the Elephant*, 29, 31.

17. Alfred Hopkins, *Magic: Stage Illusions, Special Effects, and Trick Photography* (Dover, 1976), 55–60.

18. Steinmeyer, *Hiding the Elephant*, 83–88.

19. Gunning, "We Are Here and Not Here," 54.

20. Gunning, "We Are Here and Not Here," 56.

21. Giambattista della Porta, *Natural Magick* (Thomas Young and Samuel Speed, 1658), 370.

22. Gunning, "The Long and Short of It," 28.

23. Gunning, "The Long and Short of It," 28.

24. Quoted in Laurent Mannoni, *The Great Art of Light and Shadow: Archaeology of the Cinema*, trans. and ed. Richard Crangle (University of Exeter Press, 2000), 162.

25. Jeremy Brooker, *The Temple of Minerva: Magic and the Magic Lantern at the Royal Polytechnic Institution, London 1837–1901* (Magic Lantern Society, 2013), 191.

26. David Brewster, *Letters on Natural Magic, Addressed to Sir Walter Scott* (John Murray, 1832), 5.

27. Brewster, *Letters on Natural Magic*, 5.

28. Charles Dickens, *A Christmas Carol and Other Stories* (Modern Library, 2001), 21.

29. Srdjan Smajic, *Ghost-Seers, Detectives and Spiritualists: Theories of Vision in Victorian Literature and Science* (Cambridge University Press, 2010), 29.

30. Barbara Stafford, *Artful Science: Enlightenment, Entertainment, and the Eclipse of Visual Education* (MIT Press, 1994), 47.

31. Stafford, *Artful Science*, 67.

32. William Hooper, *Rational Recreations: Volume the Second, Containing Experiments in Optics, Chromatics, and Acoustics*, 3rd ed. (L. Davis, 1787).

33. William Hooper, *Rational Recreations: Volume the First, Containing Arithmetical and Mechanical Experiments*, 3rd ed. (L. Davis, 1787), v.

34. Brewster, *Letters on Natural Magic*, 44.

35. Brewster, *Letters on Natural Magic*, 66.

36. Stafford, *Artful Science*, 67.

37. Brooker, *The Temple of Minerva*, 29.

38. Brewster, *Letters on Natural Magic*, 55.

39. Brewster, *Letters on Natural Magic*, 55.

40. Brewster, *Letters on Natural Magic*, 2.

41. Brewster, *Letters on Natural Magic*, 46.

42. Bellion, *Citizen Spectator*, 5.

43. Bellion, *Citizen Spectator*, 15.

44. Jennifer Pitts, *A Turn to Empire: The Rise of Imperial Liberalism in Britain and France* (Princeton University Press, 2006), 20.

45. Pitts, *A Turn to Empire*, 143.

46. Pitts, *A Turn to Empire*, 20–21.

47. Helen Groth, *Moving Images: Nineteenth-Century Reading and Screen Practices* (Edinburgh University Press, 2014), 96.

48. "A Shilling's Worth of Science," *Household Words* 1 (July 24, 1850): 508.

49. Arthur Sketchley, "Mrs. Brown Visits the Polytechnic," in *Mrs. Brown at the Play* (Routledge, 1871), 83.

50. Sketchley, "Mrs. Brown Visits the Polytechnic," 89–90.

51. Sketchley, "Mrs. Brown Visits the Polytechnic," 89.

52. Jeremy Brooker calls *Letters on Natural Magic* "a crucial document in articulating a philosophy" for galleries of science like the Royal Polytechnic Institution. Brooker, *The Temple of Minerva*, 17.

53. Morus, "More the Aspect of Magic," 338.

54. Elizabeth Gaskell, *Cranford* (Oxford University Press, 2011), 81. Further references to this text will be page numbers that are provided in parentheses.

55. *Cranford*'s representation of stage magic has received negligible treatment in scholarship about Gaskell. Sustained readings of magic in *Cranford* can be found in my article Amanda Shubert, "In Defense of Credulous Women: Magic and Optical Spectatorship in *Cranford*," *Victorian Studies* 63, no. 3 (Spring 2021): 377–400; Michael Jay Claxon, "The Conjurer Unmasked: Literary and Theatrical Magicians, 1840–1925" (PhD diss., University of North Carolina at

Chapel Hill, 2003). Brief discussions of magic and the figure of the magician appear in Adrienne E. Gavin, "Language Among the Amazons: Conjuring and Creativity in *Cranford*," *Dickens Studies Annual* 23 (1994): 205–25; Jeffrey Cass, "'The Scraps, Patches and Rags of Daily Life': Gaskell's Oriental Other and the Conservation of *Cranford*," *Papers on Language and Literature: A Journal for Scholars and Critics of Language and Literature* (Fall 1999): 417–33; Margaret Case Croskery, "Mothers Without Children, Unity Without Plot: *Cranford*'s Radical Charm," *Nineteenth-Century Literature* 52, no. 2 (September 1997): 198–220.

56. It is unclear whether Gaskell was aware that the "vanishing canary" trick, in which the magician made a canary vanish under a handkerchief and then reappear on a tray, really did involve killing the canary and then presenting a duplicate to the audience. An explanation of this trick can be found in Professor Hoffman, *Modern Magic: A Practical Treatise on the Art of Conjuring* (Routledge, 1894), 424–26.

57. Noam M. Elcott, *Artificial Darkness: An Obscure History of Modern Art and Media* (University of Chicago Press, 2016).

58. Signor Brunoni may have been modeled, at least in name, on Signor Blitz, a British stage magician born Antonio van Zandt who performed in London in the 1830s before settling in Philadelphia. Like Antonio van Zandt, the British Samuel Brown styles himself as a "Signor" in his stage act to present himself as an alluring and cosmopolitan foreigner. See Julie L. Melby, "Learned Birds and Other Acts," https://www.princeton.edu/~graphicarts/2012/04/broadside_1.html, accessed April 3, 2021; Bell, *The Magical Imagination*, 97.

59. Brewster, *Letters on Natural Magic*, 60.

60. Shubert, "In Defense of Credulous Women."

61. Hilary M. Schor, "Affairs of the Alphabet: Reading, Writing, and Narrating in *Cranford*," *NOVEL: A Forum on Fiction* 22, no. 3 (Spring 1989): 288–304.

62. Brewster, *Letters on Natural Magic*, 3.

63. Mary Wollstonecraft, *A Vindication of the Rights of Women, with Strictures on Moral and Political Subjects* (Cambridge University Press, 2012), 1–2.

64. Patrick Brantlinger, *Rule of Darkness: British Literature and Imperialism, 1830–1914* (Cornell University Press, 1988), 12–13.

65. Wendy Carse, "A Penchant for Narrative: Mary Smith in Elizabeth Gaskell's *Cranford*," *Journal of Narrative Technique* 20, no. 3 (1990): 326.

66. This motif of the conjurer's gaze dovetails with Hilary Schor's argument that Gaskell wrote into *Cranford* her editorial conflict with Charles Dickens, who published *Cranford* in serial in *Household Words*. In Schor's terms, "Dickens stands clearly as the male writer reading over Gaskell's shoulder as she writes *Cranford*," surveilling and censoring her work. Mary, who is herself a writer, literally fantasizes a man standing behind her and watching over her shoulder after being surveilled covertly by the conjurer. See Schor, "Affairs of the Alphabet," 293.

2. The Mirror of Ink

1. Jorge Luis Borges, "The Mirror of Ink," in *Collected Fictions*, trans. Andrew Hurley (Penguin, 1999), 60.

2. Borges, "The Mirror of Ink," 61.

3. Raymond Bellour, "Les mots-images," *Magazine Littéraire* 259 (1988): 64. My translation.

4. William Wordsworth, "Preface," in *Lyrical Ballads* (1802), in William Wordsworth and Samuel Taylor Coleridge, *Lyrical Ballads: 1789 and 1802* (Oxford University Press, 2013), 104. If anything, it is an embodiment of Wordsworth's greatest fear of "gross and violent stimulants" that "blunt the discriminating powers of the mind," examples of which for him included not only "frantic novels" but optical shows like panoramas. Wordsworth, "Preface," 99.

5. Peter Mendelsund, *What We See When We Read: A Phenomenology* (Random House, 2014), 11.

6. Mendelsund, *What We See When We Read*, 9.

7. Borges, "The Mirror of Ink," 61.

8. Susan Zieger, *The Mediated Mind: Affect, Ephemera, and Consumerism in the Nineteenth Century* (Fordham University Press, 2018), 105.

9. Zieger, *The Mediated Mind*, 90.

10. The scholarship on George Eliot and realism is too extensive to contain in a single footnote, but the following examples are representative of the ways that Victorian literary scholars have thought about Eliot's realism as constituted in visual techniques and metaphors: J. Hillis Miller, *Reading for Our Time: Adam Bede and Middlemarch Revisited* (Edinburgh University Press, 2012); Neil Hertz, *George Eliot's Pulse* (Stanford University Press, 2003); Ruth Bernard Yeazell, *Art of the Everyday: Dutch Painting and the Realist Novel* (Princeton University Press, 2009); Ruth Livesey, "George Eliot and Van Gogh: Radiant Realism," *19: Interdisciplinary Studies in the Nineteenth Century* 19 (2020): 1–26.

11. H. G. Wells, "The Remarkable Case of Mr. Davidson's Eyes," in H. G. Wells, *Short Stories* (Penguin, 1972), 182.

12. Sir John Barrow, "An Account of *Modern Egyptians*," *Quarterly Review* 59, no. 117 (July 1837): 195.

13. Edward Said, *Orientalism* (Pantheon, 1978), 149–66. Edward William Lane's substantial scholarly contributions include *Modern Egyptians* (1836), a translation of *The Thousand and One Nights* (1839–1841), *Selections from the Koran* (1843), and *Arab-English Lexicon* (1863–1893). For more on his career as an Orientalist, see Jason Thompson, *Edward William Lane, 1801–1876: The Life of the Pioneering Egyptologist and Orientalist* (American University in Cairo Press, 2010).

14. Jason Thompson, "Edward William Lane's 'Description of Egypt,'" *International Journal of Middle East Studies* 28, no. 4 (November 1996): 565–66.

15. Jason Thompson, "Edward William Lane in Egypt," *Journal of the American Research Center in Egypt* 34 (1997): 247.

16. Thompson, *Edward William Lane*, 312.

17. Said, *Orientalism*, 161–62.

18. Thompson, "Edward William Lane's 'Description of Egypt,'" 569.

19. Thompson, *Edward William Lane*, 20–21.

20. Edward William Lane, *An Account of the Manners and Customs of the Modern Egyptians* (Dover, 1973), 270. Further references to this text will be page numbers that are provided in parentheses.

21. Zieger, *The Mediated Mind*, 101.

22. See Tom Gunning, "Hand and Eye: Excavating a New Technology of the Image in the Victorian Era," *Victorian Studies* 54, no. 3 (April 2012): 495–515.

23. David Brewster, *Letters on Natural Magic, Addressed to Sir Walter Scott* (John Murray, 1832), 62, 65.

24. See Stefan Andriopoulos's discussion of Guyot's related illusion in Stefan Andriopoulos, "Kant's Magic Lantern: Historical Epistemology and Media Archaeology," *Representations* 115, no. 1 (August 2011): 49–50.

25. Brewster, *Letters on Natural Magic*, 62–63.

26. Barrow, "An Account of *Modern Egyptians*," 202.

27. However, he continued to promote Barrow's essay as essential reading on the mirror of ink, referring readers to it in his remarks on the mirror of ink in his translation of *The Thousand and One Nights*.

28. Lane, *An Account of the Manners and Customs*, 275.

29. Thompson, *Edward William Lane*, 313.

30. Jason Ananda Joseph Storm, *The Myth of Disenchantment: Magic, Modernity, and the Birth of the Human Sciences* (University of Chicago Press, 2017), 5–6.

31. Leah Price, *How to Do Things with Books in Victorian Britain* (Princeton University Press, 2012), 5–7.

32. Quoted in Thompson, "Edward William Lane's 'Description of Egypt,'" 556.

33. Anne McClintock, *Imperial Leather: Race, Gender and Sexuality in the Colonial Context* (Routledge, 1995), 22–23.

34. "What Is Reading & Writing, & What Are the Advantages Likely to Accrue from a Knowledge Thereof?," *Mirror of Literature, Amusement, and Instruction* 12, no. 1 (1842): 203–4.

35. William MacLure Thomson, *The Land and the Book, or Biblical Illustrations Drawn from the Manner and Customs, the Scenes and Scenery of the Holy Land* (Harper, 1859), 228.

36. See Mary-Louise Pratt, *Imperial Eyes: Travel Writing and Transculturation* (Routledge, 2007).

37. See Nicholas Mirzoeff, *The Right to Look: A Counterhistory of Visuality* (Duke University Press, 2011).

38. Sophia Lane-Poole, *The Englishwoman in Egypt: Letters from Cairo, Written During a Residence There in 1842, 3, & 4*, vol. 1 (Charles Knight, 1845), 168.

39. George Eliot, *Adam Bede* (Oxford University Press, 2008), 161–62. Further references to this text will be page numbers that are provided in parentheses.

40. The scholarship on Eliot and realism is extensive, but I am thinking here of key works on Eliot as a novelist of ordinary life, including Josephine McDonagh, *George Eliot* (Liverpool University Press, 1997); Harry Shaw, *Narrating Reality: Austen, Scott, Eliot* (Cornell University Press, 2004); Miller, *Reading for Our Time*; Rae Greiner, *Sympathetic Realism in Nineteenth-Century British Fiction* (Johns Hopkins University Press, 2013). Examples of scholarship that place Eliot's realism of ordinary life in the context of realist painting include Peter Brooks, *Realist Vision* (Yale University Press, 2005); Livesey, "George Eliot and Van Gogh"; Deborah Nord, "George Eliot and John Everett Millais: The Ethics and Aesthetics of Realism," *Victorian Studies* 60, no. 3 (2018): 361–89; Yeazell, *Art of the Everyday*.

41. See Alison Byerly, *Are We There Yet? Virtual Travel and Victorian Realism* (University of Michigan Press, 2012).

42. Readings of *Adam Bede*'s mirror of ink as part of the novel's theory of representation can be found in Hertz, *George Eliot's Pulse*, 97–101; Miller, *Reading for Our Time*, 12–14; Monica Fludernik, "Eliot and Narrative," in *A Companion to George Eliot*, ed. Amanda Anderson and Harry Shaw (Wiley, 2013), 21–34. A careful reading of the mirror motif in *Adam Bede* in relation to nineteenth-century optical technology can be found in Meegan Kennedy, *Revising the Clinic: Vision and Representation in Victorian Medical Narrative and the Novel* (Ohio State University Press, 2010), 119–47, although Kennedy does not discuss the mirror of ink itself. Susan Zieger correctly identifies *Adam Bede*'s mirror of ink as part of a culture of ink gazing as a "participatory visual entertainment," but she does not elaborate on the metafictional significance of the passage. See Zieger, *The Mediated Mind*, 88.

43. See Kennedy, *Revising the Clinic*, 119–47.

44. Rachel Teukolsky, *Picture World: Image, Aesthetics, and Victorian New Media* (Oxford University Press, 2019), 134.

45. Teukolsky, *Picture World*, 135.

46. Miller, *Reading for Our Time*, 13.

47. Fludernik, "Eliot and Narrative," 22.

48. Fludernik, "Eliot and Narrative," 22.

49. Hertz, *George Eliot's Pulse*, 100.

50. Jacob Romanow, "Metafiction as Reality Effect: Trollope's Quixotism and Novel Theory," *ELH* 89, no. 4 (2022): 1078–79.

51. Teukolsky, *Picture World*, 129–38; Byerly, *Are We There Yet?*, 73–80.

52. Teukolsky, *Picture World*, 135.

53. See Alison Winter, *Mesmerized: Powers of Mind in Victorian Britain* (University of Chicago Press, 1988).

54. Lane, *An Account of the Manners and Customs*, 272n2.

55. For a description of the tour, see Caroline Roberts, *The Woman and the Hour: Harriet Martineau and Victorian Ideologies* (University of Toronto Press, 2002), 139–40.

56. Harriet Martineau, *Eastern Life, Past and Present*, vol. 2 (Lea and Blanchard, 1848), 138.

57. Winter, *Mesmerized*, 122.

58. Winter, *Mesmerized*, 122.

59. Harriet Martineau to Robinson, October 6, 1844, Robinson Papers. Quoted in Winter, *Mesmerized*, 224.

60. Martineau, *Eastern Life*, 256. On the dynamics of race and blackness in Martineau's account of the mirror of ink, see Zieger, *The Mediated Mind*, 107.

61. Martineau, *Eastern Life*, 255.

62. Martineau, *Eastern Life*, 256.

63. Richard Francis Burton, *Personal Narrative of a Pilgrimage to El-Medinah and Mecca*, vol. 2 (Longman, 1855–1856), 180. Paulo Lemos Horta argues that the mirror of ink "proves uncannily prominent in Burton's self-fashioning as a cosmopolite" and allowed him to distinguish his cross-cultural and comparative ethnographic methods from Lane's monocultural approach. See Paulo

Lemos Horta, "Richard Burton, Cosmopolitan Translator of the *Nights*," in *Scheherazade's Children*, ed. Philip F. Kennedy and Marina Warner (New York University Press, 2013), 70–85.

64. Isabel Burton, *The Life of Captain Sir Richard F. Burton*, vol. 2 (Chapman & Hall, 1893), 137–58.

65. Burton, *The Life of Captain Sir Richard F. Burton*, 144.

66. "Mesmeric Phenomena," *The Era*, no. 149 (August 1, 1841): 11.

67. Wilkie Collins, "Magnetic Evenings at Home," *The Leader* (February 28, 1852): 19–20.

68. Wilkie Collins, "My Black Mirror," *Household Words* 14 (September 6, 1856): 169.

69. Vanessa Ryan, *Thinking Without Thinking in the Victorian Novel* (Johns Hopkins University Press, 2012), 47.

70. Gordon Haight, *George Eliot: A Biography* (Clarendon, 1968), 55.

71. Emily Ogden, *Credulity: A Cultural History of US Mesmerism* (University of Chicago Press, 2018), 103.

72. Ogden, *Credulity*, 103.

73. Ogden, *Credulity*, 103–4.

74. Robert H. Collyer, *Psychography, or, the Embodiment of Thought, with an Analysis of Phreno-Magnetism, "Neurology," and Mental Hallucination, Including Rules to Govern and Produce the Magnetic State* (Redding, 1843), 31.

75. For readings of *The Lifted Veil* in the context of new media, optical technology, and sciences of mind, see Kate Flint, *Victorians and the Visual Imagination* (Cambridge University Press, 2008); Jules Law, *The Social Life of Fluids: Blood, Milk and Water in the Victorian Novel* (Cornell University Press, 2011); Richard Menke, *Telegraphic Realism: Victorian Fiction and Other Information Systems* (Stanford University Press, 2008); Nicholas Royle, *Telepathy and Literature: Essays on the Reading Mind* (Blackwell, 1991); Julian Wolfreys, *Victorian Hauntings: Spectrality, Gothic, the Uncanny and Literature* (Macmillan, 2002).

76. Menke, *Telegraphic Realism*, 140.

77. Law, *The Social Life of Fluids*, 88. See also Potter's reading of Latimer's visions as dissolving views in Jonathan Potter, *Discourses of Vision in Nineteenth-Century Britain: Seeing, Thinking, Writing* (Palgrave Macmillan, 2018), 89–92.

78. George Eliot, *The Lifted Veil and Brother Jacob* (Oxford World's Classics, 1999), 9.

79. Eliot, *The Lifted Veil*, 41.

80. Hertz, *George Eliot's Pulse*, 100.

81. Mendelsund, *What We See When We Read*, 11.

82. Maxim Gorky, "The Kingdom of Shadows," in *Authors on Film*, ed. Harry M. Geduld (Indiana University Press, 1972).

83. I wish to thank Kaneesha Parsard for sharing this observation about the colonial significance of molasses.

84. Wells, "The Remarkable Case of Mr. Davidson's Eyes," 182.

85. Wells, "The Remarkable Case of Mr. Davidson's Eyes," 180.

86. Wells, "The Remarkable Case of Mr. Davidson's Eyes," 182.

87. Wells, "The Remarkable Case of Mr. Davidson's Eyes," 183.

88. It may also be inspired by the cases of traveling clairvoyants who traversed the far reaches of empire while under mesmeric influence, such as the case in which a clairvoyant "found" the lost explorer John Franklin through a mesmeric trance and saw things "only expert mariners and explorers could have known." See Winter, *Mesmerized*, 124.

89. This reading of "The Remarkable Case of Mr. Davidson's Eyes" as an exploration of realist fiction and travel writing's claim to represent the real aligns with John Plotz's account of Wells as a "realist of the fantastic," whose early scientific romances represent "various states of partial presence," with characters simultaneously anchored in reality and "drifting away." Indeed, Plotz argues that Wells offers a crucial link between Eliot's mid-century realism and the late nineteenth-century rise of speculative fiction. John Plotz, *Semi-Detached: The Aesthetics of Virtual Experience Since Dickens* (Princeton University Press, 2018), 176.

3. Mountains of Light

1. William Dalrymple and Anita Anand, *Koh-i-Noor: The History of the World's Most Infamous Diamond* (Bloomsbury, 2017), 7.

2. "London, Monday, July 1, 1850," *The Times*, no. 20529 (July 1, 1850): 4, accessed July 27, 2022, link-gale-com.ezproxy.library.wisc.edu/apps/doc/CS67666657/GDCS?u=wisc_madison&sid=bookmark-GDCS&xid=e800ba36.

3. "London, Monday, July 1, 1850," 4.

4. Danielle Kinsey, "Koh-i-Noor: Empire, Diamonds, and the Performance of British Material Culture," *Journal of British Studies* 48, no. 2 (April 2009): 392.

5. See John Plotz, *Portable Property: Victorian Culture on the Move* (Princeton University Press, 2009); Shashi Tharoor, *Inglorious Empire: What the British Did to India* (Hurst, 2017), 12–13.

6. "The Front Row of the Shilling Gallery," *Punch* 5 (July 1851): 11; "The Koh-i-Noor Cut and Come Again," *Punch* 23 (August 1852): 54.

7. "The Great Eastern Nave," *The Illustrated Exhibitor* 1 (June 7, 1851): 19.

8. See Plotz, *Portable Property*. Other cultural histories of Victorian diamonds have foregrounded their status as material culture, imperial symbols, and role in domestic life and social constructions of gender. See Kinsey, "Koh-i-Noor"; Suzanne Daley, *The Empire Inside: Indian Commodities and Victorian Domestic Novels* (University of Michigan Press, 2011); Adrienne Munich, *Empire of Diamonds: Victorian Gems in Imperial Settings* (University of Virginia Press, 2020).

9. On the concept of imperial media, see Aaron Worth, *Imperial Media: Colonial Networks and Information Technologies in the British Literary Imagination, 1857–1918* (Ohio State University Press, 2014).

10. I agree with Danielle Kinsey, Paul Young, Lara Kriegel, and others who argue that there were multiple, contradictory narratives of empire and British India at the Great Exhibition and that the Koh-i-noor must be understood as signifying in multiple ways. See Kinsey, "Koh-i-Noor"; Paul Young, "'Carbon, Mere Carbon': The Kohinoor, the Crystal Palace, and the Mission to Make Sense of British India," *Nineteenth-Century Contexts* 29, no. 2 (December 2007): 343–58; Lara Kriegel, "Narrating the Subcontinent," in *The Great Exhibition of*

1851: New Interdisciplinary Essays, ed. Louise Purbick (University of Manchester Press, 2001).

11. See Plotz, *Portable Property*; Daley, *The Empire Inside*; Kinsey, "Koh-i-Noor"; Munich, *Empire of Diamonds*; Jean Arnold, *Victorian Jewelry, Identity, and the Novel: Prisms of Culture* (Ashgate, 2011); Marcia Pointon, *Brilliant Effects: A Cultural History of Gem Stones and Jewellery* (Yale University Press, 2009).

12. Dalrymple and Anand, *Koh-i-Noor*, 19.

13. Daley, *The Empire Inside*, 62.

14. Tharoor, *Inglorious Empire*, 12.

15. Munich, *Empire of Diamonds*, 3. On the aesthetics of diamonds, see also Stefanie Markovits, "Form Things: Looking at Genre Through Victorian Diamonds," *Victorian Studies* 52, no. 4 (Summer 2010): 591–619.

16. Isobel Armstrong, *Victorian Glassworlds: Glass Culture and the Imagination, 1830–1880* (Oxford University Press, 2008), 12.

17. Pointon, *Brilliant Effects*, 44.

18. Munich, *Empire of Diamonds*, 3.

19. A. D. Morris-Low, "Brewster and Scientific Instruments," in *"Martyr of Science": Sir David Brewster 1781–1863: Proceedings of a Bicentary Symposium: Held at the Royal Scottish Museum of 21 November 1981: Together with a Catalogue of Scientific Apparatus Associated with Sir David Brewster: And a Bibliography of His Published Writings*, ed. A. D. Morrison-Low and J. R. R. Christie (Royal Scottish Museum, 1984), 60. On the jewel microscope, see Gerard L'Estrange Turner, "The Rise and Fall of the Jewel Microscope," in *Essays on the History of Microscope* (Senecio, 1980), 109–10.

20. Andrew Pritchard, *The Microscopic Cabinet of Select Animated Objects: With a Description of the Jewel and Doublet Microscope, Test Objects, &c., to Which Are Subjoined, Memoirs on the Verification of Microscopic Phenomena, and an Exact Method of Appreciating the Quality of Microscopes and Engiscopes* (Whittaker, Treacher, and Arnot, 1832), 106–7.

21. David Brewster, "On the Microphotograph," *Photographic Journal* 8 (January 15, 1864): 441.

22. Priti Joshi, *Empire of News: The Anglo-Indian Press Writes India* (State University of New York Press, 2021), 93.

23. John Tallis, *Tallis' History of the Crystal Palace*, vol. 2 (London Printing and Publishing, 1852), 150.

24. Kriegel, "Narrating the Subcontinent," 166.

25. Kinsey, "Koh-i-Noor," 406.

26. Kriegel, "Narrating the Subcontinent."

27. Joshi, *Empire of News*, 93.

28. Kriegel, "Narrating the Subcontinent," 166.

29. Dalrymple and Anand, *Koh-i-Noor*, 188.

30. Dalrymple and Anand, *Koh-i-Noor*, 185.

31. Kinsey, "Koh-i-Noor," 393; Dalrymple and Anand, *Koh-i-Noor*, 203; Joshi, *Empire of News*, 94–95.

32. Dalrymple and Anand, *Koh-i-Noor*, 191, 203.

33. Dalrymple and Anand, *Koh-i-Noor*, 6–7.

34. Dalrymple and Anand, *Koh-i-Noor*, 118, 121.

35. Kinsey, "Koh-i-Noor," 396.

36. Kinsey, "Koh-i-Noor," 396.

37. Dalrymple and Anand, *Koh-i-Noor*, 223.

38. "The Great Eastern Nave," 19.

39. "The Koh-i-Noor Diamond," *Reynolds Miscellany of Romance, General Literature, Science, and Art* 13, no. 335 (December 9, 1854): 312; "Five Shilling Days and One Shilling Days," *Illustrated London News* (July 1851): 102; "Interesting to Burglars, Philosophers, &c.," *The Leader* 2, no. 60 (May 17, 1851): 465.

40. Armstrong, *Victorian Glassworlds*, 230.

41. Armstrong, *Victorian Glassworlds*, 142.

42. Quoted in Armstrong, *Victorian Glassworlds*, 142.

43. "Interesting to Burglars, Philosophers, &c," 465.

44. Dalrymple and Anand, *Koh-i-Noor*, 3–4.

45. Dalrymple and Anand, *Koh-i-Noor*, 223.

46. Dalrymple and Anand, *Koh-i-Noor*, 216.

47. Charles King, *Antique Gems: Their Use, Origin, and Value as Interpreters of Ancient History; and as Illustrative of Ancient Art* (John Murray, 1860), 68.

48. John R. Davis, *The Great Exhibition* (Sutton, 1999), 138.

49. Charles Baggage, "Art. IX—The Exposition of 1851; or, Views of the Industry, the Science, and the Government of England. By Charles Baggage, Esq., Corresponding Member of the Academy of Moral Sciences of the Institute of France. London, 1851. Second Edition," *North British Review* 15 (1851): 542.

50. Armstrong, *Victorian Glassworlds*, 142.

51. Margaret Maria Gordon, *The Home Life of David Brewster* (Cambridge University Press, 2011), 213; Dalrymple and Anand, *Koh-i-Noor*, 225.

52. "Precious Stones in the Crystal Palace," *The Illustrated Exhibitor*, no. 6 (July 12): 94, accessed July 27, 2022, https://hdl.handle.net/2027/uc1.31175001860983?urlappend=%3Bseq=160.

53. "The Front Row of the Shilling Gallery," 11.

54. "The Koh-i-Noor Cut and Come Again," 54.

55. See Kinsey, "Koh-i-Noor."

56. "Preface," *The Parlour Magazine of the Literature of All Nations*, vol. 1, n.p.

57. Kevin Corstorphine, "Fitz-James O'Brien: The Seen and the Unseen," *The Green Book: Writings on Irish Gothic, Supernatural, and Fantastic Literature*, no. 5 (Bealtaine, 2015), 15.

58. Fitz-James O'Brien, "The Diamond Lens," in *The Diamond Lens and Other Stories* (Hesperus, 2012), 9. Further references to this text will be page numbers that are provided in parentheses.

59. O'Brien may also have been thinking of the rumor that the Pitt Diamond, the 400-carat gem acquired by Thomas Pitt in 1702 while he was serving as governor of Madras, was smuggled from its mine by an enslaved man. Tharoor, *Inglorious Empire*, 12–13.

60. Pritchard, *The Microscopic Cabinet of Select Animated Objects*, 108.

61. David Arnold, "Envisioning the Tropics: Joseph Hooker in India and the Himalayas, 1848–1850," in *Tropical Visions in an Age of Empire*, ed. Felix Driver and Luciana Martins (University of Chicago Press, 2005), 137.

62. See Meegen Kennedy, " 'Throes and Struggles . . . Witnessed with Painful Distinctness': The Oxy-Hydrogen Microscope, Performing Science, and the Projection of the Moving Image," *Victorian Studies* 62, no. 1 (2019): 85–118;

Jeremy Brooker, *The Temple of Minerva: Magic and the Magic Lantern at the Royal Polytechnic Institution, London 1887–1901* (Magic Lantern Society, 2013).

63. Rachel Teukolsky, *Picture World: Image, Aesthetics, and Victorian New Media* (Oxford University Press, 2020), 285.

64. *The Athenaeum* 1586 (March 20, 1858), 371-72.

65. See Tiago de Luca, *Planetary Cinema: Film, Media, and the Earth* (Amsterdam University Press, 2021).

66. De Luca, *Planetary Cinema*, 144.

67. I have not been able to source which world's fair this is, but handwritten notes on the back of the stereograph itself—which is in the collection of the Victoria and Albert Museum—suggest that it is either the International Exhibition of 1865 (Dublin) or the International Exhibition of 1867 (Paris).

68. Anne McClintock, *Imperial Leather: Race, Gender and Sexuality in the Colonial Context* (Routledge, 1995), 57-58.

69. Quoted in Young, "Carbon, Mere Carbon," 344.

70. Kriegel, "Narrating the Subcontinent," 155.

71. Wilkie Collins, *The Moonstone* (Modern Library, 2001), xxiv. Further references to this text will be page numbers that are provided in parentheses.

72. Arnold, *Victorian Jewelry, Identity, and the Novel*, 80. Collins likely conflates Shiva in his incarnation as Somanatha, "Lord of the Moon," who was indeed worshipped at a shrine at Somnauth, with Vishnu, who is often depicted as having four arms. See Collins, *The Moonstone*, 485n3.

73. King, *Ancient Gems*, 68n.

74. Jenny Sharpe, *Allegories of Empire: The Figure of the Woman in the Colonial Text* (University of Minnesota Press, 1993), 61-69.

75. Ian Duncan, "*The Moonstone*, the Victorian Novel, and Imperialist Panic," *Modern Language Quarterly* 55, no. 3 (September 1994): 300.

76. "What the Richer Are We?," *The Expositor: A Weekly Recorder of Inventions, Designs, and Art-Manufactures* (May 24, 1851): 59.

77. Edward Said, *Orientalism: Western Concepts of the Orient* (Penguin India, 2008), 128.

78. Collins's original title for the novel was *The Serpent's Eye*, an allusion to the gemstone serpentine. See Mark M. Hennelly, "Detecting Collins' Diamond: From Serpentstone to Moonstone," *Nineteenth-Century Fiction* 39, no. 1 (1984): 25-47.

79. Harriet Martineau, *Eastern Life, Past and Present*, vol. 2 (Lea and Blanchard, 1848), 256.

80. Susan Zieger, *The Mediated Mind: Affect, Ephemera, and Consumerism in the Nineteenth Century* (Fordham University Press, 2018), 114.

81. E. M. Collingwood, *Imperial Bodies: The Physical Experience of the Raj, c. 1800–1947* (Polity, 2001), 1.

4. Recalled to Life

1. Karl Marx, *The Eighteenth Brumaire of Louis Bonaparte* (Wildside Press, 2008), 15.

2. On ghosts in Marx, *The Eighteenth Brumaire*, see Jacques Derrida, *Specters of Marx: The State of Debt, the Work of Mourning, and the New International*, trans.

Peggy Kamuf (Routledge, 1994), 107–20; Martin Harries, "Homo Alludens: Marx's Eighteenth Brumaire," *New German Critique* 66 (Autumn 1995): 35–64.

3. Terrell Carver, "Imagery/Writing, Imagination/Politics: Reading Marx Through the Eighteenth Brumaire," in *Marx's 'Eighteenth Brumaire': (Post)Modern Interpretations*, ed. Mark Cowling and James Martin (Pluto, 2002), 121.

4. Marx, *The Eighteenth Brumaire*, 15.

5. Marx, *The Eighteenth Brumaire*, 16.

6. Marx, *The Eighteenth Brumaire*, 20.

7. Accounts of the phantasmagoria have tended to focus on three distinct areas: its relationship to the gothic, influence on German philosophy, and place in the history of cinema. On the phantasmagoria as gothic medium, see Francesco Casetti, "Rethinking the Phantasmagoria: An Enclosure and Three Worlds," *Journal of Visual Culture* 21, no. 2 (2022): 349–73; Terry Castle, "Phantasmagoria: Spectral Technology and the Metaphorics of Modern Reverie," *Critical Inquiry* 15, no. 1 (October 1988): 26–61; David J. Jones, *Gothic Machine: Textualities, Pre-Cinematic Media and Film in Popular Visual Culture, 1670–1910* (University of Wales Press, 2011), 57–78. On the phantasmagoria's legacy in German idealist and Marxist philosophy, see Stefan Andriopoulos, *Ghostly Apparitions: German Idealism, the Gothic Novel, and Optical Media* (Zone, 2013), 49–72; Margaret Cohen, "Walter Benjamin's Phantasmagoria," *New German Critique* 48 (1989): 87–107. On the phantasmagoria as precinematic visual spectacle, see Noam M. Elcott, "The Phantasmagorical Dispositif: An Assembly of Bodies and Images in Real Time and Space," in *Screen Space Reconfigured*, ed. Susanne Ø. Saether and Synne T. Bull (Amsterdam University Press, 2020), 283–316; Thomas Elsaesser, "Between Knowing and Believing: The Cinematic Dispositif After Cinema," in *Cine-Dispositifs: Essays in Epistemology Across Media*, ed. François Albera and Maria Tortajada (Amsterdam University Press, 2015), 45–72; Tom Gunning, "Illusions Past and Future: The Phantasmagoria and Its Specters," paper presented at the First International Conference on the Histories of Art, Science, and Technology, Banff New Media Institute, Canada, 2005, https://www.mediaarthistory.org/refresh/Programmatic%20key%20texts/pdfs/Gunning.pdf; Tom Gunning, "The Long and the Short of It: Centuries of Projecting Shadows, from Natural Magic to the Avant-Garde," in *The Art of Projection*, ed. Stan Douglas and Christopher Eamon (Hatje Cantz Verlag, 2009), 23–35; Tom Gunning, "The Phantasmagoria and the Manufacturing of Illusion and Wonder: Towards a Cultural Optics of the Cinematic Apparatus," in *The Cinema: A New Technology for the 20th Century*, ed. André Gaudreault, Catherine Russell, and Pierre Véronneau (Editions Payot, 2004), 32–44.

8. Simon During, *Modern Enchantments: The Cultural Power of Secular Magic* (Harvard University Press, 2002), 104.

9. See my article: Amanda Shubert, "A Bright Continuous Flow: Phantasmagoria and History in *A Tale of Two Cities*," *Victorian Literature and Culture* 48, no. 4 (2020): 693–720. Some of the research and analysis in this chapter derives from my earlier article, although the argument and approach differ substantially. I will indicate in the endnotes when my chapter corrects mistakes made in the article.

10. Max Milner, *La Fantasmagorie: Essai sur l'optique fantastique* (Presses universitaires de France, 1982), 20. My translation.

11. Mervyn Heard, *Phantasmagoria: The Secret Life of the Magic Lantern* (Projection Box, 2006), 76.

12. Heard, *Phantasmagoria*, 83. The reason I call this a possible account of his disappearance is that Tussaud is actually speaking of a man named Paul de Philipstahl, who Heard believes is the same as Paul Philidor. I am somewhat more circumspect about whether the evidence points definitively in this direction.

13. Laurent Mannoni, "The Phantasmagoria," trans. Ben Brewster, *Film History* 8, no. 4 (1996): 397.

14. Mannoni, "The Phantasmagoria," 398.

15. Mannoni, "The Phantasmagoria," 397–98.

16. Heard, *Phantasmagoria*.

17. Gunning, "The Phantasmagoria and the Manufacturing of Illusion and Wonder," 34.

18. Casetti, "Rethinking the Phantasmagoria," 356.

19. Elsaesser, "Between Knowing and Believing," 67–70.

20. Elcott, "The Phantasmagoric Dispositif," 291.

21. Elcott, "The Phantasmagoric Dispositif," 298.

22. On the phantasmagoria as gothic assemblage, see Jones, *Gothic Machine*.

23. Elsaesser, "Between Knowing and Believing," 69–70.

24. Ronen Steinberg, *The Afterlives of the Terror: Facing the Legacies of Mass Violence in Postrevolutionary France* (Cornell University Press, 2019), 128. Steinberg wrongly attributes the invention of the phantasmagoria to Robertson and therefore reads it as the product of postrevolutionary France that reflects on the legacy of the Reign of Terror, when in fact it emerged much earlier—after the formation of the republic and just a month before the execution of the king. However, his argument that Robertson's phantasmagoria offered a means of making sense of the legacy of the Terror still stands.

25. Steinberg, *The Afterlives of the Terror*, 126–28.

26. For example, Mervyn Heard and Ronen Steinberg cite this editorial as an eyewitness report, a mistake I uncritically reproduced in my essay Shubert, "A Bright Continuous Flow."

27. François Martin Poultier D'Elmotte, "Fantasmagorie," *L'Ami des Lois, par le représentant Poultier, et autres gens de lettres, sous la direction des frères Sibuet, propriétaires* 955 (March 28, 1798), 1. All translations from this editorial are my own, with assistance from Grace An.

28. The source of the error seems to be an 1871 English edition of Fulgence Marion's *The Wonders of Optics* that was translated and edited by Charles W. Quin (Scribner, 1871). Quin's translation of this line as "A decimvir of the republic has said that the dead return no more, but go to Robertson's exhibition and you will soon be convinced of the contrary, for you will see the dead returning to life in crowds" makes it difficult to identify the "decimvir" in question as Bertrand Barère. For example, Barère's aphorism was known in Victorian culture as "only the dead return not," not as "the dead return no more." Along with other scholars like Mervyn Heard, my essay, Shubert, "A Bright Continuous Flow," quoted Quin's translation without comparing it critically with the French original. I am grateful to Ellen Perry and Julie Hayes for helping me identify the quotation from Barère.

29. See Bertrand Barrère, *Memoirs of Bertrand Barère*, vol. 1, trans. De V. Payen-Payne (H. S. Nichols, 1896), 14.

30. D'Elmotte, "Fantasmagorie," 2.

31. D'Elmotte, "Fantasmagorie," 1.

32. D'Elmotte, "Fantasmagorie," 1.

33. Étienne-Gaspard Robertson, *Mémoires récreatifs, scientifiques, et anecdotiques du physician-aéronaute E. G. Robertson* (Librairie encyclopédique de Roret, 1840), 215. All translations are my own, unless otherwise marked.

34. See Casetti, "Rethinking the Phantasmagoria."

35. Robertson, *Mémoires récreatifs*.

36. Robertson, *Mémoires récreatifs*, 283–84; Heard, *Phantasmagoria*, 111.

37. Quoted in Casetti, "Rethinking the Phantasmagoria," 353.

38. Mannoni, "The Phantasmagoria," 398. Robertson was among the first to introduce Galvanism in France.

39. Jones, *Gothic Machine*, 65.

40. Jones, *Gothic Machine*, 65.

41. Jones, *Gothic Machine*, 61.

42. Jones, *Gothic Machine*, 61.

43. Robertson, *Mémoires récreatifs*, 276.

44. Suzanne Glover Lindsay, "The Revolutionary Exhumations at St-Denis, 1793," *Conversations: An Online Journal of the Center for the Study of Material and Visual Cultures of Religion* (2014), https://doi.org/10.22332/con.ess.2015.2.

45. Robertson, *Mémoires récreatifs*, 276.

46. Lindsay, "The Revolutionary Exhumations at St-Denis."

47. Joss Marsh, "Dickensian 'Dissolving Views': The Magic Lantern, Visual Story-Telling, and the Victorian Technological Imagination," *Comparative Critical Studies* 6, no. 3 (2009): 334.

48. Marsh, "Dickensian 'Dissolving Views,'" 334.

49. During, *Modern Enchantments*, 145. For a more thorough discussion of Pepper's Ghost, see chapter 1 of this book.

50. Thomas Hardy, *The Return of the Native* (Oxford World's Classics, 2005), 337.

51. See Castle, "Phantasmagoria."

52. Amy Levy, *Reuben Sachs* (Broadview, 2006), 133.

53. Marx read Carlyle's *The French Revolution: A History*, which Jean Bruhat lists among the sources Marx consulted on the history of the French Revolution. See Jean Bruhat, "La Révolution française et la formation de la pensée de Marx," *Annales historiques de la Révolution française* 184, no. 1 (1966): 125–70.

54. Castle, "Phantasmagoria," 26. For other discussions of "phantasmagoria" and "phantasmagory" as key terms in Carlyle's oeuvre, see Mark Cumming, *A Disimprisoned Epic: Form and Vision in Carlyle's* French Revolution (University of Pennsylvania Press, 1988), 131–48; Tamara Gosta, "Thomas Carlyle's 'Real-Phantasmagory': The Historical Sublime and Humanist Politics in *Past and Present*," *Studies in the Literary Imagination* 45, no. 1 (Spring 2012): 89–111; John D. Rosenberg, *Carlyle and the Burden of History* (Clarendon, 1985), 24.

55. Thomas Carlyle, *The French Revolution: A History in Three Volumes, Vol. I: The Bastille*, ed. Mark Cumming and David R. Sorensen (Oxford University Press, 2020), 146.

56. Thomas Carlyle, *The French Revolution: A History in Three Volumes, Vol. III: The Guillotine*, ed. Mark Cumming and David R. Sorensen (Oxford University Press, 2020), 22.

57. Thomas Carlyle, "On History," in *The Works of Thomas Carlyle: Volume 27: Critical and Miscellaneous Essays*, ed. Henry Duff Traill (Cambridge University Press, 2010), 88.

58. Carlyle, "On History," 90.

59. Hayden White, *Metahistory: The Historical Imagination in Nineteenth-Century Europe* (Johns Hopkins University Press, 1973), 149.

60. Thomas Carlyle, "The Diamond Necklace," in *The Works of Thomas Carlyle: Volume 28: Critical and Miscellaneous Essays III*, ed. Henry Duff Traill (Cambridge University Press, 2010), 328.

61. See Jonathan Potter, *Discourses of Vision in Nineteenth-Century Britain: Seeing, Thinking, Writing* (Palgrave Macmillan, 2018), 69–107.

62. For a more concrete description of how the phantasmagoria created this effect using slipping slides, see Shubert, "A Bright Continuous Flow."

63. Carlyle, *The French Revolution, Vol. I*, 160–61.

64. I am thinking here of what Richard Schoch identifies as an "aspiration towards the theatrical" in Carlyle's work, arguing that he adopts theatrical conventions in order to provide his readers with a "vibrant, animated, and enacted history." Building on Schoch's work, I propose that the theatrical form that history and history writing most resemble in *The French Revolution* is the phantasmagoria. See Richard W. Schoch, "'We Do Nothing but Enact History': Thomas Carlyle Stages the Past," *Nineteenth-Century Literature* 54, no. 1 (1999): 33.

65. Nora Foster, "'Free of Formulas': Innovation, Prophecy, and Truth in Thomas Carlyle's *The French Revolution*," *Carlyle Studies Annual* 24 (2008): 106.

66. On this point, see Tamara Gosta's claim that Carlyle's use of the term "real-phantasmagory" in *Past and Present* (1843) indexes the historical text's capacity to "materializ[e] a forgotten past." Gosta, "Thomas Carlyle's 'Real-Phantasmagory,'" 107.

67. Michael Goldberg, *Carlyle and Dickens* (University of Georgia Press, 1972), 161.

68. Charles Dickens, *A Tale of Two Cities* (Penguin, 2003), 117. Further references to this text will be page numbers that are provided in parentheses.

69. Sergei Eisenstein, "Dickens, Griffith, and the Film Today," in *Film Form: Essays in Film Theory*, ed. and trans. Jay Leyda (Harcourt, 1949), 213–14.

70. I develop this point more fully in Shubert, "A Bright Continuous Flow," 702–11.

71. See Robertson, *Mémoires récreatifs*, as well as Heard's translation of Robertson's program in Heard, *Phantasmagoria*, 107–10.

72. Robertson, *Mémoires récreatifs*, 283.

73. Robertson, *Mémoires récreatifs*, 327.

74. Georg Lukàcs, *The Historical Novel*, trans. Hannah Mitchell and Stanley Mitchell (University of Nebraska Press, 1983), 243.

75. Lukàcs, *The Historical Novel*, 42.

76. Fredric Jameson, *The Antinomies of Realism* (Verso, 2015), 286.

77. In my earlier publication on this topic, I was unaware of the semantic similarities between "Robertson, Artist in Ghosts" and *Mémoires récreatifs* and mistakenly attributed language to Dickens that actually has its origins in Robertson's memoir. See Shubert, "A Bright Continuous Flow," 698–99.

78. See Helen Groth, *Moving Images: Nineteenth-Century Reading and Screen Practices* (Edinburgh University Press, 2014), 100–125; Marsh, "Dickensian 'Dissolving Views'"; Christopher Pittard, "The Travelling Doll Wonder: Dickens, Secular Magic, and *Bleak House*," *Studies in the Novel* 48, no. 3 (Fall 2016): 279–300; Grahame Smith, *Dickens and the Dream of Cinema* (Manchester University Press, 2003).

79. Charles Dickens, "Robertson, Artist in Ghosts," *Household Words*, no. 253 (January 27, 1855): 557.

80. Dickens, "Robertson, Artist in Ghosts," 554, 555.

81. Dickens, "Robertson, Artist in Ghosts," 557.

82. Robertson, *Mémoires récreatifs*, 166.

83. Giacomo Leopardi, *Pensieri*, trans. W. S. Di Piero (Louisiana State University Press, 1981), 37–39.

84. Gunning, "The Long and Short of It," 28. Gunning also notes that a strikingly similar scene takes place in Bertolt Brecht's *Galileo*.

85. Because Robertson refers to it as an existing story—the reader is interpellated as "hav[ing] seen" these events take place—it is, of course, possible that both Robertson and Leopardi share a different common source, although Leopardi's dating of the event to 1831 does seem like a covert acknowledgment that his source is Robertson, *Mémoires récreatifs*, which was published that year.

86. Dickens, "Robertson, Artist in Ghosts," 557.

87. Lukàcs, *The Historical Novel*, 23.

88. Lukàcs, *The Historical Novel*, 23.

89. Linda Colley, *Britons: Forging the Nation 1707–1837* (Pimlico, 2003), 3.

90. Priti Joshi, "Mutiny Echoes: India, Britons, and Charles Dickens' *A Tale of Two Cities*," in *Global Dickens*, ed. John O. Jordan and Nirshan Perera (Routledge, 2012), 470.

91. Joshi, "Mutiny Echoes," 468.

92. David Brewster, *Letters on Natural Magic, Addressed to Sir Walter Scott* (John Murray, 1832), 46.

5. Spinning in Place

1. Michael North, *Machine-Age Comedy* (Oxford University Press, 2008), 186–87. See also Garrett Stewart, "Modern Hard Times: Chaplin and the Cinema of Self-Reflection," *Critical Inquiry* 3, no. 2 (December 1976): 295–314.

2. Stewart, "Modern Hard Times," 313.

3. Nicolas Dulac and André Gaudreault, "Circularity and Repetition at the Heart of the Attraction: Optical Toys and the Emergence of a New Cultural Series," in *The Cinema of Attractions Reloaded*, ed. Wanda Strauven (Amsterdam University Press, 2006), 227–44.

4. Stewart, "Modern Hard Times," 297.

5. Even André Gaudreault's concept of "monstration," the most elemental form of film narrative that he defines as unfolding events, is impossible when we are speaking of a loop of moving images. See André Gaudreault, "Film Narrative, Narration: The Cinema of the Lumière Brothers," in *Early Cinema: Space, Frame, Narrative*, ed. Thomas Elsaesser, with Adam Barker (BFI Publishing, 1990), 68–75.

6. The scholarship on Thomas Hardy and visual culture is more extensive than I can cover in this footnote, but for Hardy and optical technology, see especially Anna Henchman, *The Starry Sky Within: Astronomy and the Reach of the Mind in Victorian Literature* (Oxford University Press, 2014); Joan Grundy, *Hardy and the Sister Arts* (Macmillan, 1979). Grundy focuses on the "cinematic" qualities of Hardy's poetry and prose, a topic also taken up in J. B. Bullen, "Is Hardy a Cinematic Novelist? The Problem of Adaptation," *Yearbook of English Studies* 20 (1990): 48–59; David Lodge, "Hardy and Cinematographic Form," *NOVEL: A Forum on Fiction* 7, no. 3 (Spring 1974): 246–54; Paul J. Niemeyer, "Hardy and Cinema: A Plethoric Growth in Knowledge," in *The Ashgate Research Companion to Thomas Hardy*, ed. Rosemarie Morgan (Ashgate, 2010), 315–28; Roger Webster, "From Painting to Cinema: Visual Elements in Hardy's Fiction," in *Thomas Hardy on Screen*, ed. T. R. Wright (Cambridge University Press, 2015), 315–28.

7. An exception is Zena Meadowsong's analysis of industrial machinery in *Tess of the d'Urbervilles*. See Zena Meadowsong, "Thomas Hardy and the Machine: The Mechanical Deformation of Narrative Realism in *Tess of the d'Urbervilles*," *Nineteenth-Century Literature* 64, no. 2 (2009): 225–48.

8. A. Bowdoin Van Riper, "In the Shadow of Machines: *Modern Times* and the Iconography of Technology," in *Refocusing Chaplin: A Screen Icon Through Critical Lenses*, ed. L. Howe, J. E. Caron, and B. Click (Scarecrow, 2013), 85.

9. Jeffrey Vance, *Chaplin: Genius of Cinema* (Abrams, 2003), 33–34.

10. Vance, *Chaplin*, 210, 221.

11. Stewart, "Modern Hard Times."

12. Plateau's phenakistoscope is essentially identical to the stroboscope, invented at the same time by Austrian Simon Stampfer. For the complete history, see Laurent Mannoni, *The Great Art of Light and Shadow: An Archaeology of the Cinema*, trans. and ed. Richard Crangle (University of Exeter Press, 2000), 223–47.

13. While still widely in use, including by film scholars, we now know that persistence of vision is not an adequate explanation of the illusion of motion. For a fuller explanation, see Barbara Anderson and Joseph Anderson, "The Myth of Persistence of Vision Revisited," *Journal of Film and Video* 45, no. 1 (Spring 1993): 3–12.

14. Romana Karla Schuler, *Seeing Motion: A History of Visual Perception in Art and Science* (Gruyter, 2015), 33. For more on the prehistory of the modern study of retinal afterimages, see Mannoni, *The Great Art of Light and Shadow*, 202.

15. Joseph Plateau, *Dissertation sur quelques propriétés des impressions*, MA thesis, University of Liège, May 1829, quoted in Jonathan Crary, *Techniques of the Observer: On Vision and Modernity in the Nineteenth Century* (MIT Press, 1992), 109.

16. Mannoni, *The Great Art of Light and Shadow*, 215–16.

17. Plateau, quoted in Mannoni, *The Great Art of Light and Shadow*, 216.

18. David Robinson, "Animation: The First Chapter, 1833–1893," *Monthly Film Bulletin* 59, no. 4 (Autumn 1990): 251.

19. Kristin Thompson, David Bordwell, and Jeff Smith, *Film History: An Introduction*, 5th ed. (McGraw Hill, 2022), 4; Deac Rossell, *Living Pictures: The Origin of the Movies* (State University of New York Press, 1998), 19.

20. See Barbara Anderson and Joseph Anderson on how "myth of persistence of vision" posits "a *passive* viewer upon whose sluggish retina images pile up," a construction that they argue gives rise to Marxist-Lacanian theories of cinema suspicious of cinema's ideological power over the malleable film subject. Anderson and Anderson, "The Myth of Persistence of Vision Revisited," 3. An example of how this theory of passive spectatorship is applied to the analysis of the phenakistoscope can be found in Jonathan Crary's claim, in *Techniques of the Observer*, that optical toys leave the spectator "susceptible to external procedures of manipulation and stimulation that have the essential capacity *to produce experience for the subject*." Crary, *Techniques of the Observer*, 92.

21. W. G. Horner, "On the Properties of the *Daedaleum*, a New Instrument of Optical Illusion," *London Edinburgh Philosophical Magazine and Journal of Science* 4, no. 19 (January 1834): 37.

22. Tom Gunning, "Hand and Eye: Excavating a New Technology of the Image in the Victorian Era," *Victorian Studies* 54, no. 3 (April 2012): 495–516.

23. Dulac and Gaudreault, "Circularity and Repetition," 232.

24. For an overview of phenakistoscope design, see Stephen Herbert's discussion of phenakistoscope and stroboscope disks in his digital project, Stephen Herbert, *The Wheel of Life*, "The Phenakistoscope, and Stroboscopic Disc, Parts 1 and 2," https://www.stephenherbert.co.uk/phenakPartOne.htm and https://www.stephenherbert.co.uk/phenakPartTwo.htm.

25. David J. Jones, *Gothic Effigies: A Guide to Dark Visibilities* (Manchester University Press, 2008), 117.

26. Meredith Bak, *Playful Visions: Optical Toys and the Emergence of Children's Media Culture* (MIT Press, 2020), 111.

27. Herbert, "The Phenakistoscope, and Stroboscopic Disc, Part 1," https://www.stephenherbert.co.uk/phenakPartOne.htm, accessed December 7, 2022.

28. Bak, *Playful Visions*, 111.

29. Bak, *Playful Visions*, 111.

30. Bak, *Playful Visions*, 110–11.

31. Stewart, "Modern Hard Times," 311.

32. Herbert, "The Phenakistoscope, and Stroboscopic Disc, Part 2," https://www.stephenherbert.co.uk/phenakPartTwo.htm.

33. Sigmund Freud, *Beyond the Pleasure Principle*, trans. James Strachey (Norton, 1961), 24.

34. See Amanda Shubert, "'To Become a Devil': Special Effects, Magic Tricks, and the Technological Image in *Faust*," *Film Criticism* 48, no. 1 (2024). https://doi.org/10.3998/fc.5693.

35. John Plotz, "Motion Slickness: Spectacle and Circulation in Thomas Hardy's 'On the Western Circuit,'" *Studies in Short Fiction* 33 (1996): 370. As Mark Ford's biographical study *Thomas Hardy: Half a Londoner* (Harvard University

Press, 2016) reminds us, Hardy was much more metropolitan than most of his characters.

36. Margaret Kolb, "Plot Circles: Hardy's Drunkards and Their Walks," *Victorian Studies* 56, no. 4 (Summer 2014): 596.

37. Kolb, "Plot Circles," 595. Thomas Hardy, *The Mayor of Casterbridge* (Modern Library, 2002), 328. Further references to this text will be page numbers that are provided in parentheses.

38. Caroline Lesjak, *The Afterlife of Enclosure: British Realism, Character, and the Commons* (Stanford University Press, 2021), 126.

39. Thomas Hardy, *Thomas Hardy's 'Poetical Matter' Notebook*, ed. Pamela Dalziel and Michael Millgate (Oxford University Press, 2009), 15.

40. Florence Emily Hardy, *The Life of Thomas Hardy*, quoted in Lawrence J. Starzyk, "Hardy's *Mayor*: The Antitraditional Basis of Human Tragedy," *Studies in the Novel* 4, no. 4 (Winter 1972): 593.

41. Hardy, *The Mayor of Casterbridge*, 328.

42. Hardy, *The Mayor of Casterbridge*, 328.

43. This condition recalls an earlier moment in the novel, when Elizabeth-Jane wonders about the source of her own consciousness, "which spun in her that moment like a top." The physics of spinning objects and consciousness are once again metaphorically linked.

44. Elaine Scarry, "Work and the Body in Hardy and Other Nineteenth-Century Novelists," *Representations* 3 (1983): 106.

45. Scarry, "Work and the Body in Hardy," 102.

46. Scarry, "Work and the Body in Hardy," 98.

47. Scarry, "Work and the Body in Hardy," 91, 116, 92.

48. Martin Ray, *Thomas Hardy: A Textual Study of the Short Stories* (Routledge, 1997), 168.

49. Thomas Hardy, "On the Western Circuit," in *The Distracted Preacher and Other Tales* (Penguin Classics, 1979), 244. Further references to this text will be page numbers that are provided in parentheses.

50. As Ray explains, Hardy changed the title to "On the Western Circuit" quite late in the composition process. See Ray, *Thomas Hardy*, 202.

51. Michael Niblett, "'Time's Carcase': Waste, Labour, and Finance Capital in the Atlantic World-Ecology," *Atlantic Studies* 16, no. 1 (2019): 77.

52. John Plotz notes that "the description of Charles watching Anna seems to derive from the experience of watching a 'phenakistoscope.'" See Plotz, "Motion Slickness," 376.

53. See especially Isobel Armstrong, *Victorian Glassworlds: Glass Culture and the Imagination, 1830–1880* (Oxford University Press, 2008), 101, 112.

54. See Nada Al-Ajmi, "Women in Thomas Hardy's 'On the Western Circuit,'" *Hardy Society Journal* 2, no. 2 (2006): 44–51; Trish Ferguson, "Machinations Versus Mechanization: Desire in 'On the Western Circuit,'" *Hardy Review* 19, no. 2 (2017): 61–69.

55. Thomas Hardy, "The Fiddler of the Reels," in *The Distracted Preacher and Other Tales* (Penguin Classics, 1979), 286. Further references to this text will be page numbers that are provided in parentheses.

56. Armstrong, *Victorian Glassworlds*, 358.

57. Armstrong, *Victorian Glassworlds*, 350.

58. Shannon Draucker, *Sounding Bodies: Acoustical Science and Musical Erotics in Victorian Literature* (State University of New York Press, 2024), 122–24.

59. Frank R. Giordano, "Characterization and Conflict in Hardy's 'The Fiddler of the Reels,'" *Texas Studies in Literature and Language* 17, no. 3 (1975): 617–33.

60. Hardy, *Thomas Hardy's 'Poetical Matter' Notebook*, 15.

61. Lev Manovich, "What Is Digital Cinema?," in *Post-Cinema: Theorizing 21st-Century Film*, ed. Shane Denson and Julia Leyda (Reframe Books, 2016), 1.1 What Is Digital Cinema? (sussex.ac.uk), accessed November 14, 2023.

Epilogue

1. Thomas Elsaesser, "Louis Lumière: The Cinema's First Virtualist?," in *Cinema Futures: Cain, Abel, or Cable: The Screen Arts in the Digital Age*, ed. Thomas Elsaesser and Kay Hoffman (Amsterdam University Press, 1988), 57–58.

2. André Bazin, "The Myth of Total Cinema," in *What Is Cinema?*, trans. Hugh Gray (University of California Press, 1967), 21–22.

3. Bazin, "The Myth of Total Cinema," 21.

Acknowledgments

This book is the product of more than a decade of thinking and writing about Victorian media aesthetics. It is my pleasure to thank the many institutions, archives, and individuals whose support—material, intellectual, and emotional—allowed me to do my best work. I began this project as a graduate student at the University of Chicago under the exemplary direction of Elaine Hadley, Tom Gunning, and Zach Samalin. Whatever value this book offers to readers is a testament to their brilliance, generosity, and vision. I am grateful to the faculty, staff, and students of the University of Wisconsin-Madison's (UW Madison) Departments of English, Communication Arts, and Curriculum and Instruction for encouraging the development of this book. A special thank you to department chairs Christa Olson and Erica Halverson for their advocacy and leadership. I was fortunate to complete my book on a twelve-month research fellowship from the American Council of Learned Societies (ACLS); I would like to express my gratitude to the ACLS for their commitment to funding the work of junior and non-tenure-track scholars. UW Madison's Institute for Research in the Humanities offered me a home for that final year of writing and an extraordinary interdisciplinary community of scholars with whom to think and learn.

My research was also made possible by many knowledgeable and patient archivists. I wish particularly to thank Lewis Pollard at the National Science and Media Museum, Phil Whickham and Mike Rickard at the Bill Douglas Cinema Museum at the University of Exeter, and Joss Marsh and David Francis at the Kent Museum of the Moving Image. Additional thanks to the Victoria and Albert Museum's Word and Image Center, Museum of Childhood, and National Art Library; the University of Westminster Archive; and the Museum of the History of Science at Oxford University. I gratefully acknowledge the institutions that supported my archival research: the Social Science Research Council, the Midwest Victorian Studies Association, the Nicholson

Center for British Studies at the University of Chicago, and the American Philosophical Society.

Working with Cornell University Press to bring this book into the world was an honor and a pleasure. Thank you to my editor Mahinder Kingra for his confidence in me and my work, for encouraging me to trust my own instincts, and for his patience and generosity every step of the way. I am also grateful to Karen Laun, Kalie Hyatt, India Miraglia, and Kristin Ashley Gregg. Enid Zafran compiled the index and Marianne L'Abbate copyedited the manuscript; I deeply appreciate their contributions. Finally, my profound thanks to the brilliant and generous peer reviewers who improved the book through their thoughtful critiques: Rachel Teukolsky, John Plotz, and Lara Kriegel.

The companionship of so many dear friends and inspiring interlocutors made the writing of this book a joy. This book is dedicated to my writing group—Grace An, Shannon Draucker, Allyson Nadia Field, Ari Gass, Katerina Korola, and Kate Nesbit—an exceptional bunch of scholars who assembled on Zoom in the early days of the COVID-19 pandemic and were involved in every stage of this book's composition. Of all the grace and good fortune I have been the recipient of in the last five years, it is their warmth, abundant and unceasing support, and penetrating insight into my work that I value most. Shannon Draucker and Kate Nesbit deserve special recognition for reading every chapter of the book multiple times and improving both them and me. Kaneesha Parsard read an early draft and sparked new ways of thinking about the political dimensions of the project; here and in everything I write I am trying to live up to her example as a scholar and a human. Thank you to the colleagues who provided notes on the book in the final stages: Geoffrey Adelsberg, Sarah Allison, Meredith Bak, Chris Kirchgasler, and Chelsea Silva. I am also grateful to the many audiences who critiqued this project with such care, especially the Franke Institute for the Humanities, Eighteenth- and Nineteenth-Century Atlantic Cultures Workshop, and Mass Culture Workshop at the University of Chicago; and the Film Studies Colloquium and Middle Modernity Workshop at UW Madison.

My deepest thanks to the many colleagues who discussed this project with me over coffee, on long walks, around the dinner table, and curled up in the cocktail bars of conference hotels. This book was enriched by conversations with Zarena Aslami, Bill Brown, Alexis Chema, Zara Chowdhary, Kelley Conway, Pat Day, Maud Ellman, Sarah Ensor, Frances Ferguson, Edgar Garcia, Mary-Catherine Harrison, Elizabeth

Helsinger, Eric Hoyt, Priti Joshi, Andrea Korda, Josephine McDonagh, Darshana Mini, Daniel Morgan, Julie Orlemanski, Mario Ortiz-Robles, John Plotz, John Plunkett, Lisa Ruddick, Meghna Sapui, Oishani Sengupta, Bassam Sidiki, Anna-Claire Stinebring, Rachel Teukolsky, Kristin Thompson, Anne Vila, Sarah Wells, Sandy Zagarell, and David Zimmerman. A special thank you to the late David Bordwell for his friendship, conversation, and kind belief in my work. I am grateful to Ellen Perry, who solved the mystery of an eighteenth-century newspaper editorial, and to Nina Clements, who assisted me in tracking down sources. My loving gratitude to Katie and Chris Kirchgasler for accepting me as part of their family and celebrating every book milestone, and to Geoff Adelsberg and Faith Carol Newton for the blessed gift of conversation about everything *but* this book. Kate Vieira is a writing companion and a fount of wisdom and nonstop fun: I am thankful to her in too many ways to name.

Thank you to my parents, Howard and Rachelle, and my brother, Ben, for their loving and steadfast support; to Alli Carlisle for more than fifteen years of dearest friendship; and to all the kids who made me an auntie—Lincoln, Livia, Oren, Amália, Mak, and Teddy. Thank you to Zora, my dog, for taking me to the park every weekend. To Peter McDonald, who improved every page, delighted in every victory, and lovingly endured every crisis of faith: a simple thank you could never begin to cover it. But what sweet pleasure to write our books together. Let's do it again sometime.

Bibliography

Al-Ajmi, Nada. "Women in Thomas Hardy's 'On the Western Circuit.'" *Hardy Society Journal* 2, no. 2 (2006): 44–51.

Anderson, Barbara, and Joseph Anderson. "The Myth of Persistence of Vision Revisited." *Journal of Film and Video* 45, no. 1 (Spring 1993): 3–12.

Andriopoulos, Stefan. *Ghostly Apparitions: German Idealism, the Gothic Novel, and Optical Media*. Zone, 2013.

Andriopoulos, Stefan. "Kant's Magic Lantern: Historical Epistemology and Media Archaeology." *Representations* 115, no. 1 (August 2011): 42–70.

Armstrong, Isobel. *Victorian Glassworlds: Glass Culture and the Imagination, 1830–1880*. Oxford University Press, 2008.

Armstrong, Nancy. *Fiction in the Age of Photography: The Legacy of British Realism*. Harvard University Press, 1999.

Arnold, David. "Envisioning the Tropics: Joseph Hooker in India and the Himalayas, 1848–1850." In *Tropical Visions in an Age of Empire*, edited by Felix Driver and Luciana Martins. University of Chicago Press, 2005.

Arnold, Jean. *Victorian Jewelry, Identity, and the Novel: Prisms of Culture*. Ashgate, 2011.

Baggage, Charles. "Art. IX—The Exposition of 1851; or, Views of the Industry, the Science, and the Government of England." *North British Review* 15 (1851).

Bak, Meredith. "The Ludic Archive: The Work of Playing with Optical Toys." *Moving Image: The Journal of the Association of Moving Image Archivists* 16, no. 1 (Spring 2016): 1–16.

Bak, Meredith. *Playful Visions: Optical Toys and the Emergence of Children's Media Culture*. MIT Press, 2020.

Barrère, Bertrand. *Memoirs of Bertrand Barrère*, vol. 1. Translated by De V. Payen-Payne. H. S. Nichols, 1896.

Barrow, Sir John. "An Account of *Modern Egyptians*." *Quarterly Review* 59, no. 117 (July 1837).

Bazin, André. "The Myth of Total Cinema." In *What Is Cinema?* Translated by Hugh Gray. University of California Press, 1967, 17–22.

Bell, Karl. *The Magical Imagination: Magic and Modernity in Urban England, 1780–1914*. Cambridge University Press, 2012.

Bellion, Wendy. *Citizen Spectator: Art, Illusion, and Visual Perception in Early National America*. University of North Carolina Press, 2011.

Bellour, Raymond. "Les mots-images." *Magazine Littéraire* 259 (1988): 63–64.

Borges, Jorge Luis. "The Mirror of Ink." In *Collected Fictions*. Translated by Andrew Hurley, 60–62. Penguin, 1999.

Brantlinger, Patrick. *Rule of Darkness: British Literature and Imperialism, 1830–1914.* Cornell University Press, 1988.

Brewster, David. *Letters on Natural Magic, Addressed to Sir Walter Scott.* John Murray, 1832.

Brewster, David. "On the Microphotograph." *Photographic Journal* 8 (January 15, 1864): 441.

Brewster, David. *A Treatise on Optics: First American Edition, with an Appendix, Containing an Elementary View of the Application of Analysis to Reflexion and Refraction, by A. D. Bache.* Carey, Lea, & Blanchard, 1833.

Brooker, Jeremy. *The Temple of Minerva: Magic and the Magic Lantern at the Royal Polytechnic Institution, London 1837–1901.* Magic Lantern Society, 2013.

Brooks, Peter. *Realist Vision.* Yale University Press, 2005.

Brown, Bill. *The Material Unconscious: American Amusement, Steven Crane, and the Economics of Play.* Harvard University Press, 1997.

Bruhat, Jean. "La Révolution française et la formation de la pensée de Marx." *Annales historiques de la Révolution française* 184, no. 1 (1966): 125–70.

Bullen, J. B. "Is Hardy a Cinematic Novelist? The Problem of Adaptation." *Yearbook of English Studies* 20 (1990): 48–59.

Burton, Isabel. *The Life of Captain Sir Richard F. Burton*, vol. 2. Chapman & Hall, 1893.

Burton, Richard Francis. *Personal Narrative of a Pilgrimage to El-Medinah and Mecca*, vol. 2. Longman, 1855–1856.

Byerly, Alison. *Are We There Yet? Virtual Travel and Victorian Realism.* University of Michigan Press, 2012.

Carlyle, Thomas. "The Diamond Necklace." In *The Works of Thomas Carlyle: Volume 28: Critical and Miscellaneous Essays III*, edited by Henry Duff Traill, 324–402. Cambridge University Press, 2010.

Carlyle, Thomas. *The French Revolution: A History in Three Volumes, Vol. I: The Bastille*, edited by Mark Cumming and David R. Sorensen. Oxford University Press, 2020.

Carlyle, Thomas. *The French Revolution: A History in Three Volumes, Vol. III: The Guillotine*, edited by Mark Cumming and David R. Sorensen. Oxford University Press, 2020.

Carlyle, Thomas. "On History." In *The Works of Thomas Carlyle: Volume 27: Critical and Miscellaneous Essays*, edited by Henry Duff Traill, 83–95. Cambridge University Press, 2010.

Carse, Wendy. "A Penchant for Narrative: Mary Smith in Elizabeth Gaskell's *Cranford*." *Journal of Narrative Technique* 20, no. 3 (1990): 318–30.

Carver, Terrell. "Imagery/Writing, Imagination/Politics: Reading Marx Through the Eighteenth Brumaire." In *Marx's 'Eighteenth Brumaire': (Post)Modern Interpretations*, edited by Mark Cowling and James Martin, 113–28. Pluto, 2002.

Casetti, Francesco. "Rethinking the Phantasmagoria: An Enclosure and Three Worlds." *Journal of Visual Culture* 21, no. 2 (2022): 349–73.

Cass, Jeffrey. "'The Scraps, Patches and Rags of Daily Life': Gaskell's Oriental Other and the Conservation of *Cranford*." *Papers on Language and Literature: A Journal for Scholars and Critics of Language and Literature* (Fall 1999): 417–33.

Castle, Terry. "Phantasmagoria: Spectral Technology and the Metaphorics of Modern Reverie." *Critical Inquiry* 15, no. 1 (October 1988): 26–61.

Claxon, Michael Jay. "The Conjurer Unmasked: Literary and Theatrical Magicians, 1840–1925." PhD diss., University of North Carolina at Chapel Hill, 2003.

Cohen, Margaret. "Walter Benjamin's Phantasmagoria." *New German Critique* 48 (1989): 87–107.

Colley, Linda. *Britons: Forging the Nation 1707–1837*. Pimlico, 2003.

Collingwood, E. M. *Imperial Bodies: The Physical Experience of the Raj, c. 1800–1947*. Polity, 2001.

Collins, Wilkie. "Magnetic Evenings at Home." *The Leader* (February 28, 1852): 19–20.

Collins, Wilkie. *The Moonstone*. Modern Library, 2001.

Collins, Wilkie. "My Black Mirror." *Household Words* 14 (September 6, 1856): 169.

Collyer, Robert H. *Psychography, or, the Embodiment of Thought, with an Analysis of Phreno-Magnetism, "Neurology," and Mental Hallucination, Including Rules to Govern and Produce the Magnetic State*. Redding, 1843.

Corstorphine, Kevin. "Fitz-James O'Brien: The Seen and the Unseen." *The Green Book: Writings on Irish Gothic, Supernatural, and Fantastic Literature*, no. 5 (Bealtaine, 2015).

Crary, Jonathan. *Techniques of the Observer: On Vision and Modernity in the Nineteenth Century*. MIT Press, 1992.

Croskery, Margaret Case. "Mothers Without Children, Unity Without Plot: *Cranford*'s Radical Charm." *Nineteenth-Century Literature* 52, no. 2 (September 1997): 198–220.

Cumming, Mark. *A Disimprisoned Epic: Form and Vision in Carlyle's* French Revolution. University of Pennsylvania Press, 1988.

Daley, Suzanne. *The Empire Inside: Indian Commodities and Victorian Domestic Novels*. University of Michigan Press, 2011.

Dalrymple, William, and Anita Anand. *Koh-i-Noor: The History of the World's Most Infamous Diamond*. Bloomsbury, 2017.

Dames, Nicholas. *The Physiology of the Novel: Reading, Neural Science, and the Form of Victorian Fiction*. Oxford University Press, 2007.

Davis, John R. *The Great Exhibition*. Sutton, 1999.

De Luca, Tiago. *Planetary Cinema: Film, Media, and the Earth*. Amsterdam University Press, 2021.

Della Porta, Giambattista. *Natural Magick*. Thomas Young and Samuel Speed, 1658.

Derrida, Jacques. *Specters of Marx: The State of Debt, the Work of Mourning, and the New International*. Translated by Peggy Kamuf. Routledge, 1994.

Dickens, Charles. *A Christmas Carol and Other Stories*. Modern Library, 2001.

Dickens, Charles. "Robertson, Artist in Ghosts." *Household Words*, no. 253 (January 27, 1855): 553–58.

Dickens, Charles. *A Tale of Two Cities*. Penguin, 2003.

Draucker, Shannon. *Sounding Bodies: Acoustical Science and Musical Erotics in Victorian Literature*. State University of New York Press, 2024.

Dulac, Nicolas, and André Gaudreault. "Circularity and Repetition at the Heart of the Attraction: Optical Toys and the Emergence of a New Cultural Series." In *The Cinema of Attractions Reloaded*, edited by Wanda Strauven, 227–44. Amsterdam University Press, 2006.

Duncan, Ian. "*The Moonstone*, the Victorian Novel, and Imperialist Panic." *Modern Language Quarterly* 55, no. 3 (September 1994): 297–319.

During, Simon. *Modern Enchantments: The Cultural Power of Secular Magic*. Harvard University Press, 2002.

Eisenstein, Sergei. "Dickens, Griffith, and the Film Today." In *Film Form: Essays in Film Theory*, edited and translated by Jay Leyda, 213–14. Harcourt, 1949.

Elcott, Noam M. *Artificial Darkness: An Obscure History of Modern Art and Media*. University of Chicago Press, 2016.

Elcott, Noam M. "The Phantasmagorical Dispositif: An Assembly of Bodies and Images in Real Time and Space." In *Screen Space Reconfigured*, edited by Susanne Ǿ. Saether and Synne T. Bull, 283–316. Amsterdam University Press, 2020.

Eliot, George. *Adam Bede*. Oxford University Press, 2008.

Eliot, George. *The Lifted Veil and Brother Jacob*. Oxford World's Classics, 1999.

Elsaesser, Thomas. "Between Knowing and Believing: The Cinematic Dispositif After Cinema." In *Cine-Dispositifs: Essays in Epistemology Across Media*, edited by François Albera and Maria Tortajada, 45–72. Amsterdam University Press, 2015.

Elsaesser, Thomas. "Louis Lumière: The Cinema's First Virtualist?" In *Cinema Futures: Cain, Abel, or Cable: The Screen Arts in the Digital Age*, edited by Thomas Elsaesser and Kay Hoffman, 45–61. Amsterdam University Press, 1988).

Farina, Jonathan. "Dickens' 'As If': Analogy and Victorian Virtual Reality." *Victorian Studies* 53, no. 3 (Spring 2011): 427–36.

Ferguson, Trish. "Machinations Versus Mechanization: Desire in 'On the Western Circuit.'" *Hardy Review* 19, no. 2 (2017): 61–69.

Fickers, Andreas. "How to Grasp Historical Media Dispositifs in Practice." In *Materializing Memories: Dispositifs, Generations, Amaturs*, edited by Susan Aasman, Andreas Fickers, and Joseph Wachelder, 85–102. Bloomsbury, 2018.

Fickers, Andreas, and Annie van den Oeve. "Doing Experimental Media Archaeology: Epistemological and Methodological Reflections on Experiments with Historical Objects in Media Technologies." In *New Media Archaeologies*, edited by Ben Roberts and Mark Goodall, 45–68. Amsterdam University Press, 2019.

"Five Shilling Days and One Shilling Days." *Illustrated London News* (July 1851): 102.

Flint, Kate. *The Victorians and the Visual Imagination*. Cambridge University Press, 2008.

Fludernik, Monica. "Eliot and Narrative." In *A Companion to George Eliot*, edited by Amanda Anderson and Harry Shaw, 21–34. Wiley, 2013.

Ford, Mark. *Thomas Hardy: Half a Londoner*. Harvard University Press, 2016.

Foster, Nora. "'Free of Formulas': Innovation, Prophecy, and Truth in Thomas Carlyle's *The French Revolution*." *Carlyle Studies Annual* 24 (2008): 101–16.

Freud, Sigmund. *Beyond the Pleasure Principle*. Translated by James Strachey. Norton, 1961.

Friedberg, Anne. *The Virtual Window: From Alberti to Microsoft*. MIT Press, 2009.

"The Front Row of the Shilling Gallery." *Punch* 5 (July 1851): 11.

Gao, Timothy. *Virtual Play and the Victorian Novel: The Ethics and Aesthetics of Fictional Experience*. Cambridge University Press, 2021.

Gaskell, Elizabeth. *Cranford*. Oxford University Press, 2011.

Gaudreault, André. "Film Narrative, Narration: The Cinema of the Lumière Brothers." In *Early Cinema: Space, Frame, Narrative*, edited by Thomas Elsaesser, with Adam Barker, 68–75. BFI Publishing, 1990.

Gavin, Adrienne E. "Language Among the Amazons: Conjuring and Creativity in *Cranford*." *Dickens Studies Annual* 23 (1994): 205–25.

Gilbert, Robby. "The Concrete Zoetrope: Engaging Students in Pre-Cinema with an Eye to the Future." *Early Popular Visual Culture* 18, no. 1 (2020): 44–57.

Giordano, Frank R. "Characterization and Conflict in Hardy's 'The Fiddler of the Reels,'" *Texas Studies in Literature and Language* 17, no. 3 (1975): 617–33.

Goldberg, Michael. *Carlyle and Dickens*. University of Georgia Press, 1972.

Gordon, Margaret Maria. *The Home Life of David Brewster*. Cambridge University Press, 2011.

Gorky, Maxim. "The Kingdom of Shadows." In *Authors on Film*, edited by Harry M. Geduld. Indiana University Press, 1972.

Gosta, Tamara. "Thomas Carlyle's 'Real-Phantasmagory': The Historical Sublime and Humanist Politics in *Past and Present*." *Studies in the Literary Imagination* 45, no. 1 (Spring 2012): 89–111.

"The Great Eastern Nave." *The Illustrated Exhibitor* 1 (June 7, 1851).

Greiner, Rae. *Sympathetic Realism in Nineteenth-Century British Fiction*. Johns Hopkins University Press, 2013.

Groth, Helen. *Moving Images: Nineteenth-Century Reading and Screen Practices*. Edinburgh University Press, 2014.

Grundy, Joan. *Hardy and the Sister Arts*. Macmillan, 1979.

Gunning, Tom. "An Aesthetic of Astonishment: Early Film and the (In)Credulous Spectator." In *Film Theory and Criticism: Introductory Reading*, 6th ed., edited by Leo Braudy and Marshall Cohen, 862–76. Oxford University Press, 2004.

Gunning, Tom. "The Cinema of Attractions: Early Film, Its Spectator, and the Avant-Garde." In *Early Cinema: Space, Frame, Narrative*, edited by Thomas Elsaesser, 56–62. BFI Publishing, 2006.

Gunning, Tom. "Hand and Eye: Excavating a New Technology of the Image in the Victorian Era." *Victorian Studies* 54, no. 3 (April 2012): 495–516.

Gunning, Tom. "Illusions Past and Future: The Phantasmagoria and Its Specters." Paper presented at the First International Conference on the Histories of Art, Science, and Technology, Banff New Media Institute, Canada, 2005. https://www.mediaarthistory.org/refresh/Programmatic%20key%20texts/pdfs/Gunning.pdf.

Gunning, Tom. "The Long and Short of It: Centuries of Projecting Shadows, from Natural Magic to the Avant-Garde." In *The Art of Projection*, edited by Stan Douglas and Christopher Eamon, 23–35. Hatje Cantz Verlag, 2009.

Gunning, Tom. "The Phantasmagoria and the Manufacturing of Illusion and Wonder: Towards a Cultural Optics of the Cinematic Apparatus." In *The Cinema: A New Technology for the 20th Century*, edited by André Gaudreault, Catherine Russell, and Pierre Véronneau, 32–44. Editions Payot, 2004.

Gunning, Tom. "The Play Between Still and Moving Images: Nineteenth-Century 'Philosophical Toys' and Their Discourse." In *Between Stillness and Motion: Film, Photography, Algorithms*, edited by Eivind Røsaak, 27–44. Amsterdam University Press, 2011.

Gunning, Tom. "To Scan a Ghost: The Ontology of Mediated Vision." *Grey Room* 26 (2007): 94–127.

Gunning, Tom. " 'We Are Here and Not Here': Late Nineteenth-Century Stage Magic and the Roots of Cinema in the Appearance (and Disappearance) of the Virtual Image." In *A Companion to Early Cinema*, edited by André Gaudreault, Nicolas Dulac, and Santiago Hidalgo, 52–63. Wiley-Blackwell, 2012.

Haight, Gordon. *George Eliot: A Biography*. Clarendon, 1968.

Hardy, Thomas. *The Distracted Preacher and Other Tales*. Penguin Classics, 1979.

Hardy, Thomas. *The Mayor of Casterbridge*. Modern Library, 2002.

Hardy, Thomas. *The Return of the Native*. Oxford World's Classics, 2005.

Hardy, Thomas. *Thomas Hardy's 'Poetical Matter' Notebook*, edited by Pamela Dalziel and Michael Millgate. Oxford University Press, 2009.

Harries, Martin. "Homo Alludens: Marx's Eighteenth Brumaire." *New German Critique* 66 (Autumn 1995): 35–64.

Heard, Mervyn. *Phantasmagoria: The Secret Life of the Magic Lantern*. Projection Box, 2006.

Henchman, Anna. *The Starry Sky Within: Astronomy and the Reach of the Mind in Victorian Literature*. Oxford University Press, 2014.

Hennelly, Mark M. "Detecting Collins' Diamond: From Serpentstone to Moonstone." *Nineteenth-Century Fiction* 39, no. 1 (1984): 25–47.

Herbert, Stephen. *The Wheel of Life*. "The Phenakistoscope, and Stroboscopic Disc, Parts 1 and 2." https://www.stephenherbert.co.uk/phenakPartOne.htm and https://www.stephenherbert.co.uk/phenakPartTwo.htm.

Hertz, Neil. *George Eliot's Pulse*. Stanford University Press, 2003.

Hooper, William. *Rational Recreations: Volume the First, Containing Arithmetical and Mechanical Experiments*, 3rd ed. L. Davis, 1787.

Hooper, William. *Rational Recreations: Volume the Second, Containing Experiments in Optics, Chromatics, and Acoustics*, 3rd ed. L. Davis, 1787.

Hopkins, Alfred. *Magic: Stage Illusions, Special Effects, and Trick Photography*. Dover, 1976.

Horner, W. G. "On the Properties of the *Daedaleum*, a New Instrument of Optical Illusion." *London Edinburgh Philosophical Magazine and Journal of Science* 4, no. 19 (January 1834): 36–41.

Horta, Paulo Lemos. "Richard Burton, Cosmopolitan Translator of the *Nights*." In *Scheherazade's Children*, edited by Philip F. Kennedy and Marina Warner, 70–85. New York University Press, 2013.

"How to See Pictures." *National Magazine*. Edited by John Saunders and Westland Marston. (London, 1856): 23–25.

Huhtamo, Erkki. "Elements of Screenology: Toward an Archaeology of the Screen." *ICONICS: International Studies of the Modern Image* 7 (2004): 31–82.

"Interesting to Burglars, Philosophers, &c." *The Leader* 2, no. 60 (May 17, 1851): 465.

Jameson, Fredric. *The Antinomies of Realism*. Verso, 2015.

Jameson, Frederic. "Marx's Purloined Letter." In *Ghostly Demarcations: A Symposium on Jacques Derrida's* Specters of Marx, edited by Michael Sprinker, 26–67. Verso, 1999.

Jones, David J. *Gothic Effigies: A Guide to Dark Visibilities*. Manchester University Press, 2008.

Jones, David J. *Gothic Machine: Textualities, Pre-Cinematic Media and Film in Popular Visual Culture, 1670–1910*. University of Wales Press, 2011.

Jones, Graham M. *Magic's Reason: An Anthropology of Analogy*. University of Chicago Press, 2017.

Joshi, Priti. *Empire of News: The Anglo-Indian Press Writes India*. State University of New York Press, 2021.

Joshi, Priti. "Mutiny Echoes: India, Britons, and Charles Dickens' *A Tale of Two Cities*." In *Global Dickens*, edited by John O. Jordan and Nirshan Perera, 435–74. Routledge, 2012.

Kennedy, Meegan. *Revising the Clinic: Vision and Representation in Victorian Medical Narrative and the Novel*. Ohio State University Press, 2010.

Kennedy, Meegan. " 'Throes and Struggles . . . Witnessed with Painful Distinctness': The Oxy-Hydrogen Microscope, Performing Science, and the Projection of the Moving Image." *Victorian Studies* 62, no. 1 (2019): 85–118.

King, Charles. *Antique Gems: Their Use, Origin, and Value as Interpreters of Ancient History; and as Illustrative of Ancient Art*. John Murray, 1860.

Kinsey, Danielle. "Koh-i-Noor: Empire, Diamonds, and the Performance of British Material Culture." *Journal of British Studies* 48, no. 2 (April 2009): 391–419.

Kluitenberg, Eric, ed. *The Book of Imaginary Media*. Nai, 2006.

Kluitenberg, Eric. "On the Archaeology of Imaginary Media." In *Media Archaeology: Approaches, Applications, and Implications*, edited by Erkki Huhtamo and Jussi Parikka, 61–63. University of California Press, 2011.

Kolb, Margaret. "Plot Circles: Hardy's Drunkards and Their Walks." *Victorian Studies* 56, no. 4 (Summer 2014): 595–623.

Kriegel, Lara. "Narrating the Subcontinent." In *The Great Exhibition of 1851: New Interdisciplinary Essays*, edited by Louise Purbick. University of Manchester Press, 2001.

"The Koh-i-Noor Cut and Come Again." *Punch* 23 (August 1852): 54.

"The Koh-i-Noor Diamond." *Reynolds Miscellany of Romance, General Literature, Science, and Art* 13, no. 335 (December 9, 1854): 312.

D'Elmotte, François Martin Poultier. "Fantasmagorie." *L'Ami des Lois, par le représentant Poultier, et autres gens de lettres, sous la direction des frères Sibuet, propriétaires* 955 (March 28, 1798), 1–2.

Lamont, Peter. *The Rise of the Indian Rope Trick: How a Spectacular Hoax Became History*. Abacus, 2005.

Lamont, Peter, and Crispin Bates. "Conjuring Images of India in Nineteenth-Century Britain." *Social History* 32, no. 3 (August 2007): 308–24.

Lane, Edward William. *An Account of the Manners and Customs of the Modern Egyptians*. Dover, 1973.

Lane-Poole, Sophia. *The Englishwoman in Egypt: Letters from Cairo, Written During a Residence There in 1842, 3, & 4*, vol. 1. Charles Knight, 1845.

Law, Jules. *The Social Life of Fluids: Blood, Milk and Water in the Victorian Novel*. Cornell University Press, 2011.

Law, Jules. "Victorian Virtual Reality." In *BRANCH: Britain, Representation and Nineteenth-Century History*, edited by Dino Franco Felluga. https://branchcollective.org/?ps_articles=jules-law-victorian-virtual-reality. Accessed December 13, 2023.

Law, Jules. "Virtual Evidence." *Victorian Studies* 56, no. 3 (Spring 2014): 411–24.

Leeder, Murray. "M. Robert-Houdin Goes to Algeria: Spectatorship and Panic in Illusion and Early Cinema." *Early Popular Visual Culture* 8, no. 2 (May 2010): 209–25.

Leopardi, Giacomo. *Pensieri*. Translated by W. S. Di Piero. Louisiana State University Press, 1981.

Lesjak, Caroline. *The Afterlife of Enclosure: British Realism, Character, and the Commons*. Stanford University Press, 2021.

Levy, Amy. *Reuben Sachs*. Broadview, 2006.

Lindsay, Suzanne Glover. "The Revolutionary Exhumations at St-Denis, 1793." *Conversations: An Online Journal of the Center for the Study of Material and Visual Cultures of Religion* (2014). https://doi.org/10.22332/con.ess.2015.2.

Livesey, Ruth. "George Eliot and Van Gogh: Radiant Realism." *19: Interdisciplinary Studies in the Nineteenth Century* 19 (2020): 1–26.

Lodge, David. "Hardy and Cinematographic Form." *NOVEL: A Forum on Fiction* 7, no. 3 (Spring 1974): 246–54.

Loiperdinger, Martin, and Bernd Elzer. "Lumiere's Arrival of the Train: Cinema's Founding Myth." *Moving Image* 4, no. 1 (Spring 2004): 89–118. https://doi.org/10.1353/mov.2004.0014.

"London, Monday, July 1, 1850." *The Times*, no. 20529 (July 1, 1850): 4.

Lukàcs, Georg. *The Historical Novel*. Translated by Hannah Mitchell and Stanley Mitchell. University of Nebraska Press, 1983.

Mangan, Michael. *Performing Dark Arts: A Cultural History of Conjuring*. Intellect, 2007.

Mannoni, Laurent. *The Great Art of Light and Shadow: Archaeology of the Cinema*. Translated and edited by Richard Crangle. University of Exeter Press, 2000.

Mannoni, Laurent. "The Phantasmagoria." Translated by Ben Brewster. *Film History* 8, no. 4 (1996): 390–415.

Manovich, Lev. "What Is Digital Cinema?" In *Post-Cinema: Theorizing 21st-Century Film*, edited by Shane Denson and Julia Leyda. Reframe Books, 2016.

Marion, Fulgence. *The Wonders of Optics*. Translated and edited by Charles W. Quin. Scribner, 1871.

Markovits, Stefanie. "Form Things: Looking at Genre Through Victorian Diamonds." *Victorian Studies* 52, no. 4 (Summer 2010): 591–619.

Marsh, Joss. "Dickensian 'Dissolving Views': The Magic Lantern, Visual Story-Telling, and the Victorian Technological Imagination." *Comparative Critical Studies* 6, no. 3 (2009): 333–46.

Martineau, Harriet. *Eastern Life, Past and Present*, vol. 2. Lea and Blanchard, 1848.

Marx, Karl. *The Eighteenth Brumaire of Louis Bonaparte*. Wildside Press, 2008.

McClintock, Anne. *Imperial Leather: Race, Gender and Sexuality in the Colonial Context*. Routledge, 1995.

McDonagh, Josephine. *George Eliot*. Liverpool University Press, 1997.

Meadowsong, Zena. "Thomas Hardy and the Machine: The Mechanical Deformation of Narrative Realism in *Tess of the d'Urbervilles*." *Nineteenth-Century Literature* 64, no. 2 (2009): 225–48.

Melby, Julie L. "Learned Birds and Other Acts." Graphic Arts: Exhibitions, Acquisitions, and Other Highlights from the Graphic Arts Collection, Princeton University Library. April 3, 2012. https://www.princeton.edu/~graphicarts/2012/04/broadside_1.html.

Mendelsund, Peter. *What We See When We Read: A Phenomenology*. Random House, 2014.

Menke, Richard. *Telegraphic Realism: Victorian Fiction and Other Information Systems*. Stanford University Press, 2008.

"Mesmeric Phenomena." *The Era*, no. 149 (August 1, 1841): 11.

Miller, J. Hillis. *Reading for Our Time: Adam Bede and Middlemarch Revisited*. Edinburgh University Press, 2012.

Milner, Max. *La Fantasmagorie: Essai sur l'optique fantastique*. Presses universitaires de France, 1982.

Mirzoeff, Nicholas. *The Right to Look: A Counterhistory of Visuality*. Duke University Press, 2011.

Mitchell, W. J. T. *Picture Theory: Essays on Verbal and Visual Representation*. University of Chicago Press, 1995.

Morris-Low, A. D. "Brewster and Scientific Instruments." In *"Martyr of Science": Sir David Brewster 1781–1863: Proceedings of a Bicentary Symposium: Held at the Royal Scottish Museum of 21 November 1981: Together with a Catalogue of Scientific Apparatus Associated with Sir David Brewster: And a Bibliography of His Published Writings*, edited by A. D. Morrison-Low and J. R. R. Christie, 59–66. Royal Scottish Museum, 1984.

Morus, Iwan Rhys. "'More the Aspect of Magic Than Anything Natural': The Philosophy of Demonstration." In *Science and the Marketplace: Nineteenth-Century Sites and Experiences*, edited by Aileen Frye and Bernard Lightman, 336–70. University of Chicago Press, 2007.

Munich, Adrienne. *Empire of Diamonds: Victorian Gems in Imperial Settings*. University of Virginia Press, 2020.

Niblett, Michael. "'Time's Carcase': Waste, Labour, and Finance Capital in the Atlantic World-Ecology." *Atlantic Studies* 16, no. 1 (2019): 72–89.

Niemeyer, Paul J. "Hardy and Cinema: A Plethoric Growth in Knowledge." In *The Ashgate Research Companion to Thomas Hardy*, edited by Rosemarie Morgan, 315–28. Ashgate, 2010.

Nord, Deborah. "George Eliot and John Everett Millais: The Ethics and Aesthetics of Realism." *Victorian Studies* 60, no. 3 (2018): 361–89.

North, Michael. *Machine-Age Comedy*. Oxford University Press, 2008.

O'Brien, Fitz-James. "The Diamond Lens," in *The Diamond Lens and Other Stories* (Hesperus, 2012), 9.

Ogden, Emily. *Credulity: A Cultural History of US Mesmerism*. University of Chicago Press, 2018.

Otto, Peter. *Multiplying Worlds: Romanticism, Modernity, and the Emergence of Virtual Reality*. Oxford University Press, 2011.

Parikka, Jussi. *What Is Media Archaeology?* Polity, 2012.

Parikka, Jussi, and Erkki Huhtamo, eds. *Media Archaeology: Approaches, Applications, and Implications*. University of California Press, 2011.

Park, Julie. *My Dark Room: Spaces of the Inner Self in Eighteenth-Century England*. University of Chicago Press, 2023.

Pepper, John Henry. *Light: Embracing Reflection and Refraction of Light, Light and Colour, Spectrum Analysis, the Human Eye, Polarized Light*. Scribner, Welford, and Armstrong, 1876.

Pittard, Christopher. "The Travelling Doll Wonder: Dickens, Secular Magic, and *Bleak House*." *Studies in the Novel* 48, no. 3 (Fall 2016): 279–300.

Pitts, Jennifer. *A Turn to Empire: The Rise of Imperial Liberalism in Britain and France*. Princeton University Press, 2006.

Plotz, John. "Motion Slickness: Spectacle and Circulation in Thomas Hardy's 'On the Western Circuit,'" *Studies in Short Fiction* 33 (1996): 369–86.

Plotz, John. *Portable Property: Victorian Culture on the Move*. Princeton University Press, 2009.

Plotz, John. *Semi-Detached: The Aesthetics of Virtual Experience Since Dickens*. Princeton University Press, 2018.

Plunkett, John. "Optical Recreations and Victorian Literature." *Literature and the Visual Media* 58 (2005): 1–28.

Pointon, Marcia. *Brilliant Effects: A Cultural History of Gem Stones and Jewellery*. Yale University Press, 2009.

Potter, Jonathan. *Discourses of Vision in Nineteenth-Century Britain: Seeing, Thinking, Writing*. Palgrave Macmillan, 2018.

Pratt, Mary-Louise. *Imperial Eyes: Travel Writing and Transculturation*. Routledge, 2007.

"Precious Stones in the Crystal Palace." *The Illustrated Exhibitor*, no. 6 (July 12): 93–95.

"Preface," *The Parlour Magazine of the Literature of All Nations*, vol. 1, n.p.

Price, Leah. *How to Do Things with Books in Victorian Britain*. Princeton University Press, 2012.

Pritchard, Andrew. *The Microscopic Cabinet of Select Animated Objects: With a Description of the Jewel and Doublet Microscope, Test Objects, &c., to Which Are Subjoined, Memoirs on the Verification of Microscopic Phenomena, and an Exact Method of Appreciating the Quality of Microscopes and Engiscopes*. Whittaker, Treacher, and Arnot, 1832.

Professor Hoffman. *Modern Magic: A Practical Treatise on the Art of Conjuring*. Routledge, 1894.

Ray, Martin. *Thomas Hardy: A Textual Study of the Short Stories*. Routledge, 1997.

Robert-Houdin, Jean-Eugène. *Les secrets de la prestidigitation et de la magie: comment on deviant sorcier*. Michel Lévy Frères, 1868.

Roberts, Caroline. *The Woman and the Hour: Harriet Martineau and Victorian Ideologies*. University of Toronto Press, 2002.

Robertson, Étienne-Gaspard. *Mémoires récreatifs, scientifiques, et anecdotiques du physician-aéronaute E. G. Robertson*. Librairie encyclopédique de Roret, 1840.

Robinson, David. "Animation: The First Chapter, 1833–1893." *Monthly Film Bulletin* 59, no. 4 (Autumn 1990): 251–54.

Romanow, Jacob. "Metafiction as Reality Effect: Trollope's Quixotism and Novel Theory." *ELH* 89, no. 4 (2022): 1077–1105.

Rosenberg, John D. *Carlyle and the Burden of History*. Clarendon, 1985.

Rossell, Deac. *Living Pictures: The Origin of the Movies*. State University of New York Press, 1998.

Royle, Nicholas. *Telepathy and Literature: Essays on the Reading Mind*. Blackwell, 1991.

Ryan, Vanessa. *Thinking Without Thinking in the Victorian Novel*. Johns Hopkins University Press, 2012.

Said, Edward. *Orientalism: Western Concepts of the Orient*. Penguin India, 2008.

Said, Edward. *Orientalism*. Pantheon, 1978.

Saler, Michael. *As If: Modern Enchantment and the Literary Prehistory of Virtual Reality*. Oxford University Press, 2012.

Salverte, Eusèbe. *Occult Sciences: The Philosophy of Magic, Prodigies and Miracles*. Translated by Anthony Todd Thomson. Cambridge University Press, 2013.

Scarry, Elaine. "Work and the Body in Hardy and Other Nineteenth-Century Novelists." *Representations* 3 (1983): 90–123.

Schiavo, Laura Burd. "From Phantom Image to Perfect Vision: Physiological Optics, Commercial Photography, and the Popularization of the Stereoscope." In *New Media, 1740–1915*, edited by Lisa Gitelman and Geoffrey B. Pingree, 113–38. MIT Press, 2003.

Schoch, Richard W. "'We Do Nothing but Enact History': Thomas Carlyle Stages the Past." *Nineteenth-Century Literature* 54, no. 1 (1999): 27–52.

Schor, Hilary M. "Affairs of the Alphabet: Reading, Writing, and Narrating in *Cranford*." *NOVEL: A Forum on Fiction* 22, no. 3 (Spring 1989): 288–304.

Schuler, Romana Karla. *Seeing Motion: A History of Visual Perception in Art and Science*. Gruyter, 2015.

Sharpe, Jenny. *Allegories of Empire: The Figure of the Woman in the Colonial Text*. University of Minnesota Press, 1993.

Shaw, Harry. *Narrating Reality: Austen, Scott, Eliot*. Cornell University Press, 2004.

"A Shilling's Worth of Science." *Household Words* 1 (July 24, 1850): 508.

Shubert, Amanda. "A Bright Continuous Flow: Phantasmagoria and History in *A Tale of Two Cities*." *Victorian Literature and Culture* 48, no. 4 (2020): 693–720.

Shubert, Amanda. "In Defense of Credulous Women: Magic and Optical Spectatorship in *Cranford*." *Victorian Studies* 63, no. 3 (Spring 2021): 377–400.

Shubert, Amanda. "'To Become a Devil': Special Effects, Magic Tricks, and the Technological Image in *Faust*." *Film Criticism* 48, no. 1 (2024). https://doi.org/10.3998/fc.5693.

Sketchley, Arthur. *Mrs. Brown at the Play*. Routledge, 1871.

Smajic, Srdjan. *Ghost-Seers, Detectives and Spiritualists: Theories of Vision in Victorian Literature and Science*. Cambridge University Press, 2010.

Smith, Grahame. *Dickens and the Dream of Cinema*. Manchester University Press, 2003.

Stafford, Barbara. *Artful Science: Enlightenment, Entertainment, and the Eclipse of Visual Education*. MIT Press, 1994.

Starzyk, Lawrence J. "Hardy's *Mayor*: The Antitraditional Basis of Human Tragedy." *Studies in the Novel* 4, no. 4 (Winter 1972): 592–607.

Steinberg, Ronen. *The Afterlives of the Terror: Facing the Legacies of Mass Violence in Postrevolutionary France*. Cornell University Press, 2019.

Steinmeyer, Jim. *Hiding the Elephant: How Magicians Invented the Impossible and Learned to Disappear*. Da Capo, 2004.

Stewart, Garrett. "Modern Hard Times: Chaplin and the Cinema of Self-Reflection." *Critical Inquiry* 3, no. 2 (December 1976): 295–314.

Storm, Jason Ananda Joseph. *The Myth of Disenchantment: Magic, Modernity, and the Birth of the Human Sciences*. University of Chicago Press, 2017.

Tallis, John. *Tallis' History of the Crystal Palace*, vol. 2. London Printing and Publishing, 1852.

Teukolsky, Rachel. *Picture World: Image, Aesthetics, and Victorian New Media*. Oxford University Press, 2020.

Tharoor, Shashi. *Inglorious Empire: What the British Did to India*. Hurst, 2017.

Thompson, Jason. *Edward William Lane, 1801–1876: The Life of the Pioneering Egyptologist and Orientalist*. American University in Cairo Press, 2010.

Thompson, Jason. "Edward William Lane in Egypt." *Journal of the American Research Center in Egypt* 34 (1997): 243–61.

Thompson, Jason. "Edward William Lane's 'Description of Egypt.'" *International Journal of Middle East Studies* 28, no. 4 (November 1996): 565–83.

Thompson, Kristin, David Bordwell, and Jeff Smith. *Film History: An Introduction*, 5th ed. McGraw Hill, 2022.

Thomson, William MacLure. *The Land and the Book, or Biblical Illustrations Drawn from the Manner and Customs, the Scenes and Scenery of the Holy Land*. Harper, 1859.

Turner, Gerard L'Estrange. "The Rise and Fall of the Jewel Microscope." In *Essays on the History of Microscope*, 109–10. Senecio, 1980.

Van Riper, A. Bowdoin. "In the Shadow of Machines: *Modern Times* and the Iconography of Technology." In *Refocusing Chaplin: A Screen Icon Through Critical Lenses*, edited by L. Howe, J. E. Caron, and B. Click. Scarecrow, 2013.

Vance, Jeffrey. *Chaplin: Genius of Cinema*. Abrams, 2003.

Webster, Roger. "From Painting to Cinema: Visual Elements in Hardy's Fiction." In *Thomas Hardy on Screen*, edited by T. R. Wright, 315–28. Cambridge University Press, 2015.

Wells, H. G. "The Remarkable Case of Mr. Davidson's Eyes." In H. G. Wells, *Short Stories*. Penguin, 1972.

"What Is Reading & Writing, & What Are the Advantages Likely to Accrue from a Knowledge Thereof?" *Mirror of Literature, Amusement, and Instruction* 12, no. 1 (1842): 203–4.

"What the Richer Are We?" *The Expositor: A Weekly Recorder of Inventions, Designs, and Art-Manufactures* (May 24, 1851): 59.

White, Hayden. *Metahistory: The Historical Imagination in Nineteenth-Century Europe*. Johns Hopkins University Press, 1973.

Williamson, Colin. *Hidden in Plain Sight: An Archaeology of Magic and the Cinema*. Rutgers University Press, 2015.

Winter, Alison. *Mesmerized: Powers of Mind in Victorian Britain*. University of Chicago Press, 1988.

Wolfreys, Julian. *Victorian Hauntings: Spectrality, Gothic, the Uncanny and Literature*. Macmillan, 2002.

Wollstonecraft, Mary. *A Vindication of the Rights of Women, with Strictures on Moral and Political Subjects*. Cambridge University Press, 2012.

Wordsworth, William, and Samuel Taylor Coleridge. *Lyrical Ballads: 1789 and 1802*. Oxford University Press, 2013.

Worth, Aaron. *Imperial Media: Colonial Networks and Information Technologies in the British Literary Imagination, 1857–1918*. Ohio State University Press, 2014.

Yeazell, Ruth Bernard. *Art of the Everyday: Dutch Painting and the Realist Novel*. Princeton University Press, 2009.

Young, Paul. "'Carbon, Mere Carbon': The Kohinoor, the Crystal Palace, and the Mission to Make Sense of British India." *Nineteenth-Century Contexts* 29, no. 2 (December 2007): 343–58.

Zieger, Susan. *The Mediated Mind: Affect, Ephemera, and Consumerism in the Nineteenth Century*. Fordham University Press, 2018.

Index

Figures are indicated by page numbers in italics.

www.ingramcontent.com/pod-product-compliance
Lightning Source LLC
LaVergne TN
LVHW020507100826
845148LV00003B/725

* 9 7 8 1 5 0 1 7 8 4 9 4 1 *